COMMANDO CRUSADE

By the same author

THE CHURCHILL CHRONICLES

COMMANDO CRUSADE

Thomas B. L. Churchill

WILLIAM KIMBER · LONDON

First published in 1987 by
WILLIAM KIMBER & CO. LIMITED
100 Jermyn Street, London, SW1Y 6EE

ISBN 0-7183-0638-4

Typeset by Grove Graphics, Tring
Printed and bound in Great Britain by
Adlard & Son Ltd, The Garden City Press,
Letchworth, Herts

For my grandson,

Thomas III Churchill

Contents

Maps and Illustrations in the text

List of Illustrations

Facing page

CHAPTER ONE

The Burma Rebellion

To start at the beginning: I was born at Dormansland in Surrey, where my parents were on leave from Ceylon, as my father was in the Public Works Department of the Colonial Civil Service. He was a trained civil engineer, and *his* father had been Director of Public Works, Ceylon, from 1877 to 1885. At that time we were a family which served abroad in India and Ceylon; for not only my father and his father, but my *maternal* grandfather, who had been born in Ireland but who had emigrated to Ceylon in 1848, worked in the island, at first planting coffee, but when that crop failed, he stayed on in Ceylon and was appointed Police Magistrate of Dimbulla in the Central Province.

In 1910 my father was moved on promotion to Hong Kong where he was appointed Assistant Director of Public Works at the early age of 34. But unfortunately in 1914 at about the time when he was due to take over the directorship, his eyesight started to fail, and, at the same time, World War I broke out. This meant that passenger ships to England were prohibited from sailing owing to the presence in the Indian Ocean of German sea raiders, and it was not until 1917 that Churchill was able to return to England to consult a well-qualified eye surgeon. Alas! it was found that it was impossible to save his sight and he had no alternative but to retire from the Public Works Department of Hong Kong at the comparatively young age of 41. The family went to live in Crick Road, Oxford, and I and my two brothers went to the Dragon School.

After the Dragon School I went to Magdalen College School as a day-boy, but C. E. Brownrigg, the headmaster, asked me to become a boarder in 1925 'as his guest' and to become a prefect. This I did, and I remember my time at MCS as, to coin a phrase, some of the happiest days of my life.

I went to Sandhurst in 1926, passing in seventh out of an entry of 108 and gaining a scholarship, which meant that my father only had to pay my 'extras' while I was at the Royal Military College.

When I left Sandhurst in 1927, gaining the prize for Military History and passing out sixth, I joined the 2nd Battalion of the Manchester Regiment in Rangoon, Burma, in which unit my brother Jack was already serving. I remained in that country for three years, and the battalion moved to Maymyo in Upper Burma soon after I joined.

Life as a subaltern was pleasant and one was able to live on one's pay and enjoy oneself. Many officers kept horses, played polo and took part in paper-chases at the week-ends. But the major event which occurred soon after we left Burma in 1930, and were stationed in Secunderabad in the Deccan in southern India, was the outbreak of the Burma Rebellion.

In May 1930 the Commanding Officer and Adjutant departed to the Hills to inspect the Hill Detachment, and Major Charles Tuely took over temporary command of the battalion, while I became the acting adjutant. At 6.15 a.m. one Saturday morning I was riding on to the parade ground to dress the markers prior to the holding of a battalion parade, when I was surprised to see the brigade staff-car arriving at the orderly room at that early hour. I sent a runner over to find out what was the reason, and he quickly returned with a sealed envelope which contained, of all things, the order for the battalion to mobilize forthwith for active service in Burma!

Telegrams recalling officers and NCOs from leave and courses had to be despatched, and mobilisation equipment issued to the companies. The Commanding Officer and the adjutant hurried back from the Hills, and mobilisation was completed in a fortnight. My company, C Company, under the command of Major K. S. Torrance, was ordered to proceed in advance of the rest of the battalion, and we left Secunderabad by train for Calcutta on 6th June 1930, right in the middle of the hot weather.

The reason why these orders were so suddenly despatched was that the inhabitants of a large part of the Irrawaddy valley in Burma were in open rebellion. Rebellion in Burma was not unknown, but the history of Burma under the British crown had not, on the whole, been an unhappy one. The native aristocracy certainly lost some of the status that they enjoyed under pure native rule, but the great commercial enterprise of the European colonists and settlers enriched the whole country, and some part of the wealth that was acquired by the rising trade increased the revenues of the upper and middle classes of the population.

An overwhelming proportion of the people were, however, peasants, who lived in villages that clustered together in the great alluvial valleys, and to them the benefits of British rule were not so apparent. Under the *pax Britannica* they enjoyed regular, moderate taxation, which was a great improvement upon the capricious levies that Eastern princes imposed on their subjects; but in the year 1930, all the evils of native rule were forgotten, and among the peasants the government of the old native princes was talked of in a legendary way, as a period of great splendour. Also, it is doubtful whether the peasant farmers were easier or more comfortable under British rule than they had been before it, for they lived by selling the produce of land that had been so subdivided that farms were little more than plots. Populations living thus were, of necessity, poor, and this had been the structure of Burmese village society for countless generations.

In 1930 a number of influences were disturbing both the upper and lower strata of the Burmese people. First, which was the real starting point of all the subsequent trouble, the price of paddy was falling. As paddy was the principal crop, nine-tenths of the rural population were distressed and anxious, for small peasants simply could not build up reserve stocks, and only a few exceptionally favoured farmers could accumulate reserves of money. The disturbance was, moreover, not purely economic, for many Indian settlers in the country had acquired land, and they (because they had funds upon which they could draw) were actually underselling the Burmese in the falling market. The Indian settlers in the country aggravated the distress by lending money, at cruel rates of interest, to the impoverished villagers. In the towns, the presence of Indian competition was also felt by small tradesmen and native shopkeepers.

It was a further disturbing influence that the separation of India from England was being canvassed throughout the East, and that the reports of the commissions that were preparing the way for the new order in India were read and studied in the Burmese towns. Distorted versions of all this reached the peasant population, who interpreted what they heard as an indication that the British Empire was at last crumbling. Political influences were thus operating amongst a population that was severely harassed by distress and low prices.

We had learned in our previous three years in Burma that the people had many engaging qualities. In ordinary times they were friendly, cheerful and obliging. But these good points were offset by great weaknesses. The mass of the population, though nominally Buddhist, had never understood (and far less digested) the mild, philosophic doctrines of their religion, and were saturated with superstition. In addition, they could be excitable, and when excited, quarrelsome and vindictive. Feuds, murder for injuries, and murder for revenge, were so well-sanctioned by custom that the police hardly attempted to bring the miscreants to justice.

There had arisen to some prominence at this time a Burman called Saya San who was proud of his race and who kindled rebellion in distant villages, setting himself up as the leader. It was said that he hoped to become King of Burma, and he was certainly endowed with great abilities, for when he raised the flag of rebellion in the Tharawaddy district (75 miles north of Rangoon) he was at the head of a considerable force which he had raised in secret by persuading the village headmen to support and assist him, and by setting up a network of chairmen and assistant chairmen, who supplied all rebel gangs with food, collected and transmitted news of the British forces, and kept all informers under observation. His levies were equipped with such arms as could be collected (mostly breech-loading guns and fighting swords called dahs) and with magic handkerchiefs and charms for deflecting rifle bullets from their point of aim. By December 1930, considerable areas in the Tharawaddy district were virtually under the control of the native rebels.

When my company arrived in Calcutta, the temperature was over 110 degrees Fahrenheit in the shade. We had to wait for several hours until the evening, when we were due to embark in the docks for Rangoon. Walter Venour, one of the other subalterns in my company, and I spent most of the time in a galvanised tin tub full of cold water under a fan in the barrack-room to which we had been allotted, trying to keep cool.

In the evening the officers were invited to have drinks at Flagstaff House with the District Commander of Calcutta. He had a tremendous reputation for irascibility which had spread throughout the army. When commanding in the West Indies it was said that on one occasion his terrified ADC knocked on his study door to deliver some urgent message. On receiving no reply, he knocked again, but more loudly – this time to be greeted by an earsplitting roar, '*Come in*, you bloody woodpecker.' I was all agog to meet this formidable officer, but he turned out to be the soul of hospitality and helpfulness, and lent us his staff car to perform various duties before we fell in with the troops, and marched to the docks, and embarked.

On arrival at Rangoon after a restful voyage on a comfortable packet-boat we were told that the battalion was to be based on the ancient capital of Mandalay, with company detachments at Meiktila and Schwebo. C Company was to be with headquarters at Mandalay, but it was to find a detachment of two platoons at Toungoo, under

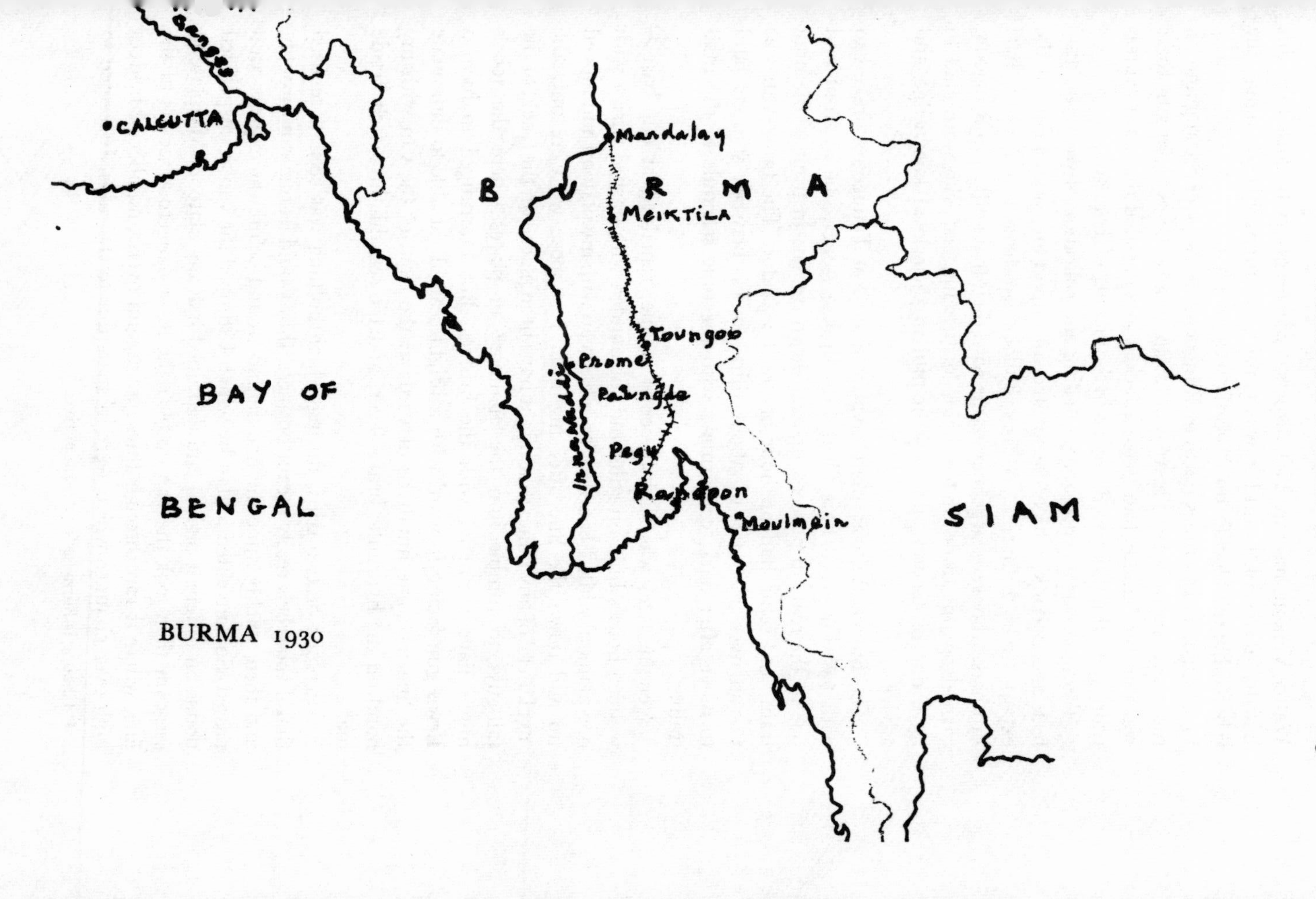
CALCUTTA
Ganges
Mandalay
B U R M A
MEIKTILA
Toungoo
Prome
Paungde
Pegu
Rangoon
Moulmein
S I A M
BAY OF
BENGAL

BURMA 1930

Walter Venour and me. This dispersal was necessary because the rains had by now broken, and it was considered impossible to engage the rebels other than locally until the dry weather set in.

Toungoo is 150 miles north of Rangoon, on the river Sittang and on the main-line railway. The reason for stationing the two platoons there was that the bandits had twice attacked and derailed the main express train from Mandalay to Rangoon in the vicinity of Toungoo.

Toungoo was a centre for the felling and collection of wood, notably teak and padauk, which constituted an important component of the export trade of Burma. Messrs Bullock Brothers and Messrs Steel Brothers, who were large merchants with their main offices in Rangoon, carried on this trade under senior local managers, who were glad to have our protection and very helpful in their local knowledge and advice.

The Burma Railway made available to us at Toungoo a brake-van with two low-sided flats filled with broken stones, one in front and one at the rear, to proceed up and down the line in front of the mail train, and some half an hour before it was due. The brake-van was to run over a stretch of about thirty miles, between stations, and to move after dark, conforming with the time schedule of the mail train.

Venour, who was slightly senior to me, remained at our base – wooden houses built on stilts and surrounded with barbed wire – with one platoon, while I boarded the brake-van with my platoon and moved up and down the line after nightfall. I suppose we were only the 'exploders' of any mines that might have been placed on the track, or the fall-guys to tumble into the chaungs* in places where the rebels might have tampered with the bridges. But I arranged to have a Lewis gun facing forward with a bright searchlight able to illuminate the line for some hundreds of yards at the front of the van with my hand on the hydraulic brake lever, and the searchlight switch beside me.

After one or two trips, during which nothing was seen, I realised that if the rebels really meant business, they would let our van through, and then quickly mine the line behind us and before the express train passed. So I invented a plan by which I stopped the van at unspecified points on different nights, and detrained half my platoon. My platoon sergeant then took the van on over the most dangerous sectors of the line, where it ran through thick jungle and over a number of bridges built over chaungs which were in spate due to the rains. It seemed to

*** Chaung is Burmese for stream or river.**

(*Right*) Alec and Nellie Churchill, the father and mother of the author – a photograph taken in the garden of their house on The Peak, Hong Kong, in about 1916, when Alec was Director of the Public Works Department on the Island (and also Adjutant of the Hong Kong Volunteer Corps).

(*Below left*) The author, aged 8, in Hong Kong

(*Below right*) The author, as a Gentleman Cadet at Sandhurst

(*Left*) Gwendolen Janie Williams in 1930. She and the author were married in 1934

(*Right*) The author after investiture at Buckingham Palace, 1930

me that if I then followed along the line on foot, I might catch the bandits removing the lines over one of the bridges with a view to derailing the train. The rain poured down in sheets – almost like a venetian blind – and the nights were very dark. Crossing the chaungs was difficult because there were gaps between the struts that supported the slippery rails, and it would have been very easy to fall through and land with a huge splash in the boiling rushing torrent which might easily result in drowning.

On one occasion I was leading my half-platoon over one such bridge when, to my dismay, I found a cow had slipped and was stuck in the middle of the line with all four feet sticking through the sleepers above the raging water fifteen feet below. The poor creature was very frightened and quite unable to move, so I called up my corporal who crawled towards me, and together we managed by superhuman effort to lift the creature and topple it over the side, into the torrent beneath. We then completed our patrol, and rejoined the van some five miles further on.

We never had the luck to catch any bandits, but during our time at Toungoo no trains were derailed, so I expect they were informed of our presence and decided not to operate in our vicinity. After two months, our two platoons were called in to Mandalay to rejoin Major Torrance and the remainder of C Company.

While we had been away, a platoon of our company went to a place called Lamaing because of reports of the presence of rebels in that area. It was thought that they were breaking southwards from the Shan States, where the steps taken by the authorities had made it too hot for them. Two platoons of D Company were ordered out to make a series of blocks along the Mandalay Canal, with C Company's platoon on their left flank.

The civil police then had a stroke of luck and arrested three men on a native bus who could give no account of themselves, and on investigation were found to be members of the major rebel Saya San's gang. One of these men consented to lead a party of military police to the rebel encampment. All posts were warned and manned, and then a party of military police, after a gruelling march of fifteen miles through the jungle, rushed the rebel camp at eight o'clock in the evening. Shots were exchanged, but owing to the darkness the rebels escaped, leaving behind their arms, documents and baggage. A few days later the rebels ran into a party of police operating in the hills to the north, and all were rushed and captured; Saya San himself was among them, and he was later tried, and executed.

The posts manned by the battalion on this occasion were part of a cordon which clearly prevented Saya San from breaking south, and contributed materially to his capture. The Burma Military Police were to make tangible recognition of this later when they presented to the officers' mess of the battalion a handsome silver *Chin-the* (the fantastic lion-dog monster which guards all Burmese temples) acquired with part of the prize money awarded for capturing Saya San.

After two months in Mandalay, my company was moved with Battalion Headquarters and D Company to Meiktila; but in early November Kenneth Torrance and C Company moved to Paukkaung, and I was sent to establish a detachment with my platoon at a place called Hmattaing, some 30 miles across country to the south. I was only too glad to be on my own.

Hmattaing was situated in a large alluvial plain lying to the east of the Irrawaddy, with Prome, some fifteen miles away on the banks of the river, as the largest town in my vicinity. Hmattaing was a small village with perhaps thirty or forty wooden houses, surrounded with paddyfields and with a broad chaung, the Wegyi chaung, flowing through it. My nearest military neighbours were a platoon of the 17th Dogra Regiment in the plain towards Prome, and a platoon of the same regiment in the hills about ten miles north-east of my post. The rebels had been active in the district, attacking villages and holding the headmen to ransom. If they were denied the food and money they demanded, the village's crops were set alight and the headman was killed. The leader of the gang was a Burman called Boh* Po Hla Gyi, a man said to be unusually tall for a Burman, and with a closely cropped head.

This man had been inciting the peasants in the hill villages to join the rebel cause, and in due course the contagion spread to the more numerous villages in the plain, many of which were situated on the banks of the Wegyi chaung. My job was to establish my platoon in a firm base at Hmattaing, and then to follow up any information which I obtained from the local civil and police authorities in the hope of catching Po Hla Gyi, or at any rate some members of his gang, unawares, in one or other of the villages in my vicinity.

I arrived from Prome by rail at a place called Paungde, a large village, where the platoon detrained. I was met by the Sub-Divisional Officer, a Burman in his late thirties called U Maung Maung, who was immaculately dressed in European-style white drill, and a white topee. He told me that Hmattaing was nine miles distant by road. There was

* The prefix *Boh* means leader in Burmese.

also present a senior inspector of police, one Hla Gyaw, a tall Indo-Burman who spoke good English and wore a khaki shirt and shorts, dark blue puttees, brown boots and a sort of floppy-brimmed boy scout's hat. These two officials were to be of the greatest help to me in the days ahead, keeping me well informed of the local news about Po Hla Gyi's movements, and frequently accompanying the platoon on its marches.

I asked U Maung Maung to arrange for the delivery of two letters which I then and there sat down and wrote, one to Subedar Wazir Singh who commanded the Dogra platoon in the plain near Paungde, and the other to Lieutenant 'Lakri'* Woods, who was the platoon commander of the Dogra platoon in the hills near Ngapaw – my two nearest neighbours. In these letters I asked them to keep me informed of their movements if they were likely to operate by night on the boundaries between their areas and mine.

I then fell the platoon in, with the followers and the mules, and marched the nine miles along the dusty but shady road to Hmattaing where we established ourselves in a dak bungalow† which was beside the Paungde road, and backed on to the Wegyi chaung. It was a wooden building on stilts, with a verandah and two large rooms upstairs, and of course nothing downstairs except a concrete floor. There were a number of trees that grew in the compound and beyond, and I set the platoon to construct a wide apron fence of barbed wire all round, with one gate only, also wired, on the road. I took some trouble to have any branches of trees which overhung the wire lopped off. I then got the men to pitch their tents on one side of the compound, and included a hospital tent, a cookhouse tent, and a tent for the Indian mule-drivers. The mules were tethered to posts at the opposite side of the compound.

I used the concrete floor under my post as the dining hall for the men, and set up trestle tables and chairs there. I issued written standing orders for the post, putting all native houses out of bounds and including shops, temples, pagodas and the police station and compound, but allowing the men to walk out in parties of not less than three, from the well from which we drew water on the south, to the well beside a Buddhist shrine on the north-east. Dress was laid down as topee, khaki shirt and shorts, puttees and boots and side arms, with khaki drill trousers and forage cap after Retreat at 6 p.m.

* *Lakri*, the word meaning wood in Urdu, is the inevitable nickname for people with such a surname.

† A Government rest-house.

A guard was mounted each evening at 5 p.m. opposite the flag-staff in the compound, the riflemen armed with twenty rounds, and revolver men with six rounds. The sentry's beat extended for twenty paces along the road in front of the gate, but from Retreat until Reveille (at 5.30 a.m.) the gate was closed and the sentry's post was inside the perimeter; and he was required to patrol the compound at least once every hour.

My platoon consisted of 28 NCOs and men, with an Anglo-Indian assistant-surgeon with a British and an Indian medical orderly; two Indian Army Service Corps mule-drivers; an Indian cook; an Indian fire-boy; an Indian water-carrier and an Indian sweeper; six contractor's followers; one Lewis gun mule, and six pack-mules – all attached to my platoon.

We spent the whole of the day after our arrival settling in. The weather was agreeable, with the temperature during the day in the high nineties (Fahrenheit), but the nights pleasantly cool. Everywhere in the plain the roads carried a coating of dust two or three inches deep, and away from the roads one had to walk on paddy-bunds two or three feet wide and often very slippery, with a several foot drop on either side into water or deep mud in which the paddy was cultivated. One was consequently continually breaking one's step, and marches of over ten miles became tiring, particularly for men who were carrying heavy loads or leading mules.

On my first operation, carried out on our second day, we visited six villages and covered seventeen miles, starting at 7 a.m. and returning at 2 p.m. The march was hard going, mostly on paddy-bunds, but for some three miles we traversed jungle-covered foothills. All the village headmen denied any knowledge of rebels. At the Buddhist temple at Shwe-Kyaung-Zaung the hpongi* professed no knowledge of a rebel meeting that took place, according to the police, at his kyaung, but on being pressed he admitted that about 100 rebels passed through about a month and a half previously.

At Kwingyi village, one of my men noticed a Burman throw something into the paddy as we entered the village. This object was found to be a fighting dah†, so we searched the house of its owner and found one dagger. We brought the man back with us and handed him over to the police. On returning to my post I found an answer to my letter to Woods at Ngapaw giving me information of rebel movements in his area.

* Chief priest.

† A Burmese sword with a flat end, the blade one-sided and wedge-shaped.

On the evening of the following day I received information from the Deputy Superintendent of police at Paungde that Po Hla Gyi had slept two nights previously at the house of one Maung Kala in the village of Kange, and that his two sons were with him. I decided to surround the village the same night, and sent a message to the subedar of the Dogra platoon asking him to line the banks of the Wegyi chaung which bordered the village's western exits.

We marched at 2 a.m. and were in position round the village two hours later. My men were disposed in groups of three at intervals of about two hundred yards in the paddy and facing inwards towards the village and about fifty yards from its edge. The men had strict orders never to fire inwards, as there had been several instances of bullets passing through a village and hitting a soldier in a post on the far side. When daylight came, the groups closed in to the edge of the village, and stayed there until the search of the houses was over.

On this occasion a gong sounded from one of the hpongyi kyaungs in the village while we were approaching, and again shortly after we had arrived. At dawn we searched the house where Po Hla Gyi was supposed to have slept, together with other houses pointed out by the police. Eight listed rebels were arrested, but there was no sign of the rebel leader or his sons. Fresh tattoo marks were found on all the rebels arrested, and in the house where Po Hla Gyi had slept we found a fighting dah with bloodstains which were verified by the medical officer with the Dogra platoon. Gurkha-style hats were also found, and this could have been significant because the rebel gang which raided a village in the vicinity three days earlier and killed an inhabitant, were all wearing such hats. Both the Dogra subedar and I were convinced that the sounding of gongs by the ponghis was probably some sort of signal, particularly as all the priests strenuously denied such action. We marched back to Hmattaing, and arrived at half past ten in the morning.

For the next two days I remained at my post writing reports and having conferences with the police and political officers. A company of Madras Sappers and Miners passed through Hmattaing on their way to a village in the hills where they were going to make a road to Ngapaw, the village where Woods's platoon was located. I agreed to use my lorry to collect their rations from Paungde.

It was now 25th November, and I had been at Hmattaing for a week. My men were fit and liking our interesting role, and we seemed to have established a workable routine whereby our rations arrived punctually at two-day intervals, and our messing, though not brilliant, was tolerable and wholesome.

Lakri Woods came in to my post to arrange for a new interpreter, and I took the opportunity to discuss with him a project which had been formulating in my mind. I felt it would be wise to search the mountain villages in the areas adjacent to his post, because I guessed that it was in these lonely hamlets, situated on the banks of the upper Wegyi chaung and its tributaries that Po Hla Gyi planned his operations. It was, I was sure, essential to keep him and the members of his gang, continually under pressure, and unable to stay for more than a night or two in one place.

The villages I had in mind, being on the banks of chaungs, were really too big to be properly surrounded at night by only one platoon, and I suggested to Woods that we should carry out some joint operations, like the one I had recently carried out with Subedar Wazir Singh, in the plain. I told him that I intended to be away from Hmattaing for several days so as to be able to cover quite a large area of territory. He readily agreed, and I said I would put the idea to the area commander, Lieutenant-Colonel Malet, who had told me that he intended to pay me a visit the following day.

Woods then set out on his return journey to Ngapaw, and I was about to have my evening meal and turn in when the Police Superintending Officer of Hmattaing arrived to say a police informer had just come to the station to report that Po Hla Gyi and his lieutenants Po Htwa and Ohn Nyun slept the previous night at Ywathitkyi and would sleep again at this village tonight. I decided to set out at a quarter past ten after the moon had risen with a column of 22 men and five policemen.

I arrived at the village after an hour's march. The head policeman pointed out three houses where Po Hla Gyi and his friends would be sleeping, and we dashed in, surrounded them, and searched them. There was no sign of the wanted rebels. However, Po Htwa's brother and also his brother-in-law were in one of the houses, and although they admitted that Po Hla Gyi had slept there the previous night, they professed not to know where he had gone. Two large cross-bows were discovered in one of the houses, together with 25 arrows, and a fighting dah. I arrested Po Htwa's relatives, and brought them back to Hmattaing and handed them over to the police. It was two in the morning when we returned, so we all went to bed.

When Colonel Malet arrived the next morning I put my plan for a five-day march with Woods's platoon in the mountains to him, and he agreed, provided I left ten men under a NCO in my post during my absence. I arranged for this, and issued orders for a start at 6 a.m. the following day, taking the mules to carry our kit and six days' hard rations.

CHAPTER TWO

Po Hla Gyi

After Reveille at 5 we duly set out an hour later before it got hot, and were soon climbing up a hilly track between bamboo bushes on our way to Gnapaw. When the country was open I generally put out advanced and flank guards of two men, as I was moving in an area which I did not know and against an enemy, however isolated or numerically inferior he might be, whom I had not yet met; and though some might think such precautions were unnecessary, I was not prepared to take risks.

The rebels, of course, were greatly under-armed, compared with us. Their normal weapons were stolen shotguns and some rifles, dahs and daggers. But they might be encountered when they least expected it, and when their situation might be desperate; and having this belief in charms as a protection against bullets, they might act in a foolhardy manner which, though it might have fatal consequences for them, might involve us in casualties by the surprising nature of their actions. They, of course, knew the countryside like the back of their hands, and here they had a major military advantage over us.

We arrived at Gnapaw at noon to find that Lakri Woods and his platoon were away on an operation, but they returned two hours later to their base. Lakri had collected a party of Chin Levies,* under their own officer, and our plan was for our two platoons and the Chins to march that night to surround the village of Pyangyidet where, it was said, Boh Nga Pyu occasionally returned to sleep; and if we didn't catch him, at least some of his gang might be found.

During the march, which the Chin Levies led, with my platoon in the middle and the Dogras in the rear, we passed through a village where the lesser wife of Nga Pyu lived, but we found her house deserted. Continuing, our march was delayed for more than an hour owing to three mistakes on the part of the guides of the column. But by doubling the rate of march for the last three miles, Pyangyidet was surrounded as the first light of dawn appeared. My platoon covered the western exits,

* An irregular force recruited from the Chin tribe in Northern Burma, by the Government of Burma.

the Dogras the northern and north-eastern faces, and the Chin Levies covered the south.

The pre-arranged signal for the completion of the encirclement was fired, and almost immediately a volley rang out from the south and south-western corner of the village. This turned out to be rifle fire from my Manchester platoon, and shotgun fire from the Chin Levies. The latter were firing at a Burman, who was killed, and the former at a man wearing a red lunghi* who was crawling in the long grass some distance to the right of the post, who suffered a like fate. One of them came from a nearby village and had been concerned in the recent attack on Padigon, while the other was a known wanted rebel.

On searching the village houses we found a charm handkerchief and a fighting dah, and we arrested three men – one the owner of the handkerchief, one who had also taken part in the Padigon attack, and one who was an absconder from another village. After prolonged interrogation, these three men divulged the name of six rebels who came from Letpangon, a village which we were intending to visit later on our march, and I noted that two of the six were brothers named Nga Tin and Nga Chaik whose parents lived at Letpangon. We were also given the names of fifteen other rebels, and the three villages from which they came.

The house-to-house search was finished at noon, and we spent the rest of the day, and the night, in the hpongi-kyaung in the village. Both platoons were tired, but the Chin Levies, not having been operating continuously for several days as we had, were fresh and energetic, so I detailed the night guards from among their number.

Next day we marched at sunrise and arrived five hours later at Thitpok, which we surrounded. Here, in the house of a doctor, we found many charms, scratched on fragments of hpongi bowls, slate and pottery, bottles of a variety of coloured inks and three books containing drawings of various charm designs, with descriptions in Burmese. These books I handed over to Woods as he was returning to Gnapaw the same day, so that they could be sent as soon as possible to Prome. In addition to this literature there was a number of books containing charms for evading illnesses and for obtaining wishes, but as they were not connected with the rebel cause, they were not confiscated. The doctor concerned was said to be absent from the village but no great distance away, so I sent some villagers to bring him in; but as they had not returned by early afternoon, I could delay no longer, and resumed my march. I learned later that he had already been arrested

* The wrap-around 'dress' which male Burmese wear.

once by Woods a fortnight previously, but as his charm industry was not then known about, he had been released. The police finally caught him a week later.

We also found a diary giving the names of five rebels and the four villages from which they came. Two of the names confirmed the statement of the men arrested at Pyangyidet. Daggers, dahs and spears were found and confiscated, and I found that many men were absent from the village. The thugyi* had gone to Prome at the summons of the District Commissioner, and the ten-house gaung was unable or unwilling to furnish any information about the rebels.

Lieutenant Woods and his platoon returned to their post taking the Chin Levies with them. I liked very much what I had seen of the Dogras, and they reinforced the impressions I had formed of Subedar Wazir Singh's men when operating with them on the plain. They were very alert and smart, very responsive to their NCOs, and capable of fast marching, and even running, for considerable distances carrying their equipment. They always wore gymshoes with puttees when on the march, so that they were both quick and silent. Otherwise, they wore a khaki turban, a drill tunic and shorts.

I continued my march soon after our mid-day meal. The path ran through dense bamboo jungle, sometimes interspersed with teak trees. A rebel gang could have hidden within fifty yards of the path with the greatest of ease and not have been detected by the platoon on the path. I experienced great difficulty in getting my nine mules across the numerous chaungs which crossed the route, since they were all very steep-sided, and the footpath was often carried across them on a two-plank bridge, sometimes with a drop of as much as 40 feet to the chaung below.

After three hours we arrived at Letpangon in the early afternoon. On a check being made of the inhabitants, I again found that a large number of men were absent. The ten-house gaung said that he was afraid of his villagers, who were all hostile to him and refused to obey him. He said that at night he hid in the jungle to avoid being murdered.

None of the rebels whose names had been given to me at Pyangyidet were present in the village, but I did arrest Po Kha, the father of the two brothers Nga Tin and Nga Chaik, whom I mentioned earlier. His wife wept bitterly at my decision and said that if I released her husband, she would promise to make her sons surrender to me in the next few days. I said that when her sons gave themselves up, I would release

* Headman.

her husband. She said she did not know where they were, but would try to find out.

I left Letpangon in the late afternoon and made for Kaingwin where I intended to spend the night, but as I had to pass through another village on the way, I assembled the people there and searched the houses, though without finding anything of interest or learning any useful information. I continued on to our destination, arriving after dark, but before settling down for the night I collected all the men and questioned them, and searched the houses. There were nine or ten men absent, but nothing else of interest, so I took over the forest bungalow and told my men to doss down in the rooms and on the open space down below, and they quickly spread their blankets and got to sleep. It had been a long day.

Next morning we were away by six o'clock having had a breakfast of boiled eggs (which we collected from the villagers, and paid for) and a brew-up of tea with powdered milk. We marched eleven miles to a village called Gyogon where we halted and carried out the usual check, but without useful results, and then continued on for seven more miles until we reached Theingon, where we spent the night in the adjacent paddyfields. I was not surprised to find that the headman had absconded since his name had been given to me as a rebel by the informers at Pyangyidet; but I arrested his nephew.

On the following day we had a march of fourteen miles to bring us back to Woods's base at Gnapaw, and we passed through four villages, making one arrest at one of them. By this time we had quite a squad of arrested men who had to be guarded on the march, and at night. We arrived at our destination at noon, and spent the rest of the day relaxing. The next day we marched back to Hmattaing, it being downhill nearly all the way. We had been marching for six days, and had slept away from our post on five nights. We had covered about 60 miles, but we had had no sickness or foot trouble, though three mules had developed slight girth-galls. We all felt we were getting to know the dimensions of our problem, as well as the countryside in which we had to operate and the people with whom we were dealing.

My chief concern as regards the efficiency and comfort of my men was to obtain a plentiful supply of boots of various sizes from the headquarters at Prome. We were covering a big mileage, and were frequently getting our boots entirely immersed in water, either in wading through chaungs, or slipping off bunds into wet paddyfields. The result was that many of the boots started to break up, the soles tore away from the uppers and the leather split open at the creases.

My platoon and I rested in our post at Hmattaing for the next two days, devoting the time to 'make-and-mend', washing our shirts, uniform and socks, and thoroughly cleaning our weapons. But our rest period was not to be long. At 5 p.m. on the second day the sub-divisional officer from Paungde came to see me to say that he had been appointed Civil Officer to Hmattaing, and in the course of our conversation he asked me if I contemplated operating the following day. I said I did, but had no particular place I wished to visit. He suggested that I should go to Sanainggon village in order to arrest one Gna Kyauk who was suspected of harbouring rebels, and also that I should visit Shabyugon village to arrest the mother-in-law of Aung Sa, Po Hla Gyi's son.

As there did not seem to be any undue urgency, I decided to leave Hmattaing in the small hours of the next morning. We duly marched at 2.30 a.m. and had surrounded Sanainggon by 4 a.m. I myself was in a post with two men at the south-western corner of the village, in tall grass about ten yards from a gate in the stockade which surrounded the village. There was a moon, but it was frequently obscured by thin clouds.

We had been in position about an hour when I heard the gate creak and two men appeared, only dimly visible, wrapped in blankets, and one of them was tall with a closely cropped head. They peered intently at the fields as if trying to decide whether to run from the village. I was holding my revolver in the aim in my right hand and was on the point of pressing the trigger when I realised that if I fired my shots might endanger my southerly post at the far side of the village. So I flashed my torch, knowing that they would either shrink back inside the village (where I could find them next morning), or make a bolt for it into the fields, in which case I could safely open fire. They chose the former alternative. It was the only time I was to have Po Hla Gyi in my sights.

A matter of minutes later volleys of rapid fire rang out from the north-western post of my platoon. They sounded very loud in the stillness of the early morning, and I longed to run to the scene of the shooting, some six or seven hundred yards away on the other side of the village, but I had issued strict instructions that posts were not to move, once posted, until dawn broke. So I possessed my soul in patience as best I could until it was sufficiently light to permit a search. I entered the village and arrested Gna Kyauk, who tried to get away through a hedge. He seemed frightened, and admitted harbouring four rebels that very night, saying that one of them was Maung* Po Hla [sic]. I collected all the males and put a guard on them, and then went to my

* *Maung* means Mister.

north-westerly post, where I found that four men had run from the village across their front, of whom one was killed instantly, a second fell, stumbled for a few yards and fell again, and then ran out of sight behind the scrub-jungle which covered the area north of Sanainggon, some ten yards behind his two remaining companions. They fired three times at my post, but the shots were heard to pass overhead.

We searched the scrub area into which the rebels had disappeared for over an hour with every available man, but could find no trace of them. Leaving Sergeant Middleton, my platoon sergeant, to continue the search, and also to arrest Ma Min Thin at Shabyugon village, I took the dead man in to Paungde to be identified by the police. He turned out to be Maung Myin, son of Po Man of Wegye village, and known to be a member of Po Hla Gyi's gang. While in Paungde I sent messages to Subedar Wazir Singh asking for his cooperation in the search, and I also signalled Area Headquarters in Prome asking for a platoon with which to continue operations that night.

Before I returned to my platoon in the fields the police brought me the news that a member of the Paungde Defence Force had been brutally murdered at half past eight that morning at a village about three miles from Sanainggon by three men, who had taken his double-barrelled shotgun and 25 rounds of ammunition. They had murdered the wretched man by severing his leg with one slash of a dah and then leaving him to bleed to death. There seemed little doubt that the murderers were the men we had fired at earlier that morning.

I returned to the scene of the search in the early afternoon, and interviewed the villagers of Sanainggon. It transpired that the four men were Po Hla Gyi, his son Aung Sa, the dead man Maung Myin and another who was thought to be Po Hla Gyi's younger son Nga Aye. All four had slept at Nga Kyauk's house. They had with them two local-made guns, and their intention in visiting the village was to collect money.

I returned with my platoon to Hmattaing in the evening, to find that another platoon of my regiment, and one platoon of Dogras, both from Prome, had arrived in response to my signals from Paungde. So I called a conference with the civil and police officials, and they gave it as their opinion that Po Hla Gyi and his two henchmen would have run on *either* to Shan That, where they committed the murder described above, and then would have gone on to the village of Ywathitkyi to spend the night, *or* would spend the night in the hpongi-kyaung at Shwe Kyaung Zaung. I therefore decided to send the Manchester platoon under its officer, Lieutenant Bob Palk, to Ywathitkyi, and to take the Dogra platoon myself under its subedar to the hpongi-kyaung, as I already knew the route and the hill on which it was situated. I decided to let my own platoon rest for the night in Hmattaing.

The Dogras and I marched out after midnight, and we were in position round the hpongi-kyaung about 4 a.m. At daylight I made the usual search and found a wealth of charms, swords and dahs, but no sign of the wanted rebel leader. The other platoon had had no better luck.

The following night I organised another search with *three* platoons – Lieutenant Wallace's and Subedar Wazir Singh's Dogra platoons, and my own, which had had a good night's sleep. We surrounded Wegyi village where we thought we might find Po Hla Gyi – but once again drew a blank. We got back to Hmattaing weary and a little discouraged at noon on 5th December; but it had become a point of honour amongst us that we must get Po Hla Gyi, and the fact that at last we had caught up with him and had exchanged shots, spurred us on in our efforts, however frustrating the process might be.

It would be tedious to relate all the marches and operations that my platoon and I undertook, sometimes augmented in strength by neighbouring platoons, over the next two months. The pattern of our activities followed very much those that I have already described. In 56 days we carried out 31 operations, and on four occasions we had no less than nine platoons involved. Coordinations of such a large number of units from different regiments was quite a complicated exercise.

From the reports that I received from the police and the civil authorities it seemed that Po Hla Gyi was wandering from village to village in the plain between the foothills and the Prome–Rangoon railway line. But when I made an analysis of the various reports that we had received concerning the rebel's movements over a period of thirty days, I found that they were so conflicting as to lead to the conclusion that he was lodging false information with the police by his friends and agents. His arm was long and his vengeance was implacable, and for this reason he recruited many individuals who performed his bidding out of fear of the consequences of disobedience. But at the same time he was undoubtedly generating much illwill amongst the villagers who blamed him for all the discomfort that they were compelled to suffer, and who had no desire to prolong a rebellion which evidently had long since failed. After a month of fruitless searching, I was inclined to think that our hero had left the district. But I never felt justified in *not* following up information, however improbable it seemed, and however much disappointment it might entail.

In the event, the end came unexpectedly and suddenly. Early one morning, an inhabitant from the village of Myo Gyi, which lies in paddyfields about seven miles south of Hmattaing, was bringing in his cattle to be milked and watered, when he saw three men sleeping under a tree. Now, Myo Gyi had an exceptionally able headman called U Po Shin who ran his village with great efficiency. I had visited the village a number of times, and had always been impressed at the authority which he exercised over his villagers. The inhabitant left his cattle and ran at once to U Po Shin in the village and told him that he thought he recognised Po Hla Gyi and two men asleep in the fields. U Po Shin, who was as keen as anyone to destroy the rebel and return to a normal way of life, armed eight of his villagers with guns, and eleven with dahs, and set out with them, but not before he had despatched an inhabitant to commandeer transport and inform me at Hmattaing of this latest development.

The men who had been asleep beneath the tree were thoroughly aroused by the time the villagers approached them, and immediately opened fire. Likewise the villagers. The rebels fled, but one was wounded and fell. He was assisted for about two hundred yards by the other two, but he made a sign to them to leave him, and run. This they did, leaving the wounded man. The villagers fell upon him, and slashed him to death with their dahs. He was Po Hla Gyi.

My platoon arrived on the scene about three-quarters of an hour after he had been killed. We followed the direction in which the two men had disappeared, and we continued the search all night. One of the two bandits gave himself up to a hpongi because his feet were torn and bleeding from his headlong flight, and the hpongi brought him to me. He was exhausted, frightened, and could no longer walk. He told me the third man was Maung Aye, Po Hla Gyi's son.

The rebel for whom we had searched for so long, and who finally had been killed by the villagers of Myo Gyi was a tall light-skinned Burman with a spare figure. He was in his late thirties, with a clean-shaven face and head, and even in death his countenance was calm and rather noble.

With the death of Po Hla Gyi, my platoon's role at Hmattaing had come to an end. Over forty gang-leaders were in prison, and the incessant harrying of the rebels that had been going on for over twelve months, coupled with the rebels' losses in killed and captured, had virtually put an end to the rebellion. I was recalled to Battalion Headquarters, at Meiktila, to take over the duties of adjutant; and so ended my first experience of active service.

CHAPTER THREE

Evidence in Camera

As soon as the rebellion in Burma had been brought under control, we were moved back to India. I was confirmed in the appointment of adjutant and almost immediately had to start preparing the regiment's move to Khartoum in the Sudan, which was going to be our next station for one year, before returning to England.

In due course we moved – another move by sea on board a troopship – and arrived at Port Sudan on the Red Sea. Thence we moved by rail to Khartoum where we established our headquarters and two companies, having dropped off one company in the Red Sea Hills at a place called Gebeit, and another company at the railway junction at Atbara. A third company had remained on board the trooper and disembarked at Cyprus.

It will be seen that the battalion was severely split up, the detachments being respectively 400, 200 and 1,300 miles distant from headquarters. This dispersion, added to the knowledge that we were only to be in our new locations for a year, disposed everyone to regard them merely as a stepping-stone to England, Home and Beauty. However, the officers and men contrived to enjoy their short stay. Those at Khartoum had the amenities of a town including cinemas and Greek-owned shops; Atbara possessed a large railway population which was very keen on sport; while Gebeit, though far more isolated a station than any of the others, was much cooler in view of its altitude in the Red Sea Hills. The Cyprus company enjoyed, of course, all the advantages of a Mediterranean island.

The memory of General Gordon* was still kept very green in Khartoum, and at a garden-party given by the Governor-General which I attended in the grounds at the Palace, there were also present a number of Egyptian and Sudanese officials who had served with General Gordon during the siege. His servant, an old man, was still employed at the Palace, and his river steamer, her decks still barricaded with railway sleepers, lay at her moorings in the Nile.

The unit we relieved was the Coldstream Guards, which rather

* Gordon was murdered on the steps of the Palace in 1885.

ght) The author on the bank of Wegyi chaung

(*Below*) Hmattaing Post

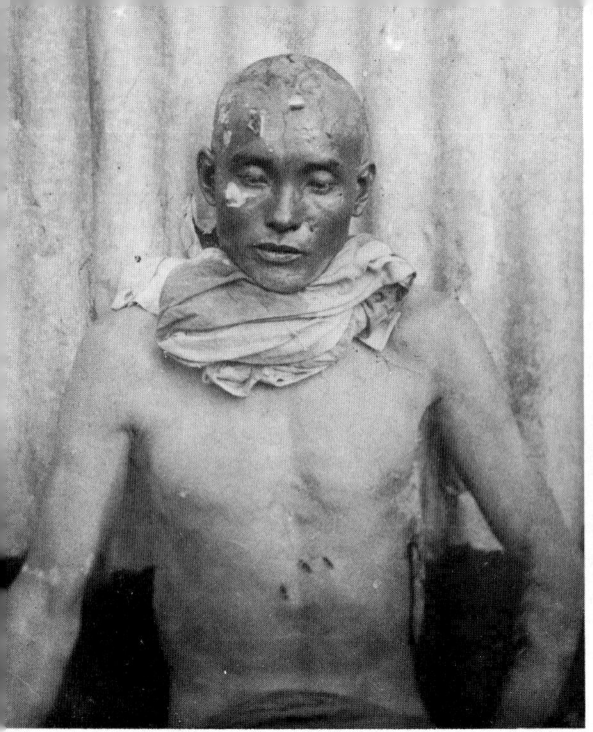

(*Left*) Po Hla Gyi – posthumous photograph (*Right*) U Po Shin, Headman of Myo Gyi Village

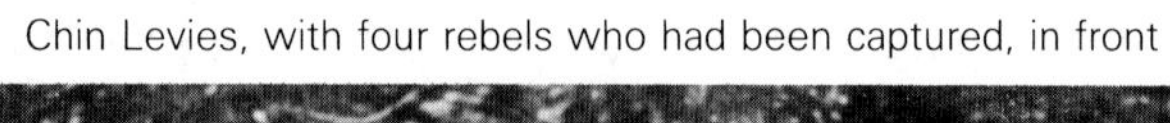

Chin Levies, with four rebels who had been captured, in front

exceptionally had been sent on two years' foreign service from their normal employment of finding guards and 'Public Duties' in London. The Guards are a wonderful body of men, and I yield to no one in my admiration for them. They observe the highest possible standards of discipline and turn-out, and they have maintained a peerless record on active service in all of England's wars. But being unused to foreign service at regular intervals, the Coldstream had to adopt ad hoc remedies to meet novel experiences. I learnt that their regimental funds were not as flush as those of most line infantry regiments, and when, for instance, they wanted to give their men a break from military duties in the dry heat of Khartoum, the officers put their hands in their pockets and paid for river steamer trips down the Nile.

When I was settling down in the adjutant's office in Khartoum, I found a bundle of papers in a drawer of my desk. It was the rough draft, written in my predecessor's hand, of a Summary of Evidence against a corporal who was being court-martialled for using obscene and threatening language to an officer. When describing the language used, I found the main offending word was genteelly spelt 'Phuck!'

But to return to Khartoum, where the battalion's tour of duty had come to an end. It was December, and we moved by troopship to Southampton, spending Christmas Day at sea. Three days later we disembarked, and moved by train to Strensall in Yorkshire, where we were accommodated in a hutted camp. We all felt the cold very much at first, but we soon settled down, and the more horsey of the officers enjoyed hunting with the Middleton, who on one occasion met at the Mess. I was soon summoned to an Investiture to receive the Military Cross which I had won in Burma. There in the drawing-rooms of Buckingham Palace I met Lakri Woods again. He was receiving the MBE, and we had a great re-union before we were shepherded off into our respective 'pens'.

When King George V hung my MC on the little hook which an attendant had previously stuck in my tunic (I was wearing scarlet full-dress) he asked me in his guttural voice, 'Where did you get it?' and I replied, 'In Burma, sir.' That was the extent of our mutual communication, though he nodded his head at my answer. Then we processed, still in single file, out of the Throne Room and into a corridor where there was a counter, and another attendant. This individual unhooked my decoration, put it in a purple leather case which he handed to me, pulled the little hook out of my tunic and said, 'Cor! Don't see many of these things nowadays! Was a time durin' the war when they was two a penny!'

When I had been on leave from India three years previously, I had become engaged to Gwendolen Janie Williams, the sister of Tony Williams who was a friend of Jack's and mine and the daughter of Dr Lewis Williams of Ferryside, South Wales. In 1934 we were married at St Peter's, Cranley Gardens in London, and Jack was my best man. My younger brother, Buster, and many of my brother-officers were there in uniform, and they formed an arch of swords outside the porch of the church.

One of the snags of returning from foreign service was that the officers were not versed in current tactical theories and were also unused to working with modern tanks and support from the air. A battalion taking part in its first annual field training in England was therefore liable to be caught out by these new-fangled practices, and officers were in consequence sent on courses whenever vacancies could be obtained, to bring themselves up to date. My colonel, Reggie Parminter, had heard that during field training units were liable to be issued with photographs taken from the air by the RAF which often contained valuable information pertaining to the military situation. He thought it would be a good idea if I went on a fourteen-day course in the interpretation of air photographs. The courses were held at the RAF School of Photography, and I attended one in January 1935. I found the work absolutely fascinating, and I was at once convinced of the value of this source of information in war.

My time as adjutant was now drawing to a close, and it was usual for officers in my situation to leave the battalion and take an extra-regimental appointment for a year or two. I was thinking of applying for some job with the Territorial Army, but suddenly my CO received a letter from the War Office saying that I had been selected to succeed Captain Peter Bickford, the army instructor in interpretation who had taught me on my course. To me it was a complete surprise, especially as the appointment had always hitherto been given to an officer of the Royal Engineers.

The School of Photography was an Air Force establishment entirely staffed by RAF personnel, which existed to train officers, NCOs and men of that service in how to fit and operate air cameras in aircraft, and how to process plate and film negatives. They were taught all the technicalities concerning such things as the size of aperture, the focal length, the speed of the aircraft in relation to the frequency of exposure when taking photographic mosaics, and all the other specialist knowledge necessary for air photography. It was at this RAF institution that the army course in the interpretation of air photographs had been held ever since the end of the First World War, presumably because the air photographs necessary for the instruction of successive courses could easily be obtained. The instructor (the only officer of the school who was not in the RAF) taught his courses in a wooden hut situated adjacent to the School buildings, and he lived as a member of the RAF Farnborough Mess.

Photographs taken from the air can be exposed either facing vertically downwards, or else facing obliquely forwards or sideways towards the ground. The former produced an unfamiliar view, and what architects call a plan view, of the ground. The latter took an easily understood photo similar to the view that one would obtain from the top of a high building, or from a mountain. In the vertical view, buildings and natural features look flat and level; only their shape as seen from above is reproduced, and they are therefore difficult to recognise, and my job as instructor was to teach officers how to recognise these unfamiliar views of man-made or natural features, and in particular, how to recognise military objects. Often, objects are too small to be seen in an air photograph taken many thousands of feet above, and then it becomes necessary to learn to recognise objects by their *associated features.*

Colour film in the thirties was still a novelty, and was never used in air cameras. Even today the existence of ground haze limits its usefulness considerably, and the chief aids to interpretation, both then as now, are *firstly*, a knowledge of the tones whereby photographic emulsions translate objects depending mostly on their properties of reflection or absorption of light; and *secondly*, the use of a stereoscope through which to examine pairs of photographic prints. This instrument enables the viewer to appreciate the vertical height of objects even though they were vertically below the camera when the photographs were taken.

Vertical and oblique views each have their characteristics and their particular uses. Although an oblique is easy to recognise, it often conceals much 'dead ground' beyond it: for instance, a view of a ridge such as the Hog's Back (near Guildford) would conceal the whole of the reverse slope of the ridge – and this could be dangerous in a military situation; whereas a vertical would reveal everything on either side of the ridge.

A photograph translates colours into tones which are graded from white to black. An interpreter becomes an expert in recognizing an object from its shape and tone. For instance, a path across a cornfield will appear lighter in tone than the cornfield itself, because the stalks are trodden down and, therefore, reflect more light than the heads of standing corn. A flat roof may appear darker in tone than the sloping face of a gable, because it may so happen that the light reflected by the gable strikes directly into the lens. Newly turned earth, such as the parapet of a trench, always appears lighter than the ground surrounding it. The presence of a belt of barbed wire can be detected, not because the wire itself can be seen, but because the vegetation underneath it tends to grow up more luxuriously owing to protection from cattle and from wind, and because of the drops of water which fall from the wire obstacle and provide additional moisture. Long grass is always darker in tone than stubble.

The air photograph gives a bird's eye view of the ground; it sees beyond hills and in between trees in a forest. It is up to date to the moment when it is taken. It shows minute detail, as, for instance, the exact width of a road, a river, or a wall. Unlike a map, it does not have to show these things by conventional signs. On a map of the southern counties, for example, the Dover road will be shown as a red line of constant thickness, but it would be useless to measure it with a pair of callipers. On the air photograph, however, this road will be shown in all its curves and variations at exactly its correct width in relation to the scale of the photograph; and one could therefore measure its width exactly. Again, an air photograph is not defaced by a number of words, such as the names of the villages. It is a straightforward document which is comparatively easy to read by someone who is trained in the art.

It frequently happens that archaeological sites, which may be nearly invisible on the ground, can be clearly discerned in air photographs. Such sites are generally most sharply defined when crops are ripening over them. If, for instance, a ditch or vallum has been dug in prehistoric times on chalk downs, and in succeeding periods the area has been ploughed level and sown, the chalk which was originally disturbed when the ditch was dug will never again congeal as compactly as the surrounding chalk which has not been disturbed. The roots of crops growing on the site of the ditch will consequently be able to penetrate more deeply, and will benefit by the more fertile humus, with the result that their colour will be a deeper green than that of surrounding crops, and the darker tone will therefore reveal the course of the ditch in air photographs.

An interpreter learns to recognise objects not so much by themselves as by their associated features. A machine gun or even a field gun will appear as so small a speck that it would be hard to differentiate it; but by the shape of the trench which may enclose it, or by the characteristic disposition of the four or five emplacements which compose a battery, or by the shape and direction of the tracks which lead up to the position, its nature will be diagnosed by the interpreter. Of course, every effort is made to thwart him by the use of camouflage. He attempts to defeat the enemy by using first and foremost his military knowledge, then by the use of the stereoscope; and by the examination of photographs of the same area taken many months earlier, or even by resort to infra-red photography which may, in certain circumstances, give a different tone value and so reveal important clues.

The scale on a vertical is not exactly constant, for two main reasons: first, that the top of a hill, being nearer to the lens of a camera, will appear to be on a bigger scale than the base of a valley; and secondly, however finely a lens is ground there will always be aberrations at the edges of a photograph due to the curvature of the lens. It follows that the photographs of comparatively flat country are less subject to scale variations than those which cover mountainous territory. The first of these disadvantages, however, can fortunately be overcome by the use of the stereoscope.

The course that I instructed at Farnborough was designed to teach battalion intelligence officers to interpret air photographs so that they would be able to extract information about the ground, and intelligence about the enemy, up to battalion requirements. The majority of officers who came on my courses were of the ranks of lieutenant and captain, though from time to time I got some officers in the next two higher ranks. Officers from the infantry predominated, though the artillery were a close second. But while I was at Farnborough, the Royal Armoured Corps started to become very interested, particularly with a view to choosing cross-country routes for tanks from air photographs. Later in my time, the appointment of Air Liaison Officer was introduced – the officers who were attached to Army Cooperation Squadrons to assist the squadron commanders and flight commanders in cooperating with and gaining visual and photographic intelligence for the army. All these ALOs came and did a course with me; and in due course when they settled down in their jobs with the Army Coop squadrons, they used to run courses themselves on army cooperation generally, and used to ask me to give a lecture or two on interpretation.

As I have indicated, the most important tool of the interpreter's trade is the stereoscope. At the time of which I am speaking, the only two stereoscopes available were one which was made of wood – a large cumbersome affair which simply incorporated four mirrors, two at each eye-piece, and which gave no magnification whatsoever. The other one was a small metal instrument which incorprated two prisms and also was without magnification. By both instruments a good impression of variations in height was obtained, provided that the variations were considerable; but for minor variations in height, some magnification was required, as also was it required for the interpretation of very small objects. There was no such stereoscope available in the army or in the Air Force, and I set about trying to invent one which might be put into mass production for the army.

I spent a lot of time visiting the Photographic Department of the Royal Aircraft Establishment at Farnborough and discussing with Henry Stringer, the director of the department, the production of a simple and inexpensive instrument which would supply the army with what it needed. With his help, I designed and had made such a stereoscope (at my own expense) which I then took up to the War Office in the hope of getting it produced. But such was the lack of interest in the subject of interpretation (and, perhaps, the lack in influence which I myself had as a junior captain) that I could raise no interest in the project whatsoever.

I think that perhaps the main reason was that for economy reasons the Treasury had persuaded the War Office to telescope the two jobs of intelligence and operations under one director – the Director of Military Operations *and* Intelligence; and this individual paid far more attention to the operational side of his duties than to the aspects of intelligence. At all events, I was always side-tracked to the Geographical Department of the War Office, who admittedly were very interested in air photographs – but only in so far as they were of use to the army in the making of maps. They invented stereoscopes, to be sure, but only the kind that were suitable to them for making maps, and these were far too large, heavy and complicated for my purposes and were not the type I wanted for extracting intelligence from air photographs. They were not prepared to press for anything purely for intelligence purposes, because it did not come within their terms of reference.

When my two years as the instructor in interpretation were up, I was asked by the War Office to extend for a further period of two years, and I agreed. This extension ran from April 1937 to February 1939 – the two years immediately preceding the outbreak of war. During this period, I was on three occasions asked to interprert batches of photographs which were sent down from the Air Ministry under conditions of great secrecy. The first batch was taken at the request of the Air Ministry by a flying boat from a squadron based at Malta, and the purpose was to discover whether the Italians were building an aerodrome and an underground air base on the island of Pantellaria. This island is strategically placed in the Narrows between Sicily and Tunisia; and the photographs had to be taken from a considerable distance out to sea to avoid infringement of Italian air space. I found that the aerodrome and associated works were practically completed, and I reported the locations of anti-aircraft and coast defence batteries that had been sited in the vicinity.

The next bundle of photographs that were sent to me were of the southern end of the Red Sea, as it was suspected that the Italians were installing heavy guns with which to control the straits between Aden and Somaliland. And the final batch had been taken at the urgent request of the Admiralty, of the Egyptian coast covering the Gulf of Sollum and including Bardia, El Adem, Tobruk, Derna, Bernice and Benghazi. In all these places I found evidence of any amount of military construction including petrol and ammunition dumps; and the aerodromes had a great many aircraft on them.

The fact that I was the only interpreter in the three Services capable of carrying out this kind of strategic interpretation is a measure of the extent to which the subject had been neglected in the inter-war years. From time to time while I was at Farnborough I taught a few RAF officers, and even fewer Naval officers, but only because they were doing the long RAF photographic course at the School of Photography.

However, in 1937 I thought it was time for me to say something to the School authorities about the advisability of the RAF training some officers to interpret the effects of bombing, because otherwise I couldn't see how they could expect to estimate the results of their raids. The approach of international tension which plainly could lead to war made them more receptive than I had found them to be before, and they must have discussed this suggestion with the Air Ministry. At all events, the Air Ministry asked me to include on my next course a wing commander nominated by them, and I found Wing Commander Wheeler, their nominee, a very sensible officer who quickly appreciated the need for intelligence officers, trained in interpretation, on each bomber station. A few weeks after Wheeler had done my course, I was asked officially if I would set up courses for RAF Intelligence Officers.

I ran three such courses, each for twenty officers, many of them retired army, or Indian army officers; and I arranged for them to visit various kinds of factories, and railway marshalling yards, and ports including the port of London and Southampton. I got the RAF to photograph these installations, and then when we visited them, we were able to compare characteristic features with their appearance in the photographs. And I also arranged for representatives of the sites visited to lecture on the work and processes carried out at the site, with reference to the effects on production of hits on vulnerable portions of the installation.

In my last year at Farnborough, the Air Ministry asked me to write a manual on the interpretation of air photographs. It was rather a tall order, as in 1938–1939 I had a lot of additional courses to instruct besides my routine army courses, and I had these batches of air photographs to interpret which suddenly turned up from various parts of the world and were obviously of the first importance. However, I managed to produce a manual, liberally illustrated with photographs, which ran to more than 200 pages and included everything that I thought was important on the subject. It was called *The Interpretation of Air Photographs*, and was designated as *Air Publication 1356*.

In the four years that I was at Farnborough I suppose I must have trained over 500 army officers in the interpretation of air photographs, so that when we mobilised and landed the British Expeditionary Force in France with an initial two divisions (to be followed later by others) there must have been a fair sprinkling of interpreters in the battalions and with the brigades and divisions. It is completely incorrect to say as did Constance Babington-Smith in her book *Evidence in Camera* published in 1958, that the army on the outbreak of war had only one trained interpreter, and that was me! I was certainly better trained and more capable of interpreting photographs exposed over the strategic areas than others, but thanks to the Farnborough courses, the army had succeeded in providing most battalions and formations with intelligence officers trained in the uses of air photographs, and the ability to put them to good use in the forward areas. This was no mean achievement.

CHAPTER FOUR

Mobilisation, and France 1939–1940

I concluded my appointment as instructor in the interpretation of air photographs on 1st March 1939. By this time the 2nd Battalion of my regiment had moved from Strensall down to Aldershot, and I rejoined the unit there, where I was given the command of A Company. The battalion was a machine gun unit, equipped with the Vickers machine gun, of which each company had twelve. I had never done a course at the Machine Gun School at Netheravon, so I had to set about learning as much as I could from officers and NCOs who had.

The international situation, after the alarms and excursions of the previous six months since Chamberlain had flown to Berchtesgarten and Munich, seemed to have stabilised, and the chances of war decreased. The steadily growing armament programme, the defence estimates and the continued organisation of air raid precaution services seemed to have reassured the nation. I took three weeks' leave and went to France with my wife, returning on 15th March. On the 16th, Hitler invaded Czechoslovakia! This plunged the whole of Europe back into an atmosphere of crisis, similar to that of September 1938. By April the Anglo-Polish Treaty of mutual assistance was signed, and then Italy invaded Albania at Easter.

The King and Queen visited the army in Aldershot, and the regiment fired a machine gun competition on the ranges against the Cheshire Regiment in their presence, which I am glad to say we won. Reservists were being recalled in batches for 12-day periods of training with the battalion, and I met a number of old friends who had left the Colours a year or two previously. Conscription was introduced towards the end of April. Practice 'black-outs' were organised, and there were periods during which gas masks had to be worn in barracks while routine work went on.

The 2nd Division, which was the 'parent formation' of the battalion in Aldershot, organised a battlefield tour in France for four days, led by General Sir Maitland (Jumbo) Wilson, its divisional commander. We made Valenciennes our headquarters, and each day motored out in coaches to study various First World War battles on the ground.

There were about 40 of us, and the studies included the 1914 battle of Le Cateau, the 1917 tank battle at Cambrai, and the 1918 breaking of the Hindenburg Line. General Wilson had arranged for a number of retired officers who had taken part in the battles to attend and describe the situations, and I found it all a very worthwhile experience.

But I suppose the thing that impressed me most was Jumbo Wilson's introductory talk at Valenciennes the night we all assembled: 'Gentlemen, I am very glad to have the opportunity of conducting this battlefield tour. I want all of you to pay particular attention to the ground, because it differs so much from that over which we normally train at Aldershot; and what you are going to see is typical of all the country in the north-east of France: and it will probably be the last opportunity any of you will have of seeing it under peacetime conditions.'

The Dunkirk campaign was exactly a year away.

The 9th Territorial Battalion of the Regiment moved down from Manchester to undergo a week's training at Mytchett, and we provided the officer and NCO instructors. I was appalled at the backward state of their training, and the lack of control in their officers. They started badly by failing to bring their machine gun dial sights, and without them the gun could hardly be used. We had of course to lend them ours, but it was an alarming indication of the happy-go-lucky attitude and lack of realism of the Territorial Army at that time.

A gloom was cast over the country by the reported sinking of the submarine *Thetis* during diving trials in the Irish Sea, with the loss of 99 men. I remember my friend Dr Willie MacPhail, of the Frimley Green Sanatorium, remarking at this time that soon casualties of this order would seem insignificant compared with the losses to be expected in war.

In the middle of the summer I learnt that having qualified in the Staff College entrance exam the previous year, I had now been given a nomination to attend the two-year course. But with the international situation as it was, it hardly looked as if I would get to Camberley before war broke out. King-Hall's *News Letter* – at that time much read – quoted a German informer as saying that those near to Hitler said, '*Er will los schlagen*'.* And the Military Attaché in Berlin said in a lecture to Aldershot Command that the German army would have a 'peak period' in August 1939, and that this would therefore be the most likely time for war to break out.

* 'He's going to let fly.'

Meanwhile, regimental life went on. A Battalion Rifle Meeting was held, and the Battalion Sports soon afterwards. My friend Tommy Woolsey was commanding D Company, and I remember congratulating him on winning 'the last Sports before the war'. Towards the end of August the news broke of the signature of a pact between Germany and Russia, which came as a great shock to everyone. We actually had in Moscow at the time senior representatives of our three services discussing the cooperation which Russia was to give Great Britain and France in the event of war with Germany! Huge troop movements in Germany towards the north-east were reported in the papers, and foreign correspondents of *The Times* all said that the fate of Europe would probably be settled that week. They forecast that the German army would be able to smash the Polish army quickly and before England and France, with their slow diplomatic procedures, would be able to do anything; and that by the time the latter countries had made up their minds, all Germany's claims on Poland and Danzig would have been settled by force of arms.

*

In the battalion, mobilisation schemes were issued to companies, and instructions were received concerning the painting of our vehicles and the fixing of identification plates. The battalion was finding a large number of working parties to dig air raid shelters, and secret orders were received regarding the posting away of senior warrant officers and NCOs to extra-regimental jobs on mobilisation. There was much speculation as to where the British Expeditionary Force would be sent, and the general consensus was that it would go to France, probably to some location on the Maginot Line. I practised riding one of the army motor cycles; and I signed my will.

A programe of 'hardening' the men was commenced, chiefly consisting of forced marches, physical training and musketry. On 31st August it was announced on the nine o'clock news that the Government had decided to complete the mobilisation of the Navy, which meant that my younger brother, Buster, rejoined the Senior Service. Officers and men of the Army Reserve and Supplementary Reserve were called up, children and invalids from the main danger areas such as London and Manchester were evacuated, and steps were taken to prevent the hoarding of food, and to restrict civil flying. The calling up of the Army Reserve directly affected my elder brother Jack, and he reported at once to the Regimental Depot at Ashton-under-Lyne in Lancashire.

My mother was delighted: all the boys again in uniform! She was not in the least apprehensive of the future. War was a fact of life, and everyone had to rally round, do their duty and defeat the enemy. No counting of the costs, no consultation of one's fears. *Aux armes, citoyens! Formez vos bataillons!*

So many reservists were reporting that the men had to double up in the barrack rooms and sleep on the flour on palliasses between the beds; and the officers' mess was full of officers reporting for duty with base and lines of communication headquarters, to which the battalion was acting as the temporary parent unit. My wife Janie, who had volunteered for ARP duties some weeks previously and had completed various short courses of instruction, was given her first task when a neighbour rang to say his mother-in-law had come to stay without her gas mask. Janie acted appropriately, and a mask was provided next morning.

Mobilisation was ordered at about 5 p.m. on 1st September, and Barty Moore, the Commanding Officer, called a conference of company commanders to discuss the putting into operation of the Mobilisation Scheme. I got home to Frimley just before midnight to find Janie's mother and sister (plus cat) had arrived from London. They had helped Janie to complete the blacking-out of the windows.

War was declared at 11 a.m. on 3rd September, and Chamberlain, the Prime Minister, had spoken on the wireless at 11.15 but I was busy with the mobilisation of my company and did not hear him. Jack arrived on 5th September from the depot on posting to the battalion, and was posted as second-in-command of D Company, under Captain Tommy Woolsey. Before Jack retired he was a year senior to Tommy, but now he had lost three years' seniority. Being engaged solely on the intensely practical problem of taking a company to war, and being spared the peacetime chores which so much irked him before, he was on the top of his form and was rightly regarded as a very valuable officer. The Commanding Officer at the time of his retirement had long since been posted elsewhere.

Various other officers arrived, including two who were posted to my company. Two air raid warnings were received, but no bombers came over and there was a wonderful crop of rumours which included the news (which turned out to be entirely erroneous) that London, Richmond, Reading, Winchester and Grimsby had been bombed. Janie motored over to Chalfont St Peter to collect my father and mother, who were to stay at a boarding-house called the Prior's Kitchen in Frimley, so as to be near Jack and Janie and me at this critical time.

The King visited Aldershot again, and we lined the route. He passed in an open car, looking very bronzed and sitting next to General Sir John Dill, the Commander-in-Chief of Aldershot Command. I called for three cheers but as the car passed so slowly I kept on cheering until we had produced five before he finally passed on to the next company.

Mobilisation was completed on 5th September, and I found it rather trying having to hang about in barracks. As the Germans had 70 divisions engaged in Poland, it seemed mad to me that we and the French were not attacking their rear, a chance which we probably would not get again.

On the 18th we loaded and secured all our vehicles with their war equipment, ammunition and stores. Long columns of 'infantry tanks' were rumbling down the roads towards Farnborough station. An expert from the Machine Gun School arrived to lecture the officers and NCOs on the new 'streamlined' ammunition, a slight snag being that the ammunition was likely to arrive before the appropriate range-tables and sights were available. On 21st September I said goodbye to Janie, my mother and father and my mother-in-law, and got a lift in a gravel lorry from Frimley to our lines in Farnborough. We were now confined to barracks, and we knew we would soon be on the move.

We sent our vehicles off four days in advance of the battalion's departure from Aldershot. Such was the secrecy imposed and observed that none of us (except the Commanding Officer, the adjutant and two confidential orderly room clerks) knew either our port of embarkation or our destination. We marched from barracks to Farnborough Station wearing greatcoats, packs and haversacks, and after the inevitable hour's wait due to military over-insurance, the train arrived and we set off. At Southampton we embarked on the SS *Biarritz*.

My brother and I had often discussed what mobilisation would be like when it finally came, and we both of us read with absorbing interest what had happened in 1914 when the battalion had mobilised at The Curragh in Ireland for the First World War. Neither of us had any doubt that it was bound to come again in our lifetime. Consequently, I observed the scene and took note of our experiences with a lively interest.

I was the company commander of A Company, and as soon as we boarded the *Biarritz* the men had their evening meal and settled down in their blankets as best they could on the mess-decks. There was quite a lot of singing, and I was disgusted with their choice of songs: 'Down

Mexico Way' was the most popular and was sung over and over again; I thought it was entirely inappropriate for the occasion, as was 'Roll out the Barrel' which they also sang.

We had breakfast on board as we were entering Cherbourg harbour on 23rd September, and we saw our transport assembled in the docks. We hoped and supposed that that meant that we should be going forward in it to our billeting area, but it was shortlived as the trucks moved off empty soon afterwards. Jack, who was with them, told me in confidence just before they left that our destination was Laval, to which we should be travelling by train. I lost no time in buying a map and found that the town lay between Le Mans and Rennes, about 110 miles from Cherbourg as the crow flies. Later I heard that Laval was the Headquarters of II Corps, and that GHQ of the British Expeditionary Force was at Le Mans.

The troops were marched over to the huge station buildings alongside the quay where the *Queen Mary* used to berth, and accommodated on the verandah. Then we took off our equipment, but found that we weren't allowed to smoke owing to petrol stores beneath the verandah. So we marched the men out of the buildings on to some waste land near the station, and there they were able to sit and smoke.

I asked Tony Fitch, my second-in-command, to go to the field cashier's office to change some money for the men. It was an awful job involving a very long wait in a never-ending queue. The HQ of the lines of communication was established at one end of the erstwhile casino, the other end doing duty as an officers' club. I visited the latter to write a letter to Janie, and met Lieutenant-Colonel Crossfield whom I had known in Burma, and who recently had attended one of my courses at Farnborough for Bomber Station Intelligence Officers in the RAF. He was now disguised as a squadron leader. I also met the ex-warrant officer from the School of Photography, now commissioned, and we all had a drink together.

After a tiring day, during the afternoon of which we let the men go into the town to have a look round the shops, we entrained at 5 p.m. and remained in our carriages until five hours later when we moved slowly out of the station. Although I repeatedly asked Axworthy, the adjutant, for the censor's stamp so that I could get my letter off to Janie, he always birked the issue and was distinctly disagreeable. I was sure he didn't want his wife to hear that Janie had received a letter when he hadn't written one! It seemed to me that both he, and the CO, made unnecessarily heavy weather of these moves, and each phase was always preceded by a company commanders' conference and a quite unnecessary flap. Perhaps it was because neither of them had seen anything but Home Service for many years.

The next day, after one or two stops when we went along to see the men and arrange for the collection of hot water so as to make tea, we arrived at Laval in bright sunlight about 11 a.m. Jack was there to meet us, and we soon moved off in our transport to our billeting areas. 'A' Company were in four farms, a platoon to each, and HQ in the fourth. They were named La Touche, Les Bois, Le Clou and La Rigourdière, all on the outskirts of the village of Soulgé-le-Bruant, about twelve miles from Laval.

I had been suffering from a very painful throat, and by the time I had finished billeting my men I felt really ill. There was yet another CO's conference at 6 p.m. so I took Tony Fitch along with me. Barty Moore, the CO, sent me straight off to see the doctor, who ordered me to bed as my temperature was 104. I remained in bed in my billet for four days, and in that time the battalion was ordered to move to its concentration area, I was ordered as soon as I was well to report to GHQ for a staff appointment connected with intelligence from air photographs; and since the battalion was moving, I was admitted into hospital in the meantime.

When I left the regiment near Laval, I was taken by military ambulance to No 9 General Hospital which had only just been set up in the beautiful Château du Grand Luce east of Le Mans and owned by the Princess de Faucigny-Lucinge. She still occupied a suite of rooms somewhere in the château, but I never saw her. All the furniture from the main salons had been removed, and replaced by army hospital beds. Mine was not nearly as comfortable as my bed in my billet at Soulgé. There were about 50 sisters and nurses, most of them non-regular QAIMNS,* and a staff of doctors drawn from the RAMC.†

I was apparently the first officer patient of the war at the hospital. As I was only convalescing (my temperature having long since returned to normal) I was allowed to get dressed and walk in the lovely grounds and formal gardens, but they were reluctant to release me altogether for at least another four days. I, however, was anxious to leave, firstly because I knew I had recovered, and secondly because I wanted to get to my new section at GHQ and start organising it as I knew it should be set up, and before anyone else could miscast the system and so involve me in a difficult operation putting it to rights. So I had a word with

* Queen Alexandra's Imperial Military Nursing Service. The name has now been changed to Queen Alexandra's Royal Army Nursing Service.

† Royal Army Medical Corps.

the CO, who was a colonel and an Irishman and, I suspect, a dug-out, but a DSO and Bar and with a thoroughly sound and helpful disposition; and he said I could report for duty the following morning.

I left the hospital by staff car at nine o'clock in the morning, and I was sorry to say goodbye to such a lovely château. In any other circumstances I should have been only too happy to have remained there being waited on hand and foot. I have often wondered who occupied it after the collapse of France, and whether now it is still kept up in the immaculate state that it was in when I first saw it on a sunny September day in 1939.

I arrived in Le Mans quite quickly and searched for, and finally found the Intelligence Branch of GHQ. My particular Section, designated as Ia (v) was presided over by Major Geoffrey Hunt of the Rifle Brigade who had been a pupil of mine at Farnborough, and was an old friend. The section dealt with intelligence provided by the RAF, and naturally I was responsible for that part of it which derived from air photographs. He was away when I first arrived, but he soon turned up, and took me to the Town Major, who allotted me a billet in the Hôtel du Saumon. Geoffrey took me there, and lent me his batman. After unpacking, I went to find the field cashier to draw some money, and practically ran into the Duke of Gloucester, who was just coming out of the cashier's office. Inside I met Lieutenant Jefferies,* also an old pupil and now ADC to the Commander-in-Chief, Lord Gort; and Lord Munster, who until recently had been Parliamentary Under Secretary of State for War, and was now also attached to Lord Gort's staff.

Hunt came back just before lunch and we went and had a vermouth at a café on the square facing Chaunzy's statue. This was followed by lunch in the hotel, and I rested until about 4.30 p.m. I then visited the shops and made a few purchases.

After a good night's sleep, I got a lift to the station about half past five in the afternoon and boarded the train which was reserved for GHQ personnel – officers, clerks, batmen, etc. Most of the brass hats and senior staff had gone by road. I shared a carriage with Captain Chamberlayne, a Reserve officer in the Scots Guards, and Lieutenant MacKenzie, a wartime officer who in peace was a member of Lloyds.

The train didn't go until eight o'clock in the evening, and it soon became apparent that I should have provided myself with food for the

* He was killed during the retreat to Dunkirk.

journey, but no one had thought to tell me so, and I imagined that there would be some arrangement on the train for an officers' mess.

'Aha!' said Chamberlayne, 'I knew there would be some foolish virgins. But I'll make you an honorary member of my personal Mess,' and he was soon unpacking a huge cooked chicken, a bottle of excellent claret, another of white wine, two flasks of brandy, some bread and butter, and several cardboard plates. Mackenzie was asked to join too, and the three of us had a most wonderful dinner party, during which Chamberlayne regaled us with stories of the First World War. We drank all the wine, and, I need hardly say, slept beautifully.

In the early morning we passed through Rouen, and then through Albert where Chamberlayne pointed out the Virgin which, all through the First War, had leaned over almost horizontally from the church spire, but never fell. The troops believed in that war that if she was to fall, the most terrible misfortunes would befall the Allies, but she never did. At the end of hostilities she was restored to her proper vertical position. After Albert, the train passed over the northern part of the Somme (1916) battlefield, and then we arrived at Arras, where we detrained.

The operations and intelligence staff of GHQ had their offices in the château in the village of Habarcq, about twelve kilometres north-west of Arras, and in surrounding farms, while the staff of other branches of the headquarters were divided between neighbouring villages. This dispersion was of course a precaution against bombing from the air, but it did obviously have attendant administrative disadvantages. Some branches were as much as ten miles away.

I soon met Browne Clayton, the officer who had been given the air photograph job, but who didn't want to do it, and was anxious to be posted back to his regiment – the 12th Lancers. He was another one who had done a course under me at Farnborough, and the fact that I knew him made matters easier. I shared a billet with him in a farm house.

In the early afternoon we went along to Ia (v), which was established in one room of a farm about 500 yards away from the Château. Habarcq itself lies on the Arras–St Pol road and consists of a number of rather smelly farms grouped round the unkempt château. The farmers were all poor, and their farms were all they had to keep them from starvation. They worked hard, with their womenfolk, and hoped for an occasional letter from their sons who had all been mobilised and were with the French armies. Here, the memories of the last war were vivid, and they seemed to regard the period of peace as merely an interlude between one great war and another.

The streets in the village were very muddy, and scored with the ruts of farm carts which were continually moving from one end of the village to the other. The farms are built round a courtyard in which are to be found a dirty green pond, a number of muddy ducks, hens and chickens, sometimes some pigs, nearly always a dog or two. The cows and horses are stalled in little sheds opening on to the courtyard, and usually forming part of the farm buildings. In the middle of the yard is a fresh mound of manure – the midden – from which drains away a stinking runnel of browny-green liquid. Hens are to be seen picking about on the midden, and once a day the farmer's wife came out to turn the dump with a fork. This was the moment to close all doors and windows.

To the ever present stench and noise of such a farmyard community the business of a great headquarters went on. Officers in gumboots, clerks and orderlies in greatcoats, despatch riders on motor bicycles, swathed in scarves and wearing balaclava helmets and leather jerkins, covered in mud and skidding from side to side, vied for road space with the farm carts, cattle and the peasants in the walled streets of the dirty little village.

The staff of my office consisted of Geoffrey Hunt, a Squadron Leader Stevens (who was responsible for keeping the order of battle of the German Air Force), a wartime gunner lieutenant called Gerald Lacoste, and two clerks. Lacoste was actually responsible for camouflage, but there wasn't too much to do under that heading, and so he was a very great help to me with air photos, and displayed an aptitude for interpretation which was exceptional in someone with so little experience of the subject. Later on we were joined by an army captain called Whittaker who had done one of my courses and was also a pilot, who had spent two years in No 4 Army Cooperation Squadron.

Once I had arrived, Browne Clayton departed and I proceeded to organise the office. The first thing to do was to file the few photographs that existed – all taken by Bomber Command, of towns, aerodromes and railway stations in Germany, and taken in the middle of September 1939. We were woefully short of office equipment, as much of our mobilisation stores had not arrived, so I got hold of a car and went in to Arras and bought paper clips, candles, waste paper baskets, file covers and coloured pencils, and ordered a filing cabinet for air photographs.

I had arranged to meet a friend from one of the other branches of the HQ for lunch at the Hôtel de l'Univers, so I went there and found Lord Munster by himself having a drink. He asked me to join him, while he waited for the C-in-C to arrive, and I found him to be very friendly and easy to get on with. He had been lord-in-waiting to Edward VIII, and as I have mentioned, Parliamentary Under Secretary of State for War until the outbreak of hostilities. He told me that the German ambassador told him a few days before war was declared, that war was impossible; and added that the wretched man was kept in complete darkness by his government as to what was happening. Munster had known the previous ambassador, Ribbentrop, quite well, and said he was pleasant enough, but a terribly dangerous and influential man. He had also known the chief German trade attaché, and lunched with him shortly before the war, when he inveighed against the Nazis in the strongest terms, and in a typical Prussian manner.

I had heard that the Duke of Windsor was in Paris, so I asked him what he was doing. He put the back of his hand to his mouth and whispered, 'I've just been meeting the So-and-So.' He said Windsor didn't like him, and vice-versa. Windsor remarked on seeing him, 'What on earth are you doing here? I thought you were at the War Office.' Munster replied, 'I was, but I chucked it up.' 'What are you doing masquerading in a Grenadier uniform?' He replied that he was ADC to the C-in-C. 'Oh, you're one of those tuppenny ha'penny soldiers, are you?' Munster replied. 'Well, there seem to be a lot of tuppenny halfpenny people about just now,' and he added that he thought that was one up to him! Windsor did not reply, and nor did he introduce his wife, who was there too.

As Munster was so forthcoming, I asked him about the feeling between the ex-King and Baldwin. He said that they were friendly and the King had never flown at the Prime Minister, and their meetings were not acrimonious. Baldwin had said that it would be perfectly all right if he had wanted to marry a cook or a housemaid, but he simply couldn't marry a divorcée. On the other hand, the King and Archbishop Lang had loathed each other like poison. The King delighted in keeping him waiting, and then puffed smoke in his face from his pipe, as he passed him on the way out!

My friend arrived, and we went off to have lunch, and shortly afterwards the C-in-C arrived, followed by Jefferies. They lunched at a table not far away, and the C-in-C looked in excellent form, and talked and laughed all through the meal. I heard that the Dukes of Windsor and Gloucester had visited the château later in the afternoon.

All of us in the office except Hunt used to feed in B Mess, in a farm near by. It was run by Chamberlayne, who had got one of the French interpreters to find a cook, who very soon was producing appetising and tasty meals. When I saw Chamberlayne that evening at dinner he said that Gort, or 'Fat Boy' as he called him, using his Brigade of Guards nickname, was so cheerful when he was at GHQ that afternoon that he was afraid that it could only mean one thing – that the prospect of a scrap was imminent.

I lost no time in arranging a visit to Grand Quartier Général, the French Supreme Headquarters, in order to contact the people in charge of their photo and interpretation sections. It was situated at La Ferté sous Jouarre, on the Marne a few miles east of Paris. I took Gerald Lacoste with me, and we went by staff car, calling at the RAF Air Component HQ near Arras, and then at Tillaloy to leave mail for the secret wireless listening station. In Paris, we went to see the Military Attaché, lunched at the Plaza Café near the Ronde Pointe, and then went on to La Ferté. There we were accommodated by the British Military Mission to GHQ in a château just across the river from the French HQ. I had a talk with Brigadier Jack Swayne who was in charge of the Mission, and then we were taken off to dinner in a French restaurant called the Epée which justly enjoyed a high culinary reputation, and which reputedly had been von Kluck's mess in 1914 when Paris was so nearly captured.

After dinner we visited the château which housed the Deuxième Bureau, and met our opposite numbers in the photographic interpretation branch. They were charming, but I suspected a little sceptical of our capabilities. They even offered to show me how to use a stereoscope! They showed us numerous photos of the Siegfried Line, and described the characteristics of the casemates and other built-in fortifications. We arranged to have another session with them the following day.

The next morning we walked to the château after breakfast. I produced a run of some eight or nine photos which had been taken by the RAF over an area well to the east of Holland. I had noticed some evidence of new work on the ground in and near woods, and as it puzzled me because it was not near any known fortifications, I wanted their views. They examined them, and diagnosed the work to be a new Reserve Line to the Siegfried Line. It caused quite a stir, and I felt our prestige had increased a point or two!

In the course of the morning they produced some little plaster-of-paris models of casemates in the line which were extremely interesting and instructive. These they produced from an inner room, of which they seemed most secretive. I thought they must have a model of a sector of the line inside, but they evidently had no intention of letting us in. They also showed me a brochure they had written on the Siegfried

Line, illustrated with air photos and architectural drawings. I asked if we could have a copy, and also if Gerald could make some drawings of the model casemates, but they said they would have to ask their chief. As we were due to call in again on our return from Paris the following day (in order to collect some photographs they had already promised us) I said we could do the drawings then, if permission was granted.

On our way back to the Epée for lunch we passed the little stone monument at the corner of a side street leading down to the river which commemorates the death of an officer of the Royal Welch Fusiliers at this spot in 1914. Someone had tied a little Union Jack to the railing in front of the stone.

In Paris we went to a shop called Flambeau and were able to buy steel cupboards, a wall fixture for displaying maps which we had seen at GHQ, a gazeteer and other office equipment. Then we returned to our friends at La Ferté, who turned out to be called Capitaine Louis Gau (Aviation) and Capitaine Pécresse. We got permission to make the drawings we wanted, and were loaded with brochures and photographs – I am sure far more than they originally intended to give us. We got back to Habarcq late that night.

Any photographs taken by the army cooperation squadrons, whether specifically demanded or not, came to my section, and Lacoste and I had to interpret them, then plot them on tracing paper with map references, and then file them, while making up Interpretation Reports summarising the information acquired which were sent to the I and II Corps, as well as to interested sections in GHQ, and to the War Office. The two of us were very hard worked, but we got some help from Corporal Hill, our clerk, who used to ink in our traces and so save us one process. When we had a big job on hand, like the making of a photographic mosaic, we needed all the space available in our farmyard office, and Geoffrey Hunt and the others had to stop work and clear out.

We arranged for the intelligence staffs of the corps and of the divisions to come in to Habarcq to examine annotated air photos of their areas, and they could demand any that they particularly wanted to have; and I used to visit the corps from time to time to advise on any problems connected with photographic intelligence. They also asked me to run some weekly photo-interpretation courses, so with Gerald's help I set up a lecture room in the Hôtel Moderne in Arras, and obtained stereoscopes and other equipment from England.

After I had been at GHQ for six months, and the 'phoney war' was still on, it was decided that those officers who would have gone to the

Staff College had the war not broken out, should now return to England and undergo a three months' staff course at Camberley. I therefore handed over my job at GHQ, and came home. As Janie and I had a house at Frimley, I could live at home, and attend the Staff College each day. After three months, when the course was practically over, I was sent to the War Office where I worked in an operations branch dealing with the campaign in Norway; but when the Germans attacked through Holland and Belgium, I was at once sent back to France to be attached to the supreme RAF Headquarters, called British Air Forces in France. It was commanded by Air Marshal Sir Arthur Barratt, universally known in the RAF as 'Ugly Barratt'; and I was posted to the Intelligence Branch, under Group Captain 'Pops' Ritchie, who had made a great reputation for himself in Intelligence circles in Palestine before the war.

The RAF HQ was at Coulommiers, about thirty miles east of Paris. I remained with them during the retreat and after Dunkirk, when we tried to stiffen the French resistance, but it was obvious that France had lost all will to win. French Grand Quartier Général left Coulommiers and retreated to Orléans, then to Tours, and finally I think to Bordeaux. But on 16th June, when the French were about to sign an armistice with the Germans, our HQ was ordered to return to England, and after various adventures we sailed from Brest and in the end docked at Plymouth.

After a week's leave, I was posted to HQ Fighter Command at Stanmore, where my job was to provide military liaison between the Commander-in-Chief and the C-in-C Home Forces, as the Battle of Britain was just beginning and invasion was expected. My brother Buster was with the minesweepers in the North Sea, and Jack had just joined the new force known as Commandos, he being one of the first to volunteer. After his excitements in France during the retreat to Dunkirk, he did not fancy the role of an infantry battalion, largely denuded of weapons, and condemned to watch the coast in expectation of invasion. At least in the Commandos there was a good chance of an offensive raid or two, and he soon found himself as second-in-command of No 5 Commando, stationed in the west of Scotland.

One of the indications that invasion might be imminent was expected to be a great concentration of the activities of the Luftwaffe in those coastal areas in England where the enemy had decided to land, and it was thought that this might be most quickly deduced from the Operations Table at Fighter Command. Consequently I had a staff of three captains who manned a 24-hour watch at the table, with direct telephone lines to the Operations Branch at HQ Home Forces established in St Paul's School at Hammersmith. I spent a good deal of my time carrying messages from Air Marshal Sir Hugh Dowding, the C-in-C, Fighter Command, to General Sir Alan Brooke, or to other army commanders, often to do with the lay-out of anti-aircraft guns so that their action could be coordinated with the tactics of day and night fighters.

The other indication of invasion would be the build-up of barges in the French Channel ports, and there was no better way to obtain this information than from air photographs. I soon reformed my links with interpretation staffs, and I must here record two important events that had occurred since the outbreak of war, each centred on the remarkable abilities and characters of two civilians, one called Cotton, and the other Hemming. Sidney Cotton had been a pilot in the Royal Naval Air Service in the First World War, and between the wars had undertaken numerous ventures involving the use of aircraft in Newfoundland, America, Canada, and I don't know where else. He had been involved in the development of colour photography and was well versed in map making from air photos; and he was a super salesman and a man of unbounded drive and initiative.

He had learnt that the RAF were having difficulty in obtaining strategic air photographs with Blenheim aircraft owing to their lack of speed and altitude, and he conceived the idea of obtaining the new Spitfire fighter, and fitting it with cameras and extra fuel tanks and denuding it of armament, in order to increase its speed and altitude. He talked his way into the offices of the Chief of the Air Staff, the First Sea Lord and the Commander-in-Chief of Fighter Command, and finally obtained the unobtainable – a Spitfire aircraft – for at that time Spitfires were more valuable than gold or diamonds.

Thanks to his initiative he took photos over Belgium, Holland and Germany from over 30,000 feet using the longest lens then available, and by positioning three cameras in the aircraft so that the central one took vertical photos, while the two flank cameras took overlapping oblique ones simultaneously, he was able to cover an immense area of country. From his pre-war activities he knew many able pilots, and he was able to form a flying unit which at first was called the Heston Flight and, after a series of other names, finally became known as the Photographic Reconnaissance Unit. This unit soon came to be used to fulfil the requirements of all three Services in strategic photographic intelligence, and used unarmed Spitfires and, in due course, unarmed Mosquitos.

Cotton himself, alas, was phased out of the RAF because his intolerance and refusal to compromise made him impossible to work with. But his tremendous contribution to strategic photographic intelligence should never be forgotten. It is a fact that on 6th May 1940 he actually obtained photographs of German tanks in the wooded area on the German side of the Luxembourg–German border in the Ardennes. This was the area which the French regarded as altogether unsuitable for tanks or armoured forces, and the whole Allied strategy was based on this assumption. It was expected that the Germans would attack further to the north, and the main French forces were disposed accordingly.

Asked by Air Marshal Sir Arthur Barratt, to whom Cotton showed wet negatives of this sortie, to obtain information of this astonishing revelation, Cotton ordered a low-level sortie to be flown on 7th May, and it fully confirmed the evidence, the interpreters estimating that there were 400 tanks visible in the area. Thus, Cotton's photographs pointed unmistakably to an imminent and major armoured thrust from the direction of the German–Luxembourg border.

Barratt at once informed the Air Staff in London, but they gave the report little credence. The Air Marshal sent them copies of the photographs, which arrived on 8th or 9th May. Barratt's suggestion was that a strong force from Bomber Command should be briefed to shower incendiaries on the forest areas that very night, 9th/10th May, to start forest fires which might develop into major conflagrations. But the Air Staff would have had to advise the War Cabinet, and the latter would have had to discuss the project with Air Marshal Sir Charles Portal, the C-in-C Bomber Command, and quite frankly, the great men in London and their staffs just were not geared to act with the requisite promptitude and resolution that the intelligence deserved. Nothing happened, and of the ten German Panzer divisions, no less than seven attacked on 10th May from the Ardennes on to the lightly held French positions in the Sedan region, and were practically unopposed.

The other civilian who made such a contribution to strategic photographic intelligence was Major H. Hemming, a friend and former colleague of Cotton, and owner of a firm engaged in aerial survey until the war broke out, with offices and a 'factory' at Wembley. It was called the 'Aircraft Operating Company', and Cotton used it to process his strategic photographs. The three Service Ministries soon got wind of this firm which turned out such excellent work, and in addition possessed a remarkable Swiss photogrammetric instrument made by a firm called Wild (pronounced 'Vilt'). This machine was of immense value in measuring accurately the dimensions of small objects on photographs, and was particularly useful therefore in identifying German Naval units; for naturally photos taken by Spitfires at a height of more than 30,000 feet were of very small scale.

Another very significant consequence of the use, and ultimately, the requisitioning of Hemming's firm was that the Service interpreters obtained the use of the excellent small magnifying stereoscope which he had invented. It was light, cheap to manufacture, and highly efficient and easy to use. This was the sort of instrument I had tried so hard but without success to get the War Office to produce before the war.

Hemming's Wembley factory in due course had its name changed to the Photographic Interpretation Unit and the Photographic Reconnaissance Unit suffered damage, and had to be moved. The PRU went to Benson Aerodrome, near Henley; and ultimately, after a search for suitable premises in which both I and Gerald Lacoste played a part, a large house called Danesfield, at Medmenham, near Marlow, was selected and requisitioned for the PIU. Here, for the rest of the war, strategic interpretation was carried out for all three Services by a staff of interpreters drawn from the three Services.

There can be no doubt that, when war became imminent, thought should have been directed to the means of obtaining strategic as well as tactical information from air photographs. The Lysander in its day was probably adequate for obtaining tactical information, both by visual and photographic reconnaissance, but the Blenheim was no good for anything but medium reconnaissance within the zone of the armies. There was no provision for an aircraft to take long-range strategic photographs over heavily defended areas, and when Blenheims were used, as they were far too frequently, and for far too long, 30% to 80% casualties resulted.

Of course, the army was not likely to get any encouragement in this matter from the RAF; they at this time were going all out for their own requirements in fighter and bomber aircraft. It was not until they themselves had a requirement for strategic photographs, and also came to realise the kudos that was to be obtained from gaining spectacular information from this source, that they took the matter seriously. Let it never be forgotten how much this country owes to Sidney Cotton and 'Lemnos' Hemming! They filled a vital need.

CHAPTER FIVE

Photographic Intelligence for Commando Raids

In December 1940, I was working in one of the Intelligence branches of Headquarters, Home Forces in London, when the telephone rang, and a voice asked for me.

'Yes, Churchill speaking,' I replied.

'Oh, thank heavens!' said the voice, 'I've been hunting you all over London.'

'Oh, have you?' I said, surprised. 'Who is that speaking?'

'Well, you won't know me, but I've been asked to get hold of you by Lieutenant-Colonel Laycock.'

'Bob Laycock?' I queried. 'What does he want me for?'

'I'm afraid I can't very well explain on the telephone' – this rather apologetically – 'but could you possibly come round and see us? We're at Richmond Terrace.'

This was all very odd, but Bob was an old friend, and I was not unduly busy at the time.

'Yes, all right,' I said, 'I'll come along after lunch. Is Bob there?'

'No, no, he's not, but if you'll ask for Room 211, we'll explain everything. Oh, and another thing – do you think you could possibly get leave from your office for a week?'

'Leave for a week!' I exclaimed. 'What *is* all this about?'

'Well, I'll explain it all when we meet, but Colonel Laycock would like you to visit him if possible, and he's out of London at present.'

'I'll do my best,' I replied. 'See you this afternoon.'

Fortunately, I knew my colleagues well, so I explained the unusual message that I had just received. I had known Bob Laycock at Sandhurst, at GHQ in France, and at the Staff College, and I knew he wouldn't ask for me like this unless there was a good reason; so I arranged for someone to answer for me for the next week, and obtained the necessary leave.

Richmond Terrace turned out to be the offices of Admiral of the Fleet Sir Roger Keyes, who had been appointed Director of Combined Operations in the preceding July. The officer who had spoken on the telephone was one of his staff, and I was introduced to several others.

They apologised for the sudden and mysterious summons, but explained that Lieutenant-Colonel Laycock, who was commanding Number 8 Commando in the Isle of Arran, had asked urgently for my services, and they had been scouring London to find out where I worked. Certain commandos, it seemed, were shortly to embark for an operation, and it would be much appreciated if I could go north and spend a few days with them looking through the air photographs of the objective, and interpreting them.

I was glad of the opportunity of getting out of London, and interested to be in contact with the commandos, of whom I had heard much, but whose exact activities were still shrouded in mystery at this time. It was explained that I would have to travel up to Scotland overnight, and while a warrant was being made out, I asked if I might be told a little more about the operation, but received the reply that the objective must remain a secret, as even the commandos themselves only knew it by the code name of 'Workshop'. In the end I elicited the fact that 'Workshop' was an island, but I could get no indication as to where it was situated.

Previous experience in Intelligence in the war had taught me that there was as yet insufficient liaison between the various branches of the three Services, and I was therefore anxious to know what the objective was so that I could collect all the photographic information which existed before burying myself in a remote Scottish island. Owing to my previous employment I probably knew more at that time about the areas which had been photographed, and the various libraries in which the air photographs were filed, than most other people in the army; and three or four hours' search would have enabled me to take North everything that existed of the particular island in which we were interested.

'Look here,' I said. 'If you'll only tell me where this island is, I can almost certainly get more photos of it from photographic libraries that I know of, as we may as well have all the dope that there is.'

'No, no, my dear Churchill,' one of them replied severely. 'No one can be told the name. But you'll find that they've got excellent photos up there – everything that's needed.'

'Have they got any obliques?' I asked.

'What are obliques?' he queried.

'Photos taken obliquely and not vertically – they would be invaluable for beach reconnaissance,' I conceded.

'Well, I'm not sure. But I tell you what, Churchill, we can show you the photos they've got, because we've got a duplicate set, and all names have been deleted for security reasons, so there's no harm in your seeing them now.'

In a few moments I recognised the island.

'That's Pantellaria!' I said.

'Good God!" they said, flabbergasted.

I explained that it was an island that I had examined in great detail, at the request of the Air Ministry, several years before the war, when Italian aspirations in the Mediterranean and on the North African coast were being studied with some attention in London. I recognised it again by a characteristic inland lake, and the shape of the harbour of the principal port, for if you work much with air photos, you develop a photographic memory of places, which seldom fails. In the end I got them to agree that I should collect the additional photographs, though they swore me to secrecy and enjoined me to take elaborate precautions to allay suspicion when selecting the photos from the library.

After a long journey, I arrived at Brodick Pier on the Isle of Arran, and was taken to Colonel Laycock's headquarters in a hotel. He had a small room reserved for his use, which was always kept locked, and in which was a mass of maps and photographs. We ensconced ourselves in this room and proceeded to examine the photos in great detail, marking the enemy's defences, and selecting the most suitable landing-places for the commandos.

I was much impressed with the secrecy which the commandos had managed to preserve; no one except Laycock knew where the place was, and the wildest guesses were being made by the junior officers as to what their destination might be. The truth would not be divulged until they were all safely embarked on the transports, and had sailed for the operation; and, in the meantime, the planning went on, while everyone referred to the island as 'Workshop'.

I spent four days in the Isle of Arran, and met Brigadier Haydon, who was commanding the Special Service Brigade. This was long enough for me to become profoundly impressed with the organisation and system of the commandos; I liked their realistic approach to the work that lay ahead of them, their absence of red tape, and their terrific enthusiasm and keenness; every officer and man was a volunteer, and their physical fitness, self-reliance and specialist training made them a corps d'élite. In an England hardly recovered from the Dunkirk retreat and hourly expecting invasion from the French coasts, it was a tonic to meet troops who had the prospect of offensive operations, and were so eager to undertake them.

I returned to London and sat uneasily at my office desk; there was no chance of my being released from my staff job just yet. But it was at this time that I decided that if it was possible, I would get into the commandos myself, and though it was to be nearly two years before I attained my ambition, I kept in touch with them, and on several more occasions was called in for consultations by Brigadier Haydon and others.

In January 1941, Bob Laycock went out to the Middle East with Numbers 7, 8 and 11 Commandos. Though the Pantellaria operation was cancelled by Whitehall, much to the annoyance of Admiral Keyes and of all the commandos, the year was to bring them active service at Bardia, Crete, the Litani River, Tobruk and at Beda Littoria, and I was not to see Bob again until he returned to this country in March 1942, to succeed Brigadier Haydon as commander of the Special Service Brigade.

A few months after my journey to Arran I was again summoned by telephone, this time to visit Number 12 Commando, then commanded by Lieutenant-Colonel Harrison and located in billets on the south coast near the Hamble River. This Commando was about to undertake a series of simultaneous small raids on the French coast north-east and south of Cape Gris Nez, and I attended the final conference which was to select the actual stretches of coastline which the various raiding parties were to assault. These raids were designed to bring back information of the state of the enemy's defences, and it was important therefore that they should get ashore with as little opposition as possible, to enable them to examine the various coastal obstacles without interference. The photographic examination showed that the enemy had recently constructed a number of concrete machine gun emplacements in one particular area which had been more or less selected as one of the landing-places; but in view of the high state of defence which was now revealed, it seemed advisable to move this projected assault to a different bit of coastline which the photographs showed to be comparatively free of defences. I was asked to travel up to London the following day with Brigadier Haydon to explain the photographs to Admiral Keyes, with whom the final decision rested.

Admiral Keyes studied the photographs and discussed the landings with Brigadier Haydon and Colonel Harrison. He listened to what I had to say, and then turned to the Colonel.

'Harrison,' he said, 'what is your opinion? Would you rather switch the attack to another beach?'

'No, sir,' replied Harrison. 'My officers and I have all studied this landing, and we'd all rather go in as planned.'

The Admiral smiled a wry smile.

'In the course of a long life,' he said, 'I have generally found that it pays to take the fence where it seems highest.' And that night the Commando moved down to the coast preparatory to embarkation at Dover.

I heard later that this operation, too, had been cancelled at the last moment when the men were actually embarked in the craft. The early days of commandos were punctuated with such disappointments at depressingly frequent intervals, which placed much strain on the nerves and credulity of the soldiers, and caused Admiral Keyes to comment most bitterly on the intervention of Whitehall Planning Committees, which were largely responsible for these cancellations. Looking back on it now, one is forced to agree with the Admiral and regret that he was not allowed to have a freer hand, for it seems certain that people were over-timid in those days, and many excellent opportunities of hitting the enemy were thrown away.

Life was not all disappointments however; a number of raids had actually been performed on the coast of France and on the Channel Islands, while an early venture in Norway had resulted in the destruction of the Hydro-Electric Power Station and Aluminium Works at Glomfjord in the early days of 1941, when Captains Black and Houghton of Number 2 Commando led a small party against this important enemy industrial objective.

By this time I had moved to the Air Ministry, where I was still dealing with my old subject of air photographs, and this meant that I was still kept in touch with commando activities, since from the earliest times it had been realised that air photographs were an essential part of the intelligence required for a raid. Thus it was that I received a visit from Captain Roger Wakefield (who was the Intelligence Officer of the Special Service Brigade, and whom I had met earlier in the year at Castle Douglas), in connection with the Vaagso project which was then in an early stage of discussion.

This operation concerned the port of Vaagso which lies on the Norwegian coast almost midway between Trondhjem and Bergen, and besides containing a number of economic targets and a German garrison, also guarded the southern approaches to Ulversund, a sheltered channel in which German coastwise shipping was wont to hide on passage between Bergen and Trondhjem.

I spent many days with Wakefield at Combined Operations Headquarters, examining large numbers of air photographs of Vaagso and the little island of Maaloy, while the experts decided whether sufficient shipping and Naval escorts could be provided to take on this remote objective. In due course the expedition sailed, and it was not to prove another false start. The operation turned out to be a complete success.

The commandos, to be sure, lost some fine officers and men, but the percentage of our losses was small compared with those of the enemy, and it clearly demonstrated that such commando enterprises offered great possibilities for the future.

About a month after the Vaagso raid, I was rung up on a Sunday morning to ask if I could come that afternoon to Richmond Terrace to discuss a new venture. When I arrived, I found Major Peter Bromley-Martin of the Airborne Division and some of the intelligence officers of Combined Operations Headquarters poring over photographs of a German radio location installation which had recently been erected on the cliffs of France at a place called Bruneval, a few miles north-east of Le Havre. This installation had attracted much interest on the part of our scientists, and it appeared that it presented certain new features of which they were anxious to know more. The cliffs on this particular bit of coastline are precipitous and unscalable, and the only point where commandos could land was some distance away from the radio location stations itself. The target seemed to offer better prospects for a parachute attack, and it was in this light that the problem was considered when I was called in for advice.

Fortunately, the ground inland of the objective seemed level and favourable for a parachute descent, but details were wanted of any overhead cables or wires which might interfere with the landing, as well as the exact number and location of barbed wire obstacles, machine gun positions anrd pill boxes which defended the installation. I took away a number of photographs from the meeting for careful study, undertaking to return them with annotations of the defences in the course of a day or so.

I should point out here that by this time the interservice Photographic Interpretation Unit was in existence and did in fact supply interpretation of enemy defences on demand, but in the case of certain raids it was the practice not to disclose the purpose for which the interpretation was wanted, in order to preserve the highest measure of secrecy. It is, however, a well established fact that if the interpreter is aware of the purpose for which it is wanted, his resulting work is often far more useful than a 'hack job' done as a routine measure. By this time I was well known to the COHQ authorities, and they therefore would frequently call me in to have a look at photographs of some project they were concerned with, having explained as much of the plan as was necessary for my purpose.

Service chiefs were watching the Bruneval raid with the keenest interest, for it was the first time that British parachutists had undertaken such an adventure in France. A previous parachute raid against Italy had been carried out exactly a year before; but it had misfired for a number of reasons, and it was much hoped that this new venture would profit by the lessons of its predecessor. The plan envisaged a drop by parachutists in the close vicinity of the objective, an attack on the defended posts lying between the radio location instrument and the small cove by which the parachutists were to be evacuated by sea, and a covering force of soldiers afloat in naval craft, who would be able to assist in the withdrawal should the need arise. At the same time a diversion had been arranged for aircraft of Fighter Command so as to minimise the danger of interference with the operation by the Luftwaffe.

The operation was carried out on the night of 27th February 1942, and in bright moonlight the Whitleys crossed the French coast just before midnight. Some anti-aircraft fire was encountered which upset the navigation of one section of the aircraft employed, but the remainder dropped their parachutists with precision, and as the men floated to the ground they were able to recognize the landmarks from their previous study of air photographs and of the model. The parachutists split up into three parties, and doubled to their objectives. One party assaulted a large isolated house which was only a hundred yards from the instrument itself, while the second party went to the cove which was to be used for withdrawal, while the third party interposed itself between the other two and some farm buildings in which enemy reinforcements were thought to be billeted.

The house and the installation were overrun in a matter of minutes, six Germans being killed and one captured, but while the instrument and certain other parts of the electrical equipment were being removed, a brisk fire was opened on the parachutists from the farm building. This fire was returned, and it was not until the engineers had taken all that they required from the site, and had destroyed the remaining equipment, that the withdrawal to the cove was commenced.

The cove was known to be defended by a number of Germans in pill boxes, and to deal with this opposition the plan had arranged for one party of parachutists to proceed straight to the cove after dropping, and thus secure the withdrawal of the remainder; when, however, the main party approached the beach, they found that the enemy had not been overcome, as the majority of those who had been detailed to go to the cove had been in those aircraft which had lost their course owing to flak fire.

Major J. D. Frost, who commanded the enterprise, at once sent a party of the parachutists who had just arrived from the main objective, to reinforce those that were in the cove already, and after a short fight, the enemy surrendered. The craft waiting on the beaches were then signalled in, and the parachutists embarked. A little firing developed from the cliffs while this was in progress, but the ships replied to it, and it failed to be effective. The expedition reached England safely, having brought back the information that was required, and having only suffered a loss of one killed, seven wounded and seven missing.

CHAPTER SIX

Joining the Commandos

By mid-1942 I was rapidly tiring of employment in Whitehall, and was anxious to get back to proper soldiering. It is true that the War Office and a number of my friends urged me to take up photographic interpretation again, suggesting that I should join the Photographic Interpretation Unit at Medmenham where I could be posted as head of the Army Section, if not as head of the PIU itself, but I was keen to join the commandos, and my friend Brigadier Bob Laycock was ready to have me in his Special Service Brigade (as the Commando Brigade at this time was officially known). I was satisfied that the provision and training of interpreters both for the army and the RAF had now been properly organised and I therefore felt no qualms of conscience in quitting the photographic interpretation scene.

And so it was that on 1st September 1942 I caught a night train for Scotland, to join the Special Service Brigade. There was no immediate appointment for me to take up so I employed my first few months being attached to the various commando units in Scotland, getting to know their work, their men and their officers. My first attachment was to No 2 Commando at Largs in Ayrshire. The St Nazaire raid had left this Commando terribly depleted in officers and men for, except for the handful of survivors who were unable to get ashore because their craft was sunk or too damaged to put alongside, and one or two men who did not take part in the raid, there was nothing left of the Commando. Their commanding officer, Lieutenant-Colonel Charles Newman, their second-in-command and their adjutant were all gone, as well as all their troop leaders.

My brother Jack had been promoted to take command in the place of Newman and he had been training the large number of new officers and recruits that had arrived during the last six months; but if they lacked experience, this Commando had an esprit de corps and a tradition which a newcomer could not help feeling in the first hours of his arrival at the unit.

The change from the office life of Whitehall was most welcome and I was pleasantly surprised to find that I was not as much out of condition as I had expected. It was true that I found the high rate of marching pretty strenuous, and was a little alarmed at the light-hearted way in which a troop would be detailed to ascend a rugged Scottish mountain as though it were a couple of miles of Salisbury Plain. The physical fitness of the officers and men astonished me, and their adaptability and quickness in executing orders were a tonic to witness. They more than demonstrated the high quality they were said to possess as picked volunteer troops.

It so happened that No 2 Commando was at this time about to undertake a series of exercises with American troops, to assist them in the final stages of the training which they had undergone in the British Isles since their arrival from America. The Americans took their training very seriously, and were quick to weed out officers or NCOs who were not up to their job. I remember that at the conclusion of one particular exercise, the brigade commander and the three lieutenant-colonels commanding the three regiments in the formation, were all relieved of their appointments, put in a train, and packed off to London, and twenty-four hours later a brand new team arrived.

The American chief umpire of the exercise was Colonel Michael O'Daniel, and it was he who was appointed as the new brigade commander. This drastic change was due to the slowness with which the combat team had dealt with a military situation brought about by the directing staff, and as No 2 Commando was acting as enemy under their orders at the time, Colonel Jack always claimed jokingly that it was to him that Colonel O'Daniel owed his promotion. The next time I saw O'Daniel was in the Anzio bridgehead, where he was second-in-command of the American 3rd Division of which he later got command. He was known to the US Army as 'Iron Mike', and I reminded him of the incident.

When these manoeuvres were over, I spent a week with Lieutenant-Colonel Charles Vaughan at the Commando Depot at Achnacarry, near Spean Bridge. Charles, after serving for over a year in No 4 Commando as Administrative officer in the early days, took on the formation and organisation of the Depot, and I think it is no exaggeration to say that the commandos owe as much to him and his hard work, vision and amazing enthusiasm, as to any other single person. He is one of the great characters of the commandos, and the stories about him and his depot are legion. An old Guards company sergeant major, he always insisted on the strictest attention to smartness and discipline, while at the same time teaching his recruits methods of river crossing, rock climbing, night marching and many other strenuous and specialised tasks in which the commandos received particular training. He had never had any illusions as to the absolute necessity for discipline in specialised troops, and time and again he was proved right in battle. There have been Commando colonels who have tried to dispense with this essential requirement, but they and their units have invariably come to grief.

This brings me to discuss the type of man that was found in a commando unit. In those days, certain rather unusual types of men were recruited because of their peculiar achievements; but I think every Commando officer would agree with me that it was the average straightforward Britisher who made the best commando leader. The unusual fellow may be outstandingly good in one particular attainment, but he is probably more trouble than he is worth. If the Commandos were admired for the work they did and were prepared to do, it was due to one fact above all others: that they were *volunteers*, and had chosen *of their own free will* to be where they were, and to do what they had to do. This, if you like, is their 'secret', and the Army commandos at any rate, always realised the value of the volunteer element in their service, and insisted upon it.

When recruits were wanted for the commandos, the fact was made known in those army formations which had been opened to them by the War Office for recruiting purposes. In the early days, they had the whole of the army to choose from, but, after a few years of war, they were only allowed to search among formations which were well up to strength. The next move was for units to call for volunteers for commandos, and those that gave in their names were interviewed at convenient centres by a Selection Board, generally composed of a Commando colonel, two or three of his officers, and a Commando medical officer.

It was explained to the recruits that in joining the commandos, they would have to be prepared to do anything, in the widest sense and application of the word. It would be pointed out to them that their training would be tough and exacting, and if they were found wanting, they would be returned to their units, and there was no appeal against this decision. At the same time they, in their turn, could request to leave the commandos at any time, and though such a request was left to the discretion of their commanding officer, I never knew one to be refused. The whole essence of army commando service was the fact that the man was a volunteer; the commandos had no wish to retain anybody who wished to be somewhere else.

When a recruit had been accepted by the Selection Board, and provided he was passed as fit for commando service by the Medical Officer, he went to Achnacarry for training at the Commando Depot. It was here that many failed to make the grade and were weeded out; while those who might have joined in order to enjoy the cachet, thinking that they would avoid hard work, soon found out their mistake and asked to return to their units. When his training was completed, the recruit was posted to a Commando, where he began his new life in earnest.

Many men who had done well in their own units, volunteered for service with the commandos, but were disappointed to find that only in exceptional cases could recruits with a rank above lance-corporal be accepted; this was because the commandos preferred to reserve promotion for those who had served them well, and whom they knew. And it was found out that if a man was really good, he would very soon be promoted in his commando unit to the rank for which his ability qualified him. It is perhaps a gratifying reflection on the quality of the British as a nation, that an enormous number of recruits, both officers and men, willingly relinquished rank in order to serve with the commandos.

Towards the end of 1942, I spent some time with No 4 Commando who were then in billets in Winchester. They had earned for themselves a great reputation for their faultless performance at Dieppe, and were always known in commando circles for their very progressive ideas in organisation, armament, and drill for battle. This was largely due to the fact that they had some excellent officers who possessed that priceless but all too rare quality – a completely realistic outlook. Under the leadership of their colonel, Lord Lovat, they had long been one of the best units in the Commando Brigade.

Full encouragement was always given to any soldier or officer who had some new idea or device to suggest, and if after examination it was found to have possibilities, the Commando would organise a demonstration to try it out under practical conditions. They owed much to the enthusiasm of their second-in-command, Major Derek Mills-Roberts, who, like his colonel, Shimi Lovat, was destined to become a Commando brigadier later on.

While I was staying with No 4 Commando, I heard that I had been appointed to Brigadier Laycock's headquarters in the rôle of the staff officer responsible for Staff Duties and Training in the rank of lieutenant-colonel. The headquarters had recently moved from Scotland and were established at Sherborne Castle in Dorset, and I moved there without further delay, to take up my work.

When the Commandos were originally formed, they were organised and equipped to carry out raids from the coasts of the British Isles, and it was not envisaged that they would be away from these shores for more than several days. It was decided therefore to organise and equip them on the assumption that when not taking part in a raid, they would be accommodated in billets, and such personnel as cooks and butchers, sanitary men, store keepers and so on were not included in their establishment. Further, this arrangement made it possible for them to move at the shortest notice, and being relieved of their own maintenance, they were able to concentrate all their attention and all their time on training for amphibious raids.

People often assume that a commando soldier received extra pay because he was a commando, but this was of course a misconception. When based in the British Isles, he received the sum of 6/8d per day as a lodging allowance; and it became his responsibility to find lodgings for himself and to pay for them with this allowance. Some men managed to save a little on it, but the arrangement they made at their billet was entirely their own affair. When a man left the British Islands for a raid, he ceased to draw the allowance for the period that he was away; and if, as was the case in Nos 1 and 6 Commandos in North Africa, he served abroad for a prolonged period, he got no more and no less, than his comrade in the infantry, or any other branch of the army.

Planning for the various small raids which were still taking place, chiefly on the French and Norwegian coasts, and in the Channel Islands, was still carried out at Combined Operations Headquarters in London, and I frequently had to attend conferences in connection with them. One such raid was the attack on the iron pyrites mine situated at Lillebo in the island of Stord about fifty miles south of Bergen.

A detachment of commandos, under the command of Major F. W. Fynn of No 12 Commando, went over to Norway in motor torpedo boats, manned by officers and men of the Norwegian Navy. Their task was to destroy the mine and re-embark when the task was completed.

As the first group of craft approached the quayside of the small fishing village of Saagvag, they were fired on from the shore by automatic weapons. Air photographs had shown that the enemy had mounted at least one gun on the jetty, so one of the MTBs fired a torpedo at it as the craft approached. There was a blinding flash and a tremendous explosion as the torpedo struck, and in the confusion which ensued, the boats came alongside and the commandos swarmed ashore. This was no easy feat, for there was a difference in level between the decks of the MTBs and the top of the jetty of some nine feet, and assault ladders and ropes had to be used to get the men on to the jetty. This first wave to land took a number of prisoners, established certain road blocks and cut all the telephone wires.

Meanwhile, the second party came in on the other side of the bay, and made straight for the mine which was two miles inland. Although they were heavily laden with explosives and demolition charges, the commandos covered the distance in 25 minutes, and as soon as they arrived, set about their work. The mine workers, who were Norwegians, realised what was happening and did nothing to impede the soldiers, but one or two quislings, who had been posted by the Germans as guards, showed fight and were dealt with.

The hoisting gear was blown up and its remains fell down the shaft, while the crushing plant, compressor house, transformer, and railway stores were demolished by explosives. A motor car full of German staff officers rushed to the scene while work at the mine was proceeding, but a road block had been posted in expectation of such a visit, and the car and its occupants were written off by three quick bursts of a bren gun.

The commandos then returned to the jetty and blew up a silo on the quayside, the conveyor system, and the enemy gun positions, before re-embarking; and to complete the day, the MTBs on the way home destroyed a low-flying Ju 88 which had evidently been sent out by the Germans to discover what it was that had hit them so suddenly and so hard. The raid had accomplished the destruction of a mine providing the Germans with 160,000 tons of iron pyrites a year, and repairs were unlikely to be completed in less than twelve months. Our losses were one NCO killed, and about a dozen men slightly wounded or injured.

Brigadier Laycock had been anxious to train a certain number of commandos in warfare in mountains, and to give men practice in movement in conditions of snow and ice. With this in view, he had been able to obtain a loan of the services of Squadron Leader Frank Smythe, the world-famous Everest climber, and the latter had organised and set up a mountain and snow warfare camp for commandos at Braemar in Aberdeenshire.

I paid him a visit soon after he had got himself established, and much enjoyed two days' climbing with him on Ben Macdhui. This must have been in January 1943, and there was quite deep snow when one got above 3,000 feet, and a howling cold wind. We issued the troops with specialist mountain equipment, including wind-proof suits, but during my stay, Frank was good enough to lend me one of his green double-thick silk Everest suits, and I was thrilled to discover in one of its pockets a small piece of stone from Everest.

Frank Smythe could tell a fascinating story of climbing and, though no rock climber myself, I have always been interested in the stories of the various Everest expeditions, and of the first ascents of the stiffer peaks of Switzerland. Frank knew them all by heart, and time passed quickly in his company. Included in the curriculum for the commando soldiers were lectures by him on climbing, many of them illustrated by exquisite coloured slides of mountains. I fear he had to contend with many difficulties in obtaining the proper mountain equipment, and I think his patience was sorely tried on more than one occasion, but we were very grateful to him for his willing help and expert knowledge.

Not long after this visit to Braemar, I had to fly up to the Shetlands with Major Eric Collins, who was then one of the Planners at Combined Operations Headquarters, to visit a camp of commandos that had been established in the islands for several months. Arrangements were going forward for another Norwegian raid, and Major Ted Fynn, who had led the attack on the iron mine at Lillebo, was in charge of the camp. The weather was bleak, and cold, and high winds swept over the peat-hags and scudded down the waters of the steel-grey lochs.

We spent a lot of time fixing up details with the Navy and with the Norwegian skippers of the MTBs, and Ted's intelligence officer and I had a certain amount of fun making a model from air photographs of the objective out of peat which we collected from the mountainside. Unfortunately, the attack never came off, for although the men sailed and reached Norwegian waters, information was received that the enemy had altered his dispositions, and it was not possible to alter our plan sufficiently at the last minute to make the attack still feasible.

When I got back to my headquarters we were already becoming involved in the planning for the invasion of Sicily, and soon it became necessary for me to move to London to take part in the daily conferences that were being held at the headquarters of the 1st Canadian Division. These were still the early days of the planning, and no final decisions had yet been taken as to where the landings would take place; we would study one part of the coastline in detail, having been given provisional objectives, and then discuss the various problems at length with the Naval Staff and with the Canadians; and just as daylight appeared to be dawning, we would be informed that the plan had changed and our new objectives were on some entirely different stretch of coastline and we would have to set to work all over again.

As usual, great precautions were taken to preserve secrecy in the planning stages. The operation was referred to by the code name of 'Husky', and an elaborate system of passes was instituted and all maps that had to be displayed on walls were covered by blinds or curtains which had hastily to be drawn if some new face appeared and asked admittance to the room. Such measures do become rather irksome at times, but they had been more than justified and were never relaxed.

This was to be the baptism of fire for the 1st Canadian Division, and after their long period of inactivity in England, they were all immensely keen and eager for the date of embarkation. It was a thrill for all of us to know that we were to land as part of the famous Eighth Army, and under the orders of General Montgomery, who was in command of the whole operation. He was, of course, at this time at his headquarters in Tunisia, and he called a preliminary conference to which Major-General Salmon, commanding the 1st Canadian Division, and Admiral Mack, the Naval Force Commnder, were flown out by air to attend. It was a great shock when we heard next morning that the aircraft had crashed and the General and the Admiral had both been killed. However, the planning had to go on, and it was soon announced that Major-General Simmonds and Admiral Vian (of *Cossack* fame) had been appointed in their places.

When General Montgomery announced his plan, we learnt that the intention was to seize the south-eastern corner of Sicily by landings on the east and south coast simultaneously, and then to advance up the eastern coast through the ports of Syracuse and Augusta to Catania, and thence onwards to Messina. Having taken Messina, we should control the Italian supply line to the island, and being cut off from supplies it was not likely that the Germans in the west of the island could hold out for long. The 1st Canadian Division was to land on beaches on the south coast of Sicily close to the south-eastern tip of the island; and they wanted two Commandos to land on their left, just ahead of them, to destroy some enemy positions on the coast which appeared to be heavily fortified, and which could bring fire to bear from the flank on the main Canadian beaches. If the landing was successful, we were to advance inland till we joined hands with the flank of the Canadian Division, and were then to conform with them and protect their southern flank.

Nos 40 and 41 Royal Marine Commandos were selected to take part in the operation, and they were moved from the Isle of Wight to Scotland to undertake special training for their part in the landing. They had, of course, no idea where they were going, or what their employment would be, but as intelligence came in at the Planning Headquarters in London concerning the enemy and our particular objectives, I would send up to the brigade major of the Special Service Brigade an outline of the tasks that had to be performed, and he would select a similar piece of country, and set exercises to give the marine commandos practice in the tasks they would have to perform.

Another of our Commandos, No 3 (Army) Commando, under Lieutenant-Colonel Durnford-Slater, was already in the Middle East, and this Commando was also taking part in the landing, but not with the Canadians; they were to land with the British XIII Corps under General Dempsey on the eastern coast just south of Syracuse. This fact, combined with the knowledge that No 2 Commando were now in Gibraltar, led Brigadier Laycock to think that once the initial landings were completed, it was quite possible that there would be as many as four Commandos in the theatre of war, and there would arise the necessity for a Commando Brigade Headquarters to control these units. He therefore sought permission to take a headquarters with him to Sicily, while leaving a second headquarters in England under the temporary command of Lieutenant-Colonel the Lord Lovat to look after the units at home.

It was not without a great deal of difficulty that this permission was obtained, and many battles on paper and in conference rooms in the War Office had to be waged before the need for this arrangement was recognised. Our friends the Canadians helped us considerably in this respect, by saying that it would make their task easier if they had a Commando Headquarters to deal with, rather than with separate units.

The great problem which was uppermost in everyone's mind at this time was the question of the depth of water off the beaches. All available evidence went to show that the beaches of Sicily had a peculiar characteristic, which seemed common to all of them, that they were all 'protected' by natural sand-bars about three hundred yards off the shore. These sand-bars appeared to run the whole length of the beaches, and it was a matter of doubt whether there was sufficient depth of water over the bar to permit the landing craft (in the first instance) to clear the bank and so approach inshore, and whether maintenance craft bringing in the stores and supplies necessary to maintain the troops would be able to discharge on the beaches.

Sometimes there were as many as three sand-bars running parallel with each other, and one of their characteristics was that the depth of water on the landward side of the bar was for a short distance deeper than on the seaward side. This meant that if the assault craft grounded on the sandbanks, and the men had to disembark and wade ashore, they were liable to find themselves out of their depth in the first few yards that they had to cover. For heavily equipped men this was a serious consideration, but so also was the maintenance problem, for even if the assault waves succeeded in landing and overcoming the enemy's coastal defence, it would be impossible to keep them supplied if the more heavily laden maintenance craft all grounded three hundred yards off the coast.

The Naval Staff spent a great deal of their time studying this awkward problem, and resort was had to every known device and method of estimating the depth of water at the vital point. Air photographs were most useful in this connection, as a method had been worked out for estimating depth by observing the frequency of wave-lines on the surface of the sea, for in calm weather there is a ratio between the depth of water and the distance between successive waves. To enable measurements to be taken, however, photography had to occur under certain conditions of light which did not obtain when the existing photographic sorties had been flown, so a new lot of photographs had to be ordered on the highest priority. They were obtained in due course, and a sapper team which was expert in working out these abstruse calculations finally produced their results, but they qualified them by saying that there was bound to be an error of plus or minus 18 inches, and it was found that if the error turned out to be a minus quantity, the beaches might prove to be unsuitable.

This risk had to be accepted, but, to minimise it, methods were devised of blowing gaps in the underwater sand-bars to make channels of approach for the craft. Although this introduced certain naval disadvantages in beach maintenance, it was the best that could be devised under the circumstances. I worked closely with Lieutenant-Commander Cameron, RNVR, of the Naval Staff on this problem, and formed a great respect for his knowledge and judgment in matters of naval intelligence, and it was a great pleasure to meet him again two months later in Algiers, when we found ourselves once again considering similar problems preparatory to the Salerno landing.

Towards the end of our planning period in London, there was a great flutter in the dovecotes because it was announced that an Important Personage would hold a conference behind locked doors in the War Office, but no one lower than the rank of brigadier was to attend, and the whole proceeding was wrapped in the closest secrecy.

The work of the more junior staff was by now concluded, and I remember lounging about with my Canadian friends of the Intelligence Branch in our Intelligence Room waiting to hear the result of the War Office conference. My opposite number was a major called Chambers of a Canadian Highland Regiment who hailed from Vancouver, and who, in addition to his military duties, was a member of the Ottawa House of Representatives. He kept me supplied with Sweet Caporals and Canadian chocolates, and regaled me with stories of shooting in the Rockies and clam picnics in the creeks on the Pacific coast. They were a very friendly staff, and I have the happiest memories of our cooperation with them in the Sicily enterprise.

It soon transpired that the mystery personage was none other than the great Monty, and he had come in person from Tunisia to outline to the Canadians his plans for the assault on Sicily, and to state simply and clearly what he required and expected of the Canadian landing. The division had known him when they had served under him in the South-Eastern Command in England, and they spoke with one voice of the frankness with which he explained the problems and the confidence which he exuded. His visit was a typical gesture, and brought to a climax the already high spirit and eagerness of the whole division.

A series of exercises had been arranged by the Naval and Army Staffs to take place on the west coast of Scotland, to rehearse the landing shortly before the convoy sailed for the Mediterranean, so Brigadier Laycock had established a temporary Headquarters in the town of Troon which we occupied from now until we sailed. I journeyed north in the train with Brigadiers Vokes and Graham, two of the Canadian brigade commanders with whom we had maintained a close liaison during the preceding month and with whom we were to land on the shores of Sicily. Brigadier Vokes had armed himself with a bottle of whisky against the journey and the three of us partook of it in tooth-mugs in his sleeping compartment before turning in for the night.

The officers of the Brigade Staff, through the good offices of Major Eric Collins, had the luck to be billeted with his father, the eminent publisher, and mother in their comfortable house outside Troon, and we all owe much to Mr and Mrs Collins for their generous hospitality in our last few weeks in Britain. I always took it as an omen that there was a painting in the hall of the Italian village of Amalfi, and I hoped that this might be taken as a pointer to our future destination and the successful conclusion of the Sicily campaign.

Apart from the two big exercises that we carried out with the

Canadians in Scotland, we held a number of commando schemes to test out our own plans for our part in the landing. While our transports were anchored in Brodick Bay in the Isle of Arran we went ashore there to do a cliff-climbing exercise at night. This was the first time that commandos had returned to the island since 1940, and we received a friendly welcome from the inhabitants who remembered our earlier visit.

Air photographs had shown that the particular cove which the commandos had selected for their landing in Sicily was fringed by a cliff which we should have to scale, in order to get inland to attack the enemy pill boxes from the rear. No one knew the exact height of this cliff, but maps and naval coastal manuals showed the general altitude of the coast to be as much as 40 feet above sea level. The photographs indicated that in the cove we had chosen, the cliff was a good deal lower, but this was based on the impression of height obtained in a stereoscopic examination of the photographs, and we were not at all certain of this fact, as we were unable to have access to the elaborate instruments and trained survey personnel who alone might have answered our problem for us. We therefore took every opportunity to practise cliff-climbing in order to insure ourselves against the worst eventuality.

At last the day of embarkation came, and Headquarters and the two Commandos went aboard the transports *Derbyshire* and *Durban Castle* that were to take them to Sicily.

CHAPTER SEVEN

Sicily

The convoy sailed on Monday, 28th June, passing through the boom across the Clyde at 8.30 p.m. The long line of merchant ships, their decks thronged with soldiers, moved rather slowly through the pale blue water. This was the start of an expedition – the beginning of an enterprise.

Our ship was the transport *Derbyshire*, and we had on board Brigade Headquarters and No 40 Royal Marine Commando. There was also the 48th Highlanders of Canada, as well as various detachments of Royal Engineers, Artillery and Beach Units.

My servant, Sapper Baldwin, was very anxious to know where we were going, and was indignant when I told him that it was still a secret. 'After all,' he said, 'we're the blokes wot 'ave got to do the fightin', and there ain't no pubs we can let it out in now.' As Admiral Vian's signal to the convoy indicated that our objective was somewhere in the Mediterranean, there were the wildest speculations being made in the mess-decks, which gave Spain, the South of France, Sicily, Sardinia, Greece, Crete and Turkey as our destination. I could only tell poor Baldwin to have patience and that tomorrow, 1st July, was the day on which all ranks would be told.

On 1st July the ship's bags were opened, and the intelligence papers that they contained were distributed to the various units on board. These included marked air photographs, maps, reports on the coastline and operation orders, as well as excellent models of the beaches. The Orders of the Day issued by General Montgomery, General Simmonds and General MacNaughten were read to the troops over the ship's loudspeaker, and briefing began and was to last for the next three or four days.

On the evening of 3rd July Brigadier Laycock spoke to all officers in the smoke-room, and outlined the main plan for the assault on Sicily, which provided the background against which each unit could see its part in the whole enterprise.

One evening we were having a practice for officers of HQ Staff in R/T procedure on the upper deck when our escort vessels detected a submarine, and dashed off in chase dropping a number of depth-charges which made a fine spectacle, though there was no evidence that a submarine had been destroyed. On 5th July in the early morning we passed through the Straits of Gibraltar, and I wished I could make a signal to my elder brother Jack who was commanding No 2 Commando on the Rock at the time.

While we were steaming one day just out of sight of the North African coast we heard and felt at luncheon the detonation of depth-charges. When we went on deck a little later, the escorts were returning and one of them passed right through the convoy flying the success signal and metaphorically wagging its tail, and later we received a signal from Admiral Vian announcing that a submarine had been destroyed.

A little later we passed between the island of La Galite and the African coast, a stretch of water which was the scene of my younger brother Buster's last air battle. He was shot down in this area while defending the famous Malta Convoy code-named 'Pedestal' on 12th August 1942, almost a year before; he had, however, destroyed two Italian twin-engined and heavily armoured Cant reconnaissance aircraft the same day. By a coincidence, the Medical Officer of No 40 Commando, Lieutenant-Commander Pride, RNVR, was serving in HMS *Victorious* with my brother at the time, and he was able to tell me a lot about the action.

By now it was generally known that 'D Day' was to be 10th July, and that the landing was to be made in the early hours of the morning. On the 8th two other convoys appeared on the horizon, the American force from Africa which was to land away to the west of us at Gela, and our own 'slow convoy' which left the Clyde two days before us, and which included the monitor HMS *Roberts* with its two enormous 15-inch guns. There was also a large number of tank landing craft, and several flotillas of motor launches. Everywhere you looked you saw ships, and all steaming steadily in the same direction. It was a most majestic spectacle, and it had in it a relentlessness of purpose – a determination and strength which warmed our hearts and sharpened our spirits.

We had enjoyed perfect weather throughout the voyage. We left the Clyde in a heat wave, and we had had calm seas the whole way. Apart from one or two submarine hunts, there had been no sign of the enemy, and we were all astonished that we had not had a single visit from the Luftwaffe or the Regia Aeronautica. Now that three large fleets from three directions were converging on Sicily, we felt sure that things would change, and expected to be bombed, or at least reconnoitred, at increasingly frequent intervals.

By 9th July, everything was ready. All the last-minute briefing was done, and the last of the signals that we had exchanged with the *Durban Castle* in which No 41 (RM) Commando was embarked had been sent. Both Commandos were content that the tasks were clear, and that all eventualities had been foreseen and catered for. The little groups of men which had monopolised the boat-deck for the last two days to prime the grenades, had disappeared, and all the heavy kitbags had been packed and stacked. These were to be brought ashore on the evening following our landing, and we had with us only what we could carry in our equipment. As always, I had the greatest difficulty in making myself get down to my own packing, though Baldwin was a great help and did a lot for me.

The wind began to freshen about noon, and by tea-time people were beginning to get alarmed at its force, and were wondering if it was likely to get too strong for the landing craft to be lowered and operated. By dinner-time the ship was rolling and pitching considerably, the wind strength was estimated at Force 6, and speculation was rife as to whether the operation would be postponed. An atmosphere of gloom prevailed. We went on deck and watched the brave little MLs being tossed about like cockleshells in the storm. The island of Gozo, off Malta, was plainly visible on our starboard beam, and seas could be seen breaking at the foot of her precipitous cliffs.

Quite suddenly the wind abated. A swell remained, but obviously conditions were improving. No word of cancellation had been received, and at 10 p.m., realising that it was then too late to cancel the operation whatever the weather, I went to my cabin to get one and a half hours' rest on my bunk before the commencement of the landing.

No 40 Commando was piped to stand by at 11.30 p.m. and Baldwin came to my cabin as arranged and helped me to get my equipment on, and then I gave him a hand with his. I tipped my cabin steward and arranged with him to send certain articles of clothing home when the ship next returned to England. He was a nice old man, a little emotional, and as he shook my hand he said, 'Goodbye, sir, and may God bless and protect you.'

On hearing the pipe 'No 40 Royal Marine Commando, stand by your craft', Baldwin and I went on deck and formed up alongside our LCA. With me, besides my batman, was Lance-Corporal Kenward, one of the headquarters clerks. We also had half the Signal Troop, No

After a conference on mobilisation at Tournai Barracks, Aldershot, September 1939. Lieut-Colonel Barty Moore, centre; author at right

(*Left*) Office of Air Intelligence Section, GHQ, BEF at Harbarcq, near Arras. The officers are, *left to right:* Major Geoffrey Hunt, Lieutenant Gerald Lacoste, Captain Whittaker, (2 clerks) and Flight Lieutenant Stevens. Photo taken by the author. (*Right*) Sidney Cotton and Air Marshal Sir Arthur Barratt at Air HQ in France, 1940

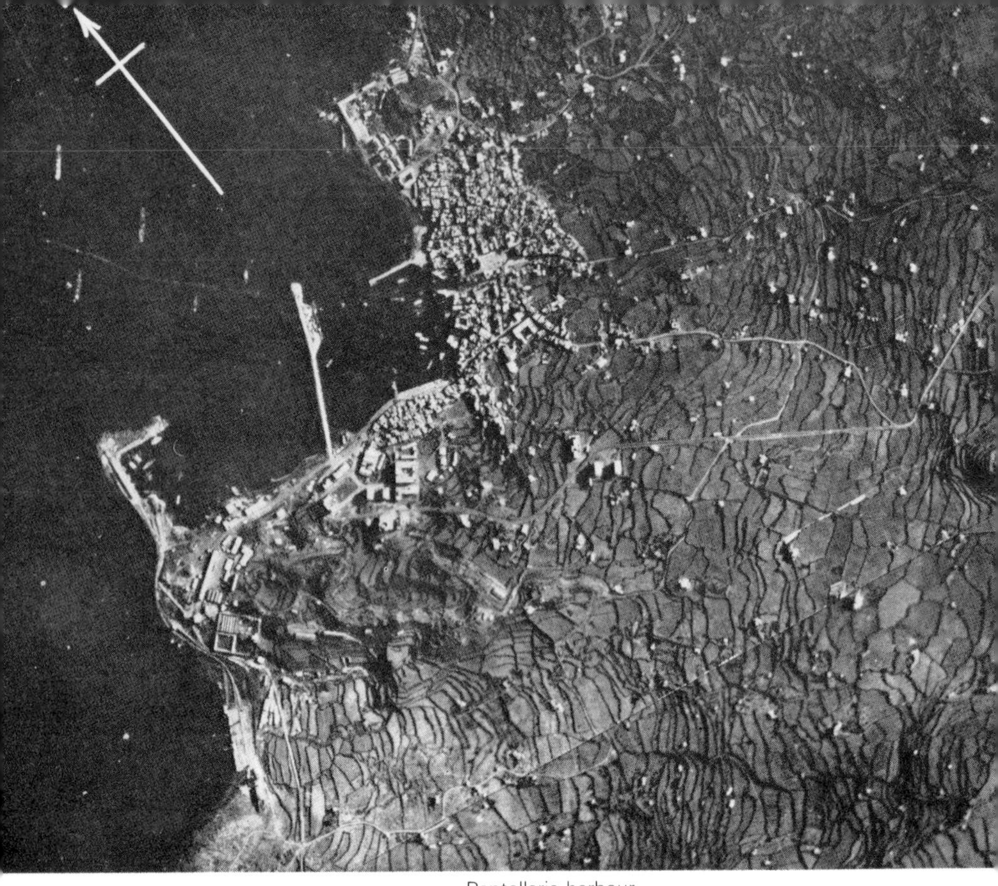

Pantellaria harbour

Bruneval RDF Station

40's 3-inch mortar team, and Lieutenant-Commander Pride and his medical orderlies.

Later came the order to embark. The LCA was hoisted at its davits on the upper deck on the port side, and the *Derbyshire* still had way on. The night was not very dark as there was a bright moon near the full. I could see the dark loom of the ship, the brilliantly clear stars and the Milky Way like a great white road in the sky. The RAF were bombing inland, and the white flare of the bomb-bursts sprang up at intervals on the horizon, for we were seven miles out and could not see the land. They were also dropping flares on the town of Pachino as arranged in the plan, to assist us in direction during the run in, and the flares hung like clusters of orange Chinese lanterns high up in the velvety darkness.

Time passed slowly, and the men were quiet. The air was balmy and consequently it was more pleasant than it had been on our exercises in Scotland, but otherwise everything seemed just the same.

At last came the order 'lower away first flight', and down went the ten LCAs from the lower decks. I heard the Canadian Military Liaison Officer add on the loudspeaker as the boats went down, 'Good luck, boys', but I doubt if any of the first flight heard it, for the falls made a good deal of noise. As soon as the first flight was clear of the sides, and their davits had been folded inboard, our turn came; we were lowered about four minutes later, and as the craft splashed on to the surface, it took up the swell of the sea. We joined up with the other LCAs which were lying off waiting for us, and then made for the rendezvous with an ML, in two columns. There we joined forces with the ten more LCAs carrying No 41 Royal Marine Commando which had been lowered from their ship, the *Durban Castle*, and the 22 LCAs, comprising the Commando Assault, headed for the coast.

There was a strong swell running and about every third wave splashed over the bows. I was drenched to the skin in the first quarter of an hour, as I was standing by the bren gunner up in the front. I thought our coxswain should have kept a bit closer to the LCAs ahead, but he was a dour Canadian Scot who resented questions or suggestions, and I thought it best to leave him to his job.

Zero hour was 2.30 a.m. At about 2 a.m. I found we were practically stationary, with about four other craft milling round us.

'What's happening now, coxswain?' I asked.

'We're waitin', sir.'

'Waiting for what?'

'Signal from the beach, sir.'

This was the procedure we had agreed upon, as No 41 were to form line abreast in front of No 40 (with whom Brigade Headquarters was moving) and close the beach. No 41 were to form a beach-head as soon as they got ashore, and signal us in; but I had my doubts if all was going according to plan, as there were not enough LCAs in company with us, and the coastline, so far as I could see, looked too flat to be our correct landing place.

'Are you sure we haven't lost the main column?' I asked.

'Dunno, sir.'

'I think we're too far to the east – those are Canadian LCAs over there.'

'Shouldn't be, sir.'

'Well, dammit, *they are*,' I replied, 'and this coast looks much too flat to be our beach. We ought to be much further over to the west.'

'Don't think so, sir.'

'Well, I do. Get under way and take me up the coast to the west. Go in close, and I'll probably be able to recognise the coastline a bit later.'

We turned to the westward and after about a mile we ran into a lot more boats; on hailing them, I found that they were from the *Circassia* and were loaded with Canadian troops. This showed that we were off the Canadian beach, so we continued on for another 500 yards; the coxswain closed the coast to about 50 yards, and I recognised Punta Castellazzo, by its peculiar shape.

As we turned to round this point, rifle shots were fired at us from the top of it, and one heard the loud shattering 'crack' of bullets passing very close. The coxswain dropped to his knees, let go the steering wheel, and the craft promptly circled round and proceeded in the direction from which we had come. At first, I thought he must have been hit, but when I realised this was not the case I made him proceed on our original course round the point.

I now recognised exactly where we were, and directed him to the second bay westwards from Punta Castellazzo, as this, I knew, would be our pre-selected 'Commando Cove'. On the way round, we were fired at again four or five times, the shots being from rifles from the pill boxes, of which I knew the position from previous study of air photographs. I was only surprised that they did not open on us with machine guns. The shots, however, told me that No 41 had evidently not yet cleared this part of the coastline, and as there was a fine old row going on a few hundred yards further down the coast, I judged that the commando landing must have missed 'Commando Cove' and have taken place somewhere near the alternative beach which we had selected.

When we were in the centre of 'Commando Cove' and about 150 yards off, I made the coxswain head straight in and increase to full speed. We grounded some fifteen yards off the beach and I ran ashore, dropping into two feet of water. Baldwin followed me and Lance-Corporal Kenward was behind him. We made straight for the base of the little cliff which bordered the beach and deposited our loads of ammunition, wireless sets, etc., and I was much relieved to find that this cliff which had caused us so much anxiety in the planning stages was in fact only about nine feet high and easily scalable.

I was expecting every moment to hear the pill boxes on the edges of the bay open up on us, so I got some men on to the road above the cliff to watch the approach from the east, and set off, with Baldwin and Kenward as scouts, towards the west to find Brigade Headquarters. The houses we had decided to occupy as Brigade Headquarters were searched, and found empty except for one cow.

Then I heard men approaching from the fields to the north-west of the road, and yelled the challenge, 'Desert Rats', and got the correct reply, 'Kill Italians'. On questioning the officer in charge, I found that this was a leading troop of No 41, which was clearing the coastline eastwards as ordered, and I pointed out to them the pill boxes that had fired at us.

We carried on down the road and then met Corporal Cook, Bob Laycock's batman, whom he had sent out to try and find me. I found Brigade Headquarters at a small house near the edge of the alternative beach and noticed a couple of dead Italian soldiers near an adjacent pill box. Bob asked me to identify their unit so that we could inform Divisional Headquarters, and this meant inspecting the divisional flash on their collars and comparing it with the identification manual. It was about 3.30 a.m. and the task of removing the collar from an Italian who had been killed by a burst of bren in the face was, to say the least of it, uncongenial at that hour of the morning. Prisoners were now coming in, and firing was audible to the east and west, where 40 and 41 Commandos were doing their job.

A conversation with an under-officer of Alpini, who could speak a little French, enabled me to identify the companies, battalions, regiments and division holding the coast in this sector, and we sent this information by wireless to the Canadian Divisional Headquarters, which was still afloat.

The landing had been made in the face of machine-gun fire, and

Major McCann, the second-in-command of No 41, and Lieutenant Hervey had been killed on the beach. The wounded were being brought in and tended by the medical section at the side of the house near which our headquarters was established. They were very patient and uncomplaining, and I spoke to Captain Tamplin, who had been hit in the thigh.

Pops Manners reported in due course to say that all his sector to the west had been mopped up, but about the same time sniping started from the low hills lying inland from the beach, and this slowly increased in intensity. Bob spoke to Pops, who sent a troop out under Captain Mike Ephraums to clear the hills. Captain Cooper, the troop leader of No 41's beach-head troop, was brought in wounded. Ephraums did a very good job quickly, by using hand grenades and brens, and killed or drove off the opposition, which consisted of coastal troops who had retired from the coast on our landing, and had taken up positions inland.

Meanwhile, messages were coming in at intervals from No 41 Commando, who were dealing systematically with enemy positions in the east. They had their toughest fighting in the neighbourhood of Punta Castellazzo, where one particularly nasty trick was played by an Italian, who put up his hands and then threw a red hand grenade which killed one of our men and seriously wounded an officer in the foot. He was promptly killed by another marine and 41 went on to clear the area, giving the enemy no more opportunities for treachery. They had learnt their lesson.

Lieutenant-Colonel Bertie Lumsden, the commanding officer of No 41 Commando, reported that he had established contact with the Seaforth Highlanders of Canada, who were the unit on our right flank, and that all opposition in his sector had been overcome. Brigade then ordered the two Commandos to take up a defensive position in accordance with the operation order and Headquarters moved up to a house on a hill overlooking the bay. The sun was now well up (it was approximately 9 a.m.) and much shipping could be seen in the bay. No single enemy aircraft appeared.

At this house, which had been the Italian Signal Headquarters, Bob and I had a shave and opened a tin of self-heating soup for breakfast. I went through the papers of some of the prisoners, and we set up our Tactical Headquarters in the shade of an olive tree in a field. I then went off to see Lieutenant-Colonel Hoffmeister, who was commanding the Seaforths of Canada, and on from him to Bertie Lumsden and 41 Commando. Some Canadians gave me a lift for part of the way in a bren-gun carrier which had just been landed. The roads were very white and dusty, and the sun was getting hot.

When I got back about two hours later I found that Brigadier Laycock had moved his headquarters to a house which had been the private residence of a wine dealer, and there was an enormous barn adjacent to the house filled with hogsheads and firkins of Marsala. We tasted this and found it to be rough but not unpleasant, though, in the heat, I thought it best when diluted with water. Bob and Philip Dunne insisted on being photographed beside the barrels because they wanted to annoy Evelyn Waugh by sending him the photograph, as Evelyn, who had been at our headquarters in England, had professed a partiality for Marsala.

About 2 p.m. No 41 reported that they were being sniped and shot up by enemy mortars and what seemed to be 6-pounder anti-tank guns, and said they were uncertain if their outpost position could be maintained in the face of it. As the brigadier was away at the time visiting the Canadian 2nd Brigade, I went to 40 Commando taking Bertie Lumsden of 41 with me, and we had a conference where we arranged for the two Commandos to assist each other forward to eliminate the enemy position. Philip Dunne came with me and we accomplished the first part of the journey in a small Fiat car which he had found and which Clifford James (our signal officer) got working with the help of one of our wireless batteries. We were sniped a little and mortars were shelling one or two fields which we had to cross between 41 and 40. It was not, however, very alarming.

I returned to our house and contacted Divisional Headquarters and asked for assistance by fire from the Seaforths, but this did not in fact amount to very much as they were having a private battle of their own in which they seemed to be using a good deal of smoke. I could see the battle from our headquarters, and the mortaring and shelling was increasing.

The heaviest weapon the commandos were armed with was a 3-inch mortar, and this was out-ranged by the German 4-inch, which they were using against 40 and 41 Commandos. The four anti-tank guns were also out of range to our mortars and the position looked a little difficult, when by chance No 41's mortar officer met an officer of the Canadian Division's 4.2-inch mortar detachment on the road. This weapon could reach the enemy guns, and the officer was longing to let off some rounds, so he said he would be delighted to help. The target was indicated to him and, in a remarkably short time, he put a burst slap in amongst the enemy anti-tank guns. Only a few more rounds were necessary to eliminate the position, and the commandos advanced to find the guns abandoned with full limbers amidst a gruesome heap of dead horses and dead and wounded Italians. It appeared that some Germans who were with them had retired as soon as our mortars found the range.

Brigadier Laycock went to a divisional conference that evening, at which it was decided to move forward by moonlight into the plain in front of Ispica. Late that night No 41's padre came in to Headquarters to say that all our wounded had been finally evacuated to the Canadian beach hospital, though we were sorry to learn that they had had a long and uncomfortable wait in the hot sun before transport arrived so that they could be moved. The padre had also buried most of our dead on the coast. Our casualties at the end of the day were two officers and five other ranks killed, and five officers and 31 other ranks wounded.

The commandos advanced that night some two thousand yards to a ridge position on the left of the Canadians, and we moved our headquarters forward about a couple of miles. In going up, we passed the scene of the battle of the previous afternoon, and saw the dead horse team at the side of the road, various dead Italians in the ditch, and the abandoned guns with their limbers.

Sniping was continuing spasmodically, but was diminishing. In the afternoon, I went off to contact Divisional Headquarters, the advanced elements of which had by now landed, and I also had a pleasant bathe on the Canadian beach. We slept at our headquarters in a farmhouse with jasmine growing outside the windows.

The two big towns of Ispice and Rosolini had now surrendered, chiefly due to the 15-inch bombardment of the monitor *Roberts*. The commandos were taken out of the line and given a rest area in reserve near the centre of the Canadian beach. During the previous night most of us had been badly bitten in our farmhouse by fleas and bugs of every description, and I was horrified to count 123 bites on my left leg between knee and ankle alone.

Brigadier Laycock had heard that General Montgomery wanted to see him, so he and I went off to the beach in a borrowed jeep and then got a craft to take us out to Admiral Vian's headquarters ship the *Hilary* which was still lying in the bay. We saw General de Guingand, Monty's Chief of Staff, who said the latter was expected, and advised us to wait. General Eisenhower came aboard, and also Admirals Ramsay and McGrigor. We heard that Admiral Mountbatten, the Chief of Combined Operations, was ashore with Monty, but later it was announced that the latter was not visiting the headquarters ship after all, and we returned to Brigade, having a bathe on the way.

That evening we received a signal that General Montgomery wanted to see Brigadier Laycock at the headquarters of XXX Corps at Pachino, so we set off again in a jeep. When we arrived at the headquarters, which was established in an olive grove, General Montgomery was busy in his caravan, so General Oliver Leese, who was commanding the corps, took us into his own caravan and told us the form while we were waiting to be sent for by General Montgomery. In due course, his ADC came across and asked us to go to his caravan.

The General was in shirt-sleeves and shorts, and was sunburnt to a dark mahogany colour as a result of his desert campaigns. He told us to come in and sit down, congratulated Brigadier Laycock on the commando landing, and outlined to us his plan and how he proposed to use us in the coming advance. This he did on a small map-board covered with talc, pointing out that our probable role would be raids on the corniche road in the rear of the enemy, as he fell back.

The General radiated confidence as usual, and we were delighted to find that our future employment accorded so exactly with the tasks for which we had been trained. I noticed that the General only had two photographs in his caravan, one was of a schoolboy who was presumably his son, and the other was of himself.

The Italian General of the Coastal Division had been captured in Syracuse, and was at XXX Corps Headquarters where he had been invited to dine. As we left we saw him under a tree, assiduously polishing his boots with his handkerchief.

Next morning, Bob went off to XXX Corps again and had another interview with General Monty, who spoke of the storming of the Straits of Messina by the Commando Brigade: 'All the Eighth Army artillery wheel to wheel covering the landing, with violent air bombing. Nothing can stand up against it,' said Monty. 'Nothing can live.' They met the Chief of Combined Operations and brought him and Colonel Anthony Head back to our headquarters. Lord Louis spoke to the troops and gave them Monty's congratulations on the landing. He outlined their future employment – all in amphibious operations – and his speech had a very good effect on the men. They clustered round him for autographs afterwards, and he signed 'British Military Authority' notes for them, the currency with which we had been issued.

I went down to the scene of our landing and inspected in detail the defences which the Italians had constructed, comparing them in my mind with the impressions we had derived before the landing from the air photographs we had studied.

I photographed the graves of our fellows down on the beaches. 'Pathetic' is the only adjective which seems to convey the sight they presented. Sandy graves with a cross made of thin bamboo staves, the cross not even a true one but at an angle, because there were no nails or string to keep the cross-pieces in place. The man's tin hat on the cross when it was robust enough to bear the weight, otherwise a British rifle, with bayonet fixed, stuck into the ground, and the tin helmet on the butt. The Italians whom they had fought were buried close by, and I thought of A. E. Housman's lines:

> In the nation that is not
> Nothing stands that stood before;
> There revenges are forgot,
> And the hater hates no more.*

Bob, Brian and I motored off to Syracuse to see General Dempsey, commanding XIII Corps, and on the way passed near Avola, the scene of the 'eastern' landing, in which No 3 Commando had played its part. There were the usual scenes of the fight, dead beside the road, walls and houses knocked down by shell fire, etc. General Dempsey's headquarters was in an almond orchard, dispersed and orderly. Both these Eighth Army Corps Headquarters impressed me very much. They were so shorn of frills of any sort. They seemed quiet, smooth-working organisations, where no one got excited and no one ran about or looked as if his job was too much for him. I wondered if the hot wind of battle were to breathe over Whitehall, whether a change for the better would result.

General Dempsey arrived from the front about an hour after we got to his HQ. I had not seen him since 1927, sixteen years previously, when he was a captain and a platoon commander in No 1 Company at Sandhurst, and I was a cadet there with Bob Laycock. He did not look a day older, and as Bob remarked, we were only surprised not to see 'Bim', his small Sealyham of those days, trotting along about four yards behind.

He told Bob of the good work done by Durnford-Slater and No 3 Commando. He said he would have work for us to do, and once again we noticed the clear conception of the role of commando troops that these hardened commanders had.

* From *A Shropshire Lad*, Jonathan Cape Ltd.

No 3 Commando were away on a raid at this time. No word had been received of them, and there was some apprehension at Corps Headquarters. They had been landed behind the enemy's lines at a place called Agnone, at the southern end of the long Catania bay, whence they were to have advanced to hold a bridge six miles inland until our forces joined up with them. The advance of the main forces had however been slower than was expected, and it was not known if the Commando were still holding out. Wireless communication with them had failed.

General Dempsey arranged to see us again at 8.30 the next morning, and Brigadier Laycock decided to move the two Commandos up to Syracuse, so as to be on the spot for the next job, whatever it might be. We made the necessary arrangements for this with the Naval Staff in Syracuse, and then motored back to Pachino.

Early the next morning we were off again, followed by Clifford James in a second jeep. We had to drive fast, to get to XIII Corps by 8.30 a.m. but Clifford stuck firmly on our tail, in spite of the dust, and we got to our destination with a minute to spare. At the end of any motor drive in Sicily, one's hair, face, moustache, and neck are completely coated with a fine white layer of dust, so that one looks like a clown made up for a circus performance. We divided our time between Corps Headquarters and the docks at Syracuse waiting for Nos 40 and 41 to arrive by LCIs. There was to be no decision as to our future employment until 5 p.m. when General Dempsey was to hold a conference with Admiral McGrigor, the flag officer, Sicily.

While waiting on the jetty, we spoke in French to the general commanding the Napoli Division, who had been captured the previous day with his entire staff. He had four rows of medals and was a typical voluble Italian. He produced the theory that if the Prince of Wales had remained King, we should never have had war, and was obviously proud of the fact that he had dined once or twice in the same mess as the Prince of Wales on the Piave front in the First World War. He was waiting for a ship that was to take him off to a prison camp in North Africa.

We bathed from the Old Fort at Syracuse at about 4 p.m. and went along to the conference at 5 p.m. On the way, we passed over the bridge for the defence of which a brigade of the Airborne Division had been dropped on the night before D-Day. A broken glider in an adjacent field and some graves with parachute helmets on the crosses bore witness to the gallantry of the small band that got to the bridge and fought so fiercely. We met General Hopkinson of the Airborne Division at Corps, when we arrived, and heard the whole story. They had over a thousand casualties that night due to the enemy's flak and the stormy weather.

At the conference it was decided to use us the following night. XIII Corps were held up in front of Catania, and could not get forward owing to the Hun positions in the plain and on the high ground west of the town. We were, therefore, to land some six miles north of the town and turn south moving down the railway line, till we came to Catania, where we were to fight our way in, and seize a beach-head in the harbour. 17th Brigade were then to land in our beach-head, and pass through Catania to attack the enemy positions in the flank.

There were many details to be worked out, so we left the conference as soon as possible, and went on board the *Prince Albert* in the harbour, where Bob, Brian and I worked out a rough plan for the operation. The two Commandos were billeted in the town for the night and were to embark in the *Princess Beatrix* and *Princess Emma* as soon as these ships arrived in harbour the next morning.

I slept on deck next to John Durnford-Slater who had returned that afternoon with about 25 men from 3 Commando's raid after some hair-raising experiences. They had got through the enemy lines, but had had severe casualties, although it was hoped that many more men would dribble in in the course of the next few days. During the night, there was an air-raid on the harbour, and an intense flak barrage was put up by the ships and the shore guns. Bombs were dropped in the harbour, but no damage was done. The bomb bursts in the water were quite impressive. Being in one of the ships in the centre of the harbour, it seemed as if one was inside a tent, the walls of which were made up of red-tracered AA shells; and the din reached a crescendo when the AA gun on the steel platform just above our head joined in the barrage. I cannot describe the intensity and ferocity of the noise.

Next morning Bob and I went on board HMS *Largs*, and immediately went into conference with Admiral McGrigor, planning the battle that was to take place that night. Meanwhile, we sailed round to Augusta, being followed later by Nos 40 and 41 Commandos and the Special Raiding Squadron commanded by Major Paddy Mayne.

We had no accurate information of the beaches, as photos had not yet arrived, so we had to select them from the map. Good supporting fire was arranged from either two or four battleships and we got, in addition, three cruisers, some destroyers, two rocket ships and several LCGs and LCFs. On arrival at Augusta the brigade commander of 17th Brigade (Brigadier Tarleton) and his brigade major came on board, and we co-ordinated plans with him. Then Bob and I retired to Captain Faulkner's cabin where we produced an operation order in three-quarters of an hour. The Commandos arrived at Augusta at 5.30 p.m. and the brigadier called a conference at once on board the *Prince Albert.*

Brigadier Laycock proceeded to give out his orders, as soon as the commanding officers and adjutants of the Commandos were assembled. These had to be given out verbally, as there had been no time for the preparation of written ones, and the adjutants took notes while the brigadier pointed out objectives, etc., on the map. The plan was, briefly, for No 40 Commando to land first and form the bridgehead. The SRS was to pass through them and make for Catania, while No 41 followed them down the railway.

The SRS was to form a beach-head in Catania Harbour, provided it was not deflected en route by enemy action; if this occurred, 41 Commando was to by-pass them and form the beach-head instead. Headquarters and 40 Commando were to follow by the same route, the latter becoming rearguard and brigade reserve. Once the beach-head in Catania was formed, one of the Commandos to be detailed later, according to circumstances, was to clear a passage through the town to help 17th Brigade to get on to their objective.

Bob had just completed his orders regarding the method of the operation and was dealing with administrative problems, when a signalman burst in with a message from XIII Corps, saying, 'Operation cancelled'. Even in Sicily, we were to be dogged by last-minute cancellations! There is no need to describe everyone's feelings – we had all gone through similar disappointments too often before. Later we heard that the reason for the cancellation was that the enemy had been heavily reinforced and our task was no longer practicable.

During the evening, we heard better news of No 3. Peter Young, their second-in-command, was back, and so were a number of other officers and men, and more driblets were expected. It appeared that they had got to the bridge and held on to it for about an hour and a half. But the enemy brought up a self-propelled gun which lay just out of range of their mortars and shelled their position very thoroughly. In the end they had to split up into small parties to avoid being surrounded, and these were now coming in, having had to fight their way back. A number of the wounded were taken prisoner by the enemy, and then freed later on by XIII Corps when the latter advanced. The men said the German soldiers treated them very well, but the Italians were swine. One officer had his wallet taken from him by an

Italian officer, who proceeded to pocket all the money, when a German officer came up, saw what was happening, and knocked the Italian out by a punch in the face.

I slept on deck again as it was hot down below. I was very tired and rather disappointed. At about midnight, there was a heavy raid on the harbour, and though the noise was considerable, it was not as bad as at Syracuse, as there was a smaller AA lay-out on shore. A lot of bombs were dropped, one particular stick falling in a straight line across us and the *Princess Emma.* I was lying beside Pops Manners, and we both put our tin hats on. After the stick that had just missed us, we thought we saw a light showing out of the side of the *Emma*, low down on the water-line.

At 6.30 a.m. the next morning, Peter Hellings came on board from the *Emma* and brought the shattering news that they had had four near misses in the raid from anti-personnel bombs, which had penetrated the side of the ship, and caused many casualties. The commando losses were three officers, and thirteen other ranks killed, and 64 other ranks wounded; in addition, one officer and thirteen ratings of the ship's crew had been killed.

The scene on the mess decks was apparently pretty grim. Confusion was added by the explosion of some of the grenades which had been primed ready for the operation which was cancelled at the last minute. Poor 'Doc' Pride of 40 was killed, and also John Stiebel and 'Florrie' Ford who had only just come out. As the ship's doctor was also killed, the medical staff was seriously handicapped, but No 40's team of sick bay attendants did magnificent work and everyone also spoke of the splendid work of the ship's first officer.

Our dead were buried at sea, and then the commandos disembarked and went into bivouacs in areas on the shore. I was very upset about Pride who was a splendid MO and had done so well tending our casualties on the day of the landing. The Canadian medical authorities had told us of how well our men had been looked after in spite of a long day in the sun, waiting for evacuation to hospital.

The headquarters chosen for us was a huge power house near the port. It was a squalid and untidy place with a quantity of glass windows, and an overgrown compound around it. I disliked it instinctively and even more when during the night the port was bombed again and a stick of whistling bombs dropped four hundred yards from us. This stick nearly wrote off Philip Dunne, our liaison officer, who was returning from Syracuse with a convoy of three-ton lorries, and was on the road at the time. I went off next day to find a new area for the two Commandos further away from the port, as it was obvious that we were going to be disturbed pretty frequently at night, if we remained near the harbour. After various unsuccessful attempts, owing chiefly to shortage of water, I discovered an area near the village of Brucoli. There was a certain amount of shade, but very few buildings, though both Commandos managed to find houses to accommodate their headquarters. We put Brigade Headquarters in a railway building at the level crossing, a well-built house with tiled floors, and a kitchen.

There was quite a good bathing place in Brucoli bay nearby, and we looked across the water to Catania nestling at the foot of the imposing mass of Etna. On the plains and foothills to the south we could see and hear the main battle quite plainly.

CHAPTER EIGHT

Planning for Salerno

We were now in reserve under orders of XIII Corps, and we kept in touch with them by wireless, telephone, and by keeping a liaison officer with them. The men spent their days on routine tasks and improving their bivouac area, and used to go down to the sea to bathe at least once a day. It was very hot indeed and Sicily gets extremely dusty at this time of the year.

Our new mess was proving a success, and we had the luxury of an ante-room as well as a dining-room. The brigadier had an office and we used the rooms upstairs as dormitories. Randolph Churchill (who is not a relation of mine) had arrived to stay with us from North Africa. He had been in No 8 Commando in the early days when Bob had commanded it, and at present was a liaison officer with the 2nd SAS Regiment. Bob told Randolph to go and find an Italian cook, and later in the day he returned with a very unwashed-looking specimen whom he had found in Syracuse, and said he was the chef of an hotel there. The batmen at once built up a 'front' against him, as they regarded themselves as the keepers of the kitchen, and we had continually to keep an eye on them as they were inclined to make things as difficult as possible for the cook. His first effort that night was a splendid soup consisting of fresh vegetables with a cheese crust on the top.

I went in to Augusta with Brian Franks, the brigade major, to contact the local town major and the AMGOT officials, and to ask if we could borrow any tables and chairs to make our mess a little more comfortable. The town major was out, but his second-in-command and the AMGOT people gave us a signed paper giving us authority to collect certain articles from the damaged and empty houses in Augusta, which, at this time, was completely evacuated. While we were doing this, the town major himself passed in a motor car, stopped, and came charging down on us, accusing us of looting. We showed him the paper signed by his own second-in-command and by AMGOT, and he calmed down, but not before Brian and he had had a spirited passage at arms. About a week later, Brian announced with great glee that the town major had been sacked.

'What for?' said I.

'Looting,' said Brian triumphantly, and we both laughed a good deal.

I thoroughly enjoyed the sea bathing at Brucoli and we all used the little stone jetty opposite the village for this purpose. One day Bob and I were bathing, when somebody started firing at us from the hill behind. There were a lot of stray Italian soldiers still wandering about Sicily in civilian clothes, and it may have been one of these, but we both suspected a local AA gun-site, whose discipline was poor, and who were probably doing it to amuse themselves. When we had dressed, we accused the lance-corporal in charge, who had been away from his gun-site at the time. He denied the allegation rather unconvincingly, and, on looking down his rifle, we found that it had been recently fired. We could prove nothing, so we had to leave the matter, but we never had any similar trouble again.

About this time, No 2 Commando arrived in Sicily from Gibraltar, and I was delighted to see my brother Jack again. I had not been with the Commando since I spent some days with them in Scotland in September of the previous year, and it was nice to meet their officers again. They went into bivouac in an almond grove beyond No 41 Commando. Jack, Randolph and I used to bathe together and argue a good deal. Randolph on the whole preferred talking to listening, and criticised everything and everybody, but he had an excellent fund of anecdotes and a splendid memory for poetry, which endeared him to me. We were discussing wartime poets on one occasion, and I remember he quoted with relish the pent-up bitterness and irony of Siegfried Sassoon's verse:

> I'd like to see a Tank come down the stalls,
> Lurching to rag-time tunes, or 'Home, sweet Home', –
> And there'd be no more jokes in music-halls
> To mock the riddled corpses round Bapaume.*

On 22nd July a conference was called in HMS *Largs* in Augusta harbour by General Dempsey, at which Admiral McGrigor was present, and to which Bob, Brian and I went. It appeared that a new division was to be brought in to turn the flank of the German Catania position on the landward side, and in order to try to prevent the movement of enemy reserves from the coast in order to meet this attack, a deception plan was being hatched in which we and the Navy were to

* From 'Blighter's, *Poems, Newly Selected* 1916–1935, Faber and Faber. Reproduced by kind permission of Mr George Sassoon.

play a big part by simulating an intention to carry out a landing on the coast north of Catania.

The general idea was for the Navy to sail a convoy consisting of a large force of landing craft, escorted by destroyers, in the afternoon, on a course which seemed to threaten the German coast in the rear of their Catania position. Then, when night fell, the landing craft were to make back to harbour, while the destroyers went on and bombarded the coast. Meantime the Commandos, with their wireless sets on the destroyers, were to fill the ether with the sort of signals that might be made during a landing; we were then to call the landing off for some reason or other and announce the fact on the wireless. A few nights later, we were to do the same thing again, and it was hoped that this would make the enemy thicken up his forces on the coast.

I went out in the destroyer *Quantock* (Lieutenant-Commander Pennell) to carry out a feint landing as part of this deception plan, and Brian Franks went out on another night with a force of MLs which sailed into the Messina channel and carried out a bombardment of the coast-line. On a third night, Brigadier Laycock went out with Admiral McGrigor with a rather bigger force which included rocket ships, and shelled the coast at Aci Reale, causing a big fire which we could see from our headquarters 27 miles away.

We heard that in the raid on Augusta a few nights previously, the monitor *Roberts* had received a near miss in which splinters had penetrated her blister and caused some forty casualties. The only snag to our headquarters site was the fact that the nightly raids on Augusta invariably woke us up, as the aircraft passed over our heads on the outward and return journeys, and because we were surrounded by AA sites. A large number of whistling splinters and nose-caps came down in our vicinity and, whereas I used to sleep out of doors for the sake of coolness, I now decided to sacrifice the night air for the protection afforded by the roof.

About this time Randolph left us for Malta. He sought interest as a bee seeks honey, and we had become rather dull. Being quick to 'catch the wind of the moment', he 'sinks his nets where the fishing seems best'. He was to come and visit us again on a number of occasions and I must say that I was always glad to see him.

On 31st July, Brigadier Laycock was summoned to Eighth Army Headquarters to attend a conference. We went by jeep to Lentini and found them in the park of an estate about two miles beyond the town. While Bob was attending the conference, I went to see Lieutenant-Colonel Williams, who was in charge of General Montgomery's Intelli-

SS Derbyshire. Sitting: Lieut-Colonel Pops Manners, Brigadier Bob Laycock and the author. *Standing:* Canadian LCA Flotilla leaders

(*Left*) Author on day of landing in Sicily. (*Right*) Rear-Admiral Lord Louis Mountbatten and Brigadier Bob Laycock on day after landing on Sicily.

A British and an Italiar
shortly after landing o

The landing beach at

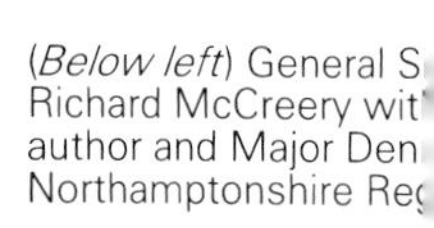

(*Below left*) General S
Richard McCreery wit
author and Major Den
Northamptonshire Reg

(*Below right*) Colonel
Darby, US Rangers

gence Branch, and learnt that they had just captured a German order which described the formation of a new Fighting Group, which included tanks, for the purpose of watching the coast near Riposto, so it looked as if our deception plan was working. This was rather gratifying news. When Bob rejoined me, he said that he would have to fly to North Africa the following day as he had received orders to report to General Horrocks in Algiers in connection with a new operation.

The next day we motored to Cassibili aerodrome between Augusta and Syracuse, where the brigadier had asked John Durnford-Slater to meet us, as he was to command the brigade during Bob's absence. The aerodrome had been made since our landing by clearing away a lot of olive trees and vines, and it had a rather loose dusty surface of red earth. It was being used chiefly to evacuate wounded by air to North Africa. We found our aircraft was not leaving till 2.45 p.m. so John took us to his Commando Headquarters not far away, and the brigadier walked round his lines and spoke to a number of the troops. Their bivouac area was very clean and orderly, and each man had dug a little hole for his bed, and erected a mosquito net over it. Then we had a quick cold lunch at their officers' mess, which was in the courtyard of a farm, with a vine trellis for walls and roof, and were given some excellent Spumanti to drink.

At the aerodrome we found our aircraft, a DC3, and sat under the wings in the shade while they unloaded wounded from ambulances and set them down on their stretchers. I spoke to several of the men and gave them cigarettes. One had a bad thigh wound and looked very ill, another was a Canadian who had come out in our ship and had been hit in a bombing raid by a Focke Wulf fighter-bomber. Finally they were put on the plane, eighteen of them, all lying on stretchers, and we took off. As the aircraft was so crowded, Bob and I were given seats up forward with the pilots and crew.

We flew over the beach at which we had landed in the assault, and it was most interesting seeing it from the air. During the flight we passed quite close to Pantellaria, our old friend 'Workshop' of earlier days, and its highest mountain, Monte Grande, was sticking up out of a cloud of haze. We landed at Tunis at 5.15 p.m. and had the nearest shave from crashing I have yet had. There was a 30 mph cross wind and we did three enormous bumps each bigger than the last, and all on one wheel; at the third, I really thought we were 'for it'. Bob cut his hand hanging on to a strut, and mine was bruised, but we didn't overturn, though it was a near thing. I felt sorry for the man with the wounded thigh.

We motored to an area headquarters, where we were given tea fixed our passage for the following morning to Algiers, and then went to a leave hotel and got rooms for the night. That evening, we dined with Lieutenant-Colonel Andrew Scott, who was commanding the Irish Guards and was a friend of Bob's. He gave us an excellent dinner, and there was much amusing talk.

The next day we flew on to Algiers in another DC3. They were not comfortable, as one had to sit on aluminium bucket seats, like benches, on each side of the fuselage, and you had to screw your neck round to see out of the rather small port-holes. The journey took three hours and was uneventful, though it was interesting flying over the appallingly rocky and mountainous country that the First Army had had to fight over, and in which Nos 1 and 6 Commandos had such a gruelling time during the North African campaign. We arrived at 1 p.m., got a lift in to Algiers and went to the Aletti Hôtel, where we were informed that only Bob could stay as no one under a full colonel was allowed in.

The hotel authorities were not very helpful, it was hot and damp and we were both very tired. We noticed how the further you get from the front, the less people are disposed to help, and how the official and officious atmosphere increases as you progress along the lines of communication. As Bob had been given a room with two beds, we decided to risk sharing it, and hoped that when we came in after dinner I should not be noticed.

We met Lieutenant-Colonel Bill Stirling by chance, just outside the hotel, and he was most helpful and promised to provide us with a jeep and driver during our stay. He was commanding the 2nd Army SAS Regiment, and knew his way about Algiers and gave us much useful information.

We dined at a strange small restaurant called Chez Cosmopolitaine which was run by a Mme Brasse, a Dutch or Belgian woman, where the food was quite good but the surroundings rather squalid. When we went back to the Aletti, we found that the hotel authorities had allotted Bob's spare bed to an American officer, who was already in possession; so I had to collect my things and wander out into the night to find other accommodation. I was suffering from a mild go of malaria at the time, and felt rather sorry for myself, but I managed to find a bed at the Hôtel Oasis. Apparently, when they were dressing next morning, after some preliminary conversation the American asked Bob:

'You'll pardon me, General, but what outfit are you with?'

'Oh, I'm in the commandos,' said Bob.

'Gee, is that so?' said the American. 'Have you just come from Sicily then?'

'Yes, we have. We flew over yesterday as a matter of fact.'

Then a thought struck him.

'Say, are you telling me that that guy I turned out last night was a commando?'

'Well, yes,' said Bob. 'He came over with me.'

'Gee,' said the Yank, 'if I'd known that, I'd gladly have slept in the gutter!'

Bill Stirling's jeep duly arrived and we went up to the Ecole Moderne where a huge conference was being held at which General Horrocks, commander of X Corps, presided. He explained that the next big operation was to be carried out by two separate landings, one by the Eighth Army across the Straits of Messina, and the other by a mixed force of Americans and British, the British component being General Horrocks' X Corps, which comprised the 46th and 56th Divisions. It was this second landing with which we were concerned, but it was complicated by the fact that it was not yet decided whether it would take place in the neighbourhood of Salerno, or on another part of the coast a good deal further south; and we were told that the plans we made must be applicable to either area.

We all started off by examining the southerly beach in detail, and Bob and I studied the Commando task, which was for a landing on the flank of 128th Brigade commanded by Brigadier James, VC, whom I had known when he was a staff officer at Aldershot before the war. However, about a week later, we heard definitely that Salerno had been selected and we re-started work on the maps and photographs of this area.

There is a technique in planning which can only be learned by experience, and the work is greatly facilitated if some, at any rate, of the interested staffs have worked together before on similar problems. This is particularly true in the planning of a Combined Operation, where the work is much accelerated if the army staff appreciates beforehand the naval considerations and vice versa. We were fortunate in having Commodore Oliver as Chief of the Naval Planning Staff, and on the whole the work proceeded very smoothly.

The Salerno plan, in broad outline, was for an American and a British corps to land on the long stretch of sandy beaches south of Salerno town, the Americans being on the right, and the British on the left. Of the two British divisions which were to land with the British X Corps, 56th was to be on the right, and 46th on the left. The commandos were to land on the left of 46th Division some four or five miles further north, leaving Salerno town between them and the British landing. Our task was to come ashore at the little fishing village of Marina, knock out a coast defence battery on the cliff above the village, clear another village called Vietri, and then hold a pass between high mountains, through which the road to Salerno and Vietri ran, towards the plain of Naples. We were to hold on to the pass for some 24 hours, until the British landing was established and 46th Division joined up with us. Then the two corps, British and American, would advance on Naples.

The American Rangers had also been allotted a task in the landing. They were to come ashore about five miles further to our left and get into the high mountains which dominated the other pass on the edge of the Naples plain. Thus the road to Naples as it passed through the belt of mountains which lay between Salerno and the Naples plain would be held by Allied troops at both its Salerno and Naples end. Our commando planning therefore had to be carefully co-ordinated both with 46th Division (who would be on our right) and the American Rangers who would be on our left.

Fortunately for us, the latter were commanded by Colonel Bill Darby who was a very old friend of ours. He had brought the 1st Ranger Battalion to Britain over a year before, and Colonel Charles Vaughan had trained them at our Commando Depot in Scotland. The Rangers are, of course, the American counterpart of Commandos, and there had always been a tremendous liaison between us. Later, the Americans raised two more Ranger battalions and Bill Darby had command of all three for the Salerno landing. He and his Rangers had been through the North African campaign and were now fresh from the fighting in Sicily. They were a splendid body of fighting men and we were very glad to be with them in this new operation.

There was excellent bathing to be had at Sidi Farouche some miles outside Algiers, while there were cinemas and restaurants in and near the town, the latter providing quite good food though at rather exorbitant prices. I met a number of friends who were passing through Algiers. One day I met Tommy Whittaker, whom I had not seen since we were together in Arras in 1939. He had got himself the extraordinary job of escorting a German general to England in an aeroplane, but Tommy always did extraordinary things. He achieved great fame in France by obtaining compassionate leave to visit his pig farm in Hampshire, apparently because the pigs were dying of some disease, and he wanted to arrange their medical attention.

Another day I met a Lieutenant-Colonel Lovell who had commanded the Royal West Kents in Tunisia until he had been blown up by a mine. We had a meal together and it transpired that he had known my elder brother at the Senior Officers' School where, he said, he admired his complete contempt for the directing staff, which he made no attempt to conceal!

While we were in Algiers, we heard that No 2 Commando had carried out a landing on the coast of Sicily south of Messina at a place called Scaletta. The purpose of this raid was to cut the east coast road, down which the Germans were retreating, while the Americans attacked by way of the north coast. When I met him later, Jack told me that the Navy had some difficulty in finding the beach and, in the end, had put them ashore at the wrong place. After a bit of a fight, the Commando advanced with some tanks of an armoured brigade that had been landed, and got right into Messina. They met the Americans, who had come in from the north, in the centre of the town. The capture of Messina marked the end of the campaign of Sicily.

When most of the planning was over, General Horrocks left Algiers to attend an exercise which was being carried out on the North African coast as a rehearsal for the Salerno landing, but he was badly wounded in an air raid on Bizerta, and General McCreery was flown out from England to take command of X Corps in his place. At the same time, we heard that General Freeman-Attwood had been replaced by a new general in command of 46th Division. It is extraordinary how often in the war commanders of expeditions had had to be appointed at the last minute. The same thing occurred before the Canadian landing in Sicily, due to a plane crash, and I remember the 'flap' just before the Norwegian campaign in early 1940 when two accidents in quick succession, to Generals Hotblack and Burney-Ficklin respectively, occasioned similar changes at the last moment.

As both the Eighth Army and X Corps wanted commandos to help them in their landings, Brigadier Laycock split his brigade, giving the Eighth Army No 3 Commando, No 40 (RM) Commando and the SRS, all under command of Lieutenant-Colonel Durnford-Slater, while he allotted No 2 Commando and No 41 (RM) Commando to X Corps. He decided to take command of the commando landings at Salerno, keeping me with him as his staff officer, and allotting Brian Franks to John Durnford-Slater. What Brigadier Laycock had anticipated in England was now coming to pass, and it was just as well that his foresight had resulted in our bringing out an headquarters to Sicily, though the splitting of the brigade put a severe strain on our small brigade staff.

By this time, Philip Dunne had arrived from Sicily to join Bob Laycock, so I flew off to Palermo, where the Rangers were in camp, to select a site for Nos 2 and 41 Commandos somewhere near the town; it had been arranged that both the Commandos and the Rangers should embark at Palermo and sail from there to the Salerno beaches, joining up with the North African convoys during the voyage. At Catania aerodrome I had to change aircraft and, as the weather was bad, the ordinary service was suspended. I was determined to get on that night if I could, as I had a lot to do, and not much time in which to do it.

I noticed a DC3 at the far end of the run-way by itself with a sentry on it and, on making inquiries, was told that it was a private aircraft of five American generals. I asked the authorities if there was any chance of my cadging a lift in it to Palermo, where the generals were going, and was told I should have to make my own arrangements with them, so I hung about talking to the pilot till they arrived. The only one I knew by sight was General Patton, but I tackled the one with the least number of stars on his shoulder. He was charming, and in that engaging American way said, 'Sure, come along, glad to have you with us,' so in I climbed.

I wondered what business had brought such an important plane-load together, and was to wonder still more when we circled the Palermo landing ground and I saw that it had been cleared, and that there was a line of onlookers clustered round the control tower. We landed, and our machine at once taxied out of the way, and I thanked my generals briefly and made myself scarce because obviously something.unusual was happening. The next scene was an eye-opener, an Italian aircraft came in from over the sea without a shot being fired by our AA guns, circled the aerodrome and came down making a perfect landing. It was then that I noticed that it had the Royal Italian markings, and I could just see where the Fascist emblems had been painted out. I realised that this must mean Armistice negotiations or something very near to them. Two or three people got out of the plane and were at once motored away in a closed car, and a guard was mounted on the aircraft.

This gave me food for thought as I went off into the town to fix up accommodation for the night. Luckily, I met Bill Darby and two of his Ranger COs, Lieutenant-Colonels Dammer and Murray. We dined at an hotel, and Dammer arranged to motor me out to their camp some miles above Palermo. On the way there next morning I selected a site for our commandos on a hillside some six miles out of the town.

I stayed with the Rangers for a night, and they did me proud as usual. They had an American Red Cross mobile canteen with them for about a week, and their men were enjoying the luxury of newly made doughnuts, which the two Red Cross girls cooked. I envied them this excellent Red Cross service, and wished most heartily that our own was allowed to do as much and on as large a scale for our men. While we were at Palermo we were offered their mobile cinema, and were issued with their rations.

I have the highest admiration for American military organisation and I like the way they put the comfort of their men and officers on a high priority, both in the line and out; I am convinced that we are completely out of date in thinking so little about it, and failing to go in for it in a big way. It always seems to me that we practise discomfort to a ridiculous degree, and there is still the feeling in certain official quarters that comfort in the theatre of war is indicative of 'softness'. Anyone who knows the discomforts of a campaign should have the sense and the desire to reduce them for the men as much as possible, particularly when all that can be done is more often in the nature of the removal of discomfort rather than the provision of luxury. I have yet to meet the man who does not benefit by it nor appreciate it.

In due course the Commandos arrived from the other side of the island, and settled in to the new area. They were to be there for about a week, before embarking for Salerno. Bob arrived from North Africa also, and we arranged the necessary practices in signal procedure and carried out one brigade exercise to give the two Commandos a run-through of their immediate tasks on landing. I remember this exercise had one great merit: it was carried out without the issue of a single piece of paper. The whole thing was done orally, and seemed to produce as much good, and teach as many lessons, as any other exercise I have taken part in.

While we were at Palermo I made a point of visiting the wonderful Basilica of Monreale, of which I had read in Guides to Sicily, and I was overcome by the richness and purity of the twelfth-century mosaics. They had been pasted over with cheesecloth to protect them from harm in the bombing, but fortunately the entire church had been spared, and the coverings were now being removed. The church also had a fine Byzantine exterior and a very lovely cloister. Many of our officers managed to see the church, and I made two more visits, one with Jack and the other with Bob, Philip and Randolph Churchill, who had turned up again.

Lord Rennell of Rodd, who was the head of the Allied Military

Government in Sicily, had very kindly invited Bob and any others of Headquarters who liked to accept, to make use of his bathroom and the luxury of hot water to bathe in. He was living in a very comfortable villa on the edge of Palermo, and Randolph was staying with him.

One evening, after having drinks there, we went in to Palermo for dinner and, returning to the camp about midnight our rather overcrowded jeep got a puncture. Jack and Randolph set about mending it with terrific zeal but with little coordination of effort, so that they were soon quarrelling over spanners and abusing each other roundly in a flow of backchat and cross-talk and temper that sent Bob and Philip and me into fits of helpless laughter. Finally these two Churchills completed their work and we continued our journey, but they were not now on speaking terms. As Jack left our tent after we got back, he fired his parting shot by saying to Bob, who was seeing him off, 'Oh would you say "goodnight" to *that Spencer fellow* for me?'

We had a great many details to fix up with the Rangers before we set sail, and there were many visits to each other's camps at this time. I think we both realised that the coming landing might be rather a tough proposition. We never worried unduly about our actual touchdown and primary tasks, but what always caused us anxiety was our role later on, if things did not go as planned. In cooperating with the infantry divisions we seldom found that they appreciated how much weaker we were in strength than an infantry battalion, and how much more lightly equipped we were than they. Further, we knew how little we could rely on promises of help from them given in the planning stages, for though they made these promises with the best will in the world, they always presupposed that matters would develop as planned. When people were hard-pressed, however, we had found that that alone was considered sufficient reason to absolve them from their promises. The Rangers knew all this as well as we did, and Bill Darby, who is nothing if not resourceful, had managed to borrow some semi-tracked vehicles with a gun mounted in the front. He couldn't get any drivers or gunners so while he was at Palermo he trained a team of his own Rangers to man each vehicle. They were a kind of armoured car, and he always referred to them as 'My Half-Tracks'. They were to prove very useful to him, and he still had them four months later at Anzio.

Bill had another card up his sleeve, and this was a company of American Chemical Mortars, which he had somehow managed to acquire in Sicily and on which he still appeared to have some sort of undefined lien. In spite of their name, this company was actually a unit equipped with the new 4.2-inch mortar which fired either high explosive or smoke bombs, and it was able to compete with the range of the German heavy mortar, whereas none of our mortars could. It is true that our infantry had some of these longer-ranged weapons, but they were normally too heavy for us in landings, as we at this time had no transport on our establishment to enable us to carry them and their ammunition. Bill very kindly offered us the loan of a platoon of these mortars for the Salerno operation, and we accepted them gratefully. They were to be invaluable in the hard days ahead.

At length the day for embarkation came, and we went on board in Palermo harbour. Headquarters and No 2 Commando were in a landing ship, while No 41 were in LCIs. The Rangers were in two landing ships and, I think, some LCIs also. We made quite a little convoy on our own, and we sailed away to join the main convoys which were on their way over from North Africa. We were to keep with them until shortly before zero hour, when we were to separate and make for our own 'release position' which was some distance to the north.

This position would be at least seven miles from the beaches, as it was unsafe for the landing ships to approach in shallow water owing to the possibility of mines. We had, however, decided to dispense with the chances of a completely silent landing by bombarding the beach with a destroyer just before our LCAs touched down. To effect this, we were to be led from the release position to within a mile of the shore by two minesweepers which were to sweep a channel for the destroyer, and when the latter had completed her shooting, she and the sweepers were to haul away to the south, while we went in and landed.

There was a great deal of discussion as to whether it might not be better to do without the destroyer and hope for an undetected approach; but there is nothing so devastating as an enemy that lets you approach and holds his fire until your craft touches down, and then lets you have it as you get out of the craft and try to get over the beach. I argued that even if we were undetected until the destroyer started firing, the time that elapsed between the cessation of her fire and our touch-down was short enough to make it difficult for the enemy to man his defences before we arrived, and the effect of the bombardment might be invaluable in destroying at any rate some of the defences.

CHAPTER NINE

The Salerno Battle

We arrived off the Italian coast in daylight the following evening, and could see the coastline clearly, and also the island of Capri. The horizon was black with ships, and it seemed to us that the enemy could not fail to see us. There had been one or two reconnaissance planes over the convoy during the day, so the chances of a surprise landing were pretty remote.

That evening it was announced on the wireless that the Italians had thrown their hand in, and this gave rise to a lot of wishful thinking. Many people seemed almost to expect that this would mean that we should be met on the beaches by the local mayor with a reception committee and a brass band. Everything depended on how the Germans would react, and whether they were forewarned of the coming Italian surrender in time to man the defences on the coastline. If they did so, our plight would be worse than before, for while we knew from our experience in the Sicily landing that the Italian was nothing to be frightened of, the German was quite another proposition.

About an hour after dark we were heavily bombed by the Luftwaffe, which dropped a large quantity of flares all over our convoy, and then bombed by the light of them and the bright moon. It was very unpleasant and we had two near shaves when we were straddled twice. This lasted about half an hour, and then the bombers went away and left us in peace. I went down below with Philip Dunne, who had been damnably cheerful all through the bombing, and had a drink in which Randolph joined us. He was attached to our headquarters for the operation.

Jack and his Commando were to land first, and climb the cliff and assault the coast defence battery. Headquarters were to come ashore ten minutes after No 2, and then 41 Commando were to land ten minutes after us. They were to clear the village of Vietri which was up above Marina, the little village on the beach. When Vietri was cleared, they were to go on up into La Molina pass and take up a defensive position.

The sea was calm and the LCAs were lowered without difficulty and made for the coast. We saw the destroyer out in front, and as No 2's craft followed her in, we hung back in our two headquarters craft until we had given them ten minutes start, and then followed on. When we were about half way in to the shore, Amalfi lay on our port beam, and I suddenly thought of the picture in the Collins's house at Troon. Soon we heard and saw the gun-fire begin over to our right on the main beaches. Battleships and monitors were loosing off and we could see tracer streaming towards the shore, and the white flare of the shellbursts. There was a tremendous rumble of gun-fire, which later increased when the rocket ships let off their terrifying projectiles. These are fired in salvos, and, when they burst, sound like a roll of drums which continues for ten or fifteen seconds.

I was standing up in the craft straining my eyes to pick out the beach ahead, but it was still too dark and all I could see was the faint outline of the mountains high above, silhouetted against the star-lit sky. Suddenly the silence and darkness was shattered by the vivid flash and crash of our destroyer's guns which had opened fire on the enemy battery and shore defences at point blank range. The gun-fire on the main beaches had obviously disclosed that a major landing was in progress, if that was not known already from the previous day's aerial reconnaissances and bombing, and now the gun-fire on our beach would show the enemy that this point also was being attacked.

I searched anxiously for signs of retaliation from the shore and, shortly after the destroyer ceased fire, some enemy mortars did open up, but their bursts fell away to our left in the sea and at the base of a steep peninsula which lay to our flank. This indicated that the enemy may have thought that the destroyer's shells had been fired from the coast road north of Marina; at any rate, nothing came at us, and by now 2 Commando would have touched down.

As always in a night landing, the beach suddenly loomed up in front before I realised how close we were, and the craft grounded with a crunch on the gravel. The ramp went down with a bang and we were out and over the beach in a matter of seconds and, having got to the sea wall, proceeded to organise ourselves and set up the wireless sets.

There was no fire on the beach, but we could hear the rattle of tommy-guns and brens on the cliff, where 2 Commando must have been going in to the assault. Their mortar officer, Captain Brunswick, had set up his 3-inch mortars on the beach and they were firing like mad on to the battery position high up over our heads. While all this was going on, 41 Commando's LCIs came on to the beach and the men piled out in long files and moved straight on past us into Marina and

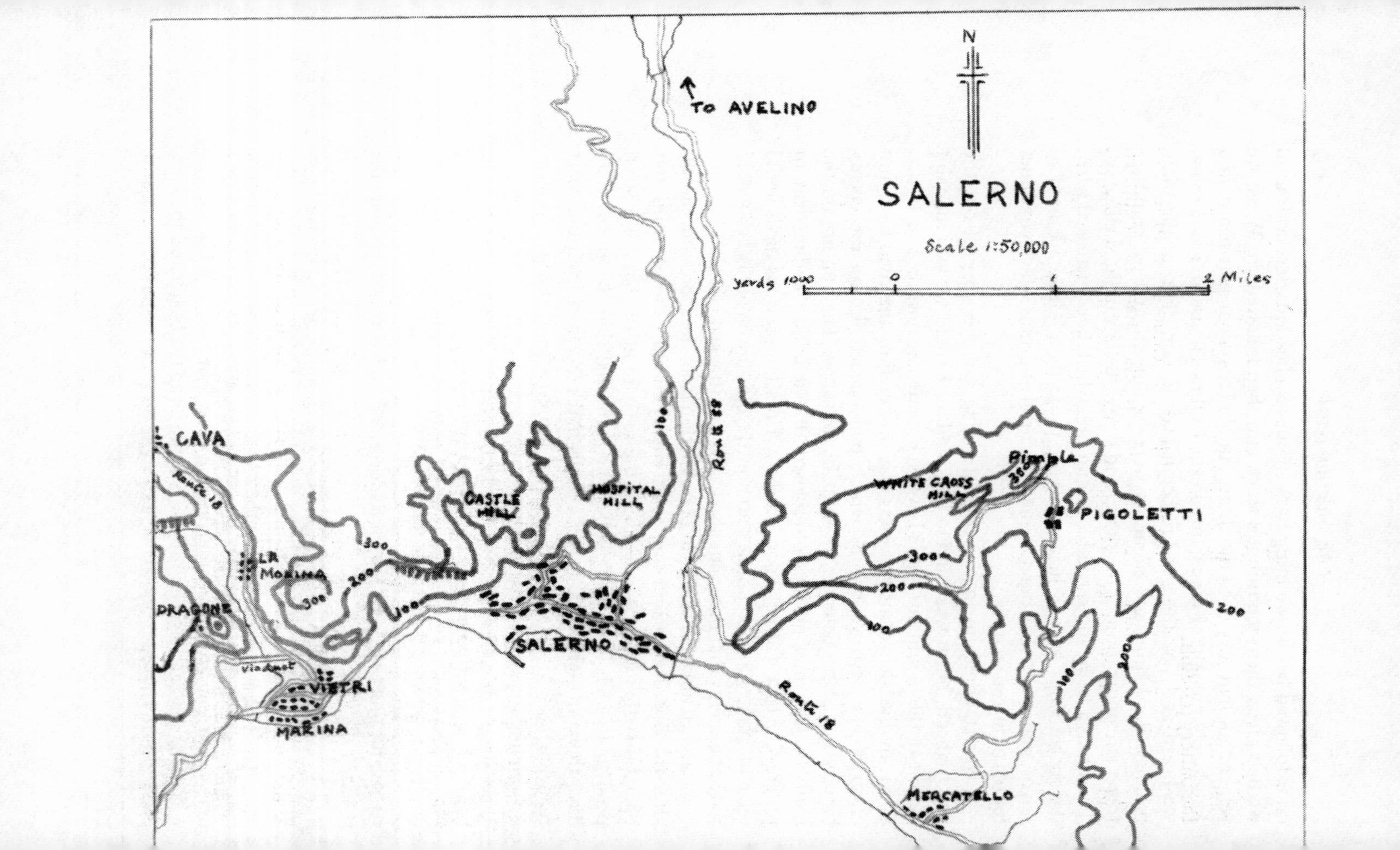
N
TO AVELINO
SALERNO
Scale 1:50,000
yards 1000
0
1
2 Miles
Route 88
CAVA
Route 18
LA MORINA
DRAGONE
Viaduct
VIETRI
MARINA
CASTLE HILL
HOSPITAL HILL
SALERNO
WHITE CROSS HILL
Pimple
PIGOLETTI
MERCATELLO
300
200
100

up towards Vietri. The Hun, in his usual way, was firing off Very lights all up and down the coast, but shortly we were to recognise No 2 Commando's success signal, which was five green rockets fired from the battery position.

Philip Dunne, who had landed with No 2, came down to us and reported to the brigadier that the battery position had been captured and several prisoners taken. He said that the Commando had captured the German barracks and the officers' mess, and it appeared that the enemy had bolted soon after the destroyer had opened fire.

Brigadier Laycock decided to move on through the village and set up his headquarters close to the two Commandos; so I gave Clifford James a rendezvous to make for with the rest of headquarters, and we set off to have a word with Jack up on the cliff. It was very dark and, as stray enemy patrols were liable to be encountered, challenges rang out every few seconds as small parties of commandos passed each other carrying up ammunition and stores from the beach. Our men by now were very quick to make and answer challenges, but the American mortar platoon seemed rather dopey, and we nearly shot three of them who were standing in a doorway and didn't answer our challenge.

Suddenly, out of the road in front, an enormous Hun rose up muttering, and I saw his ugly helmet silhouetted against the sky. A moment later he levelled his schmeiser, but in a flash Baldwin, who was just in front of me, dropped him with two bullets in his stomach, and wounded a second Hun who appeared behind. There was a scuffle on the other side of the road, and we all went to ground amongst some wooden sleepers. Baldwin had evidently accounted for the two leaders of a Hun patrol but it was too dark to see across the road and I expected a Boche stick grenade to arrive at any moment.

However, a scratch team of signallers and batmen were rapidly collected and sent off under Captain Randolph Churchill to outflank the Germans beyond the road. Some movement occurred and Bob let off his pistol; the Germans withdrew, and were eventually rounded up trying to hide in a house on the seashore.

When we met Jack, he was at a road junction with Harry Blissett, his adjutant, and Dick Laurie, his second-in-command. There were some sullen-looking German prisoners sitting down at the side of the road under a sentry. Jack explained that the enemy were not manning their guns at the time of the assault, and from the signs of confusion in the officers' mess and in the barracks, it appeared that he had beat a disorderly retreat as soon as 2 Commando arrived. They had captured a German order which appeared to give the plan for the defence of

Vietri, and Lance-Corporal Stern, the 2 Commando intelligence corporal, was already translating it by the light of an oil lamp, in a room close by. It was dated 4th September, only five days before, and commenced:

> With a landing taking place in the Salerno sector, a landing can be expected in Vietri at the same time. According to past experience, the enemy will land in the following manner:
> 1. Bombardment with heavy artillery, on the landing beaches.
> 2. The setting out and speedy arrival of landing craft. Very dark conditions, landing effected rapidly.
> 3. After bridgehead has been formed, the landing of further troops.
> 4. Speed of landing 15 kilometres in the hour.

Under the heading 'Defence of Vietri' the following orders were issued:

> a. Men will keep under cover during artillery fire and bombardment. Observation to be divided between various groups. After the bombardment and the commencement of the smokescreen, great alertness! Now comes the landing!
> b. Allow landing craft to come in undisturbed until within best range.
> c. At the landing, heavy fire, if possible from 50 to 100 metres from the shore. Very strict fire discipline is essential.
> d. Fire opens on a red Verey light fired by the section leader. Section leader will give verbal commands.
> e. The enemy landing must fail, under well controlled and aimed fire. Pay no attention to single men who have taken cover.
> f. After the enemy's attempt at landing has failed, he will probably retire and artillery fire will be renewed. Again take cover, and prepare for new landing.
> g. In the meantime, reserve platoon will be used to clear the village of Vietri. At renewal of bombardment, take cover as before.

If the enemy had carried out his orders, we should have had a difficult time, and I was glad that I decided to open fire from the destroyer at short range. Had he bombarded from, say, the release position, we should have given him time during the long run in to recover himself and oppose us on the beaches.

The first streaks of dawn were now beginning to show in the sky, and as I looked towards the pass where 41 Commando were taking up a defensive position, after having cleared Vietri, a great black column of smoke mushroomed up from the road. The Germans had sent forward a tank to find out what was happening, and the marines had knocked it out. I walked through Vietri and saw an abandoned

210-mm field gun on its limber drawn by a half-track vehicle at the big road junction at the southern end of the village. The crew were lying dead in the roadway, bearing witness to 41 Commando's mopping up activities.

Vietri village was a jumble of houses built on the southern side of the valley which, higher up, formed the pass which the marines were holding. The houses were painted in gay colours – yellow and pink and white – and presiding over their uneven tiled roofs was the green copper dome of the church. A modern viaduct spanned the valley carrying the coastal road, within a few hundred yards of a Roman aqueduct which also crossed the valley. The viaduct was always under fire, as the Germans had a clear view of it from their positions higher up the pass, and kept it covered with machine-gun and mortar fire. We used it constantly to get from one side of the valley to the other. Its Vietri end was protected by a large building, under the walls of which we used to collect while sumoning up courage for the dash across.

On one occasion Clifford James was laying a cable across it from a jeep when the latter broke down plumb in the middle. The enemy at once increased his fire, and mortar bombs were bursting on the parapet. Clifford calmly unloaded the cable-drums, and continued to lay the cable on foot. It was a miracle that neither he nor any of the three signallers he had with him were hit.

Brigadier Laycock ordered two troops of 2 Commando to move down to the northern outskirts of Salerno town to bring pressure to bear on the enemy there, as 46th Division, after landing, were to advance on Salerno from the south, and this action by 2 Commando would assist their advance. The two troops moved off under Captain the Duke of Wellington and Captain Pat Henderson, and reported enemy tanks milling about in the streets of Salerno. Morny Wellington sent small patrols into the town to snipe the enemy and test his strength, and Pat ensconced himself in an upper window with a Piat mortar. He had not long to wait as the enemy, seeing British troops about, sent a tank out to reconnoitre. It sent two shells through the wall of Pat's house, but Pat waited till it was about ten yards away and then replied with two bombs from his Piat mortar, the first of which knocked him over backwards with its recoil, but the second of which jammed the tank's turret. It withdrew, and we heard later that all the tanks had retreated eastwards in the direction of Avellino.

Meanwhile the rest of 2 Commando were held in reserve, and both they and Brigade Headquarters established themselves in the large school building in Vietri which had been the German barracks. The school was a large three-storeyed yellow building with a flat roof. There was a vineyard behind, in which the Germans had placed their coast defence battery. The rooms were full of German clothing and there were beds in most of them. There was also a great number of packing cases containing tinned food and a large quantity of glass and crockery, all marked with the sign of the Wehrmacht. Everything was in a state of confusion and papers were strewn all over the floors. There was also that characteristic German smell which, I have always noticed, pervades any house or room which they have occupied.

The brigadier and Randolph and I installed ourselves in one room which had a table, while the clerks occupied an adjacent one down the corridor. Our signallers set themselves up with their wirelesses in the yard outside, and 2 Commando Headquarters was in a room at the end of a passage. Their doctor, Captain Brian Lees, had taken over a large room as a hospital and was already tending the early casualties.

At about 11 o'clock in the morning the Germans started to mortar the beach rather heavily from their positions in the pass beyond No 41 Commando, and this caused a number of casualties in our carrying parties, who were still bringing up stores. Jack's batman, Guardsman Stretton, got a splinter in his neck which very luckily narrowly missed the jugular vein and also his backbone. He had it bandaged up and remained at duty.

The LCAs that had brought us in had made the seven-mile journey back to the transports to collect our heavy packs. As we had lost these in the Sicily landing, because the transports had sheared off owing to bombing before they could be landed, we were determined that this should not happen a second time. We had therefore left sufficient soldiers on board the transports to load the kit into the LCAs and come in with them on the second journey. As they touched down, however, they met the German mortar concentration on the beach, and no sooner had our soldiers disembarked than the craft put to sea without giving our men a chance to unload them. This was exceedingly annoying, because, for the second time, it meant that none of us had any change of clothing; and we knew, from bitter experience, that if we ever did see our packs again they would have been thoroughly looted in the meantime.

About an hour later, a staff officer of 46 Division called me up on the wireless:

'Why have you abandoned the town?'

'Do not understand,' I replied. 'We still hold the town.'

'It has been reported that the enemy have taken Vietri. You must counter-attack and get it back immediately.'

'Your report is false. I am speaking from the centre of the town. Suggest you check up source of your report.'

'OK. Off.'

This was an extraordinary conversation and we were most puzzled as to who could have passed this false information. I thought that the Germans must be putting out false reports on our wavelength; but the brigadier took the matter up very thoroughly, and it transpired later that the miserable LCA crews, not content with failing to deliver our kit because of some mortar bombing, went back and reported that the Germans were in the town, and this was passed on to Division. It made us extremely angry, and must have caused Divisional Headquarters considerable anxiety. In the afternoon the Germans shifted their mortar concentrations from the beach to La Molina pass where 41 Commando were, and to Vietri. The civilians were all very frightened, and would scuttle into their basements when the concentrations began.

We were supposed to be relieved that evening and, just after dusk, some tanks arrived and, after contacting us, went on towards the pass. We expected the infantry, therefore, to arrive during the night, but at dawn next morning we found that there was no sign of them, and that the tanks had not gone beyond 41's position. Later in the morning, the tanks withdrew from Vietri altogether and halted on the road between us and Salerno.

We already suspected that things were not going too well on the main beaches, but we did not realise till later quite how bad the situation was. General Hawkesworth, the divisional commander, paid us a visit during the afternoon and told us that our relief would have to be delayed owing to the severe opposition on the beaches.

The enemy's resistance on 41 Commando's front was steadily increasing and mortar fire became more intense. One burst fell in the road outside Headquarters, severely wounding an entire family, the mother, father and two daughters. Our men carried them in to 2 Commando's hospital where Brian Lees operated on them, but I am sorry to say that they all died. It was impossible to pick out the enemy observation posts from which he was directing his mortar fire, owing to the thick scrub which covered the steep slopes of the pass. They also had machine-gun posts on the slopes which were almost as hard to locate, but we used to search suspected areas with our machine-guns and mortars in an endeavour to knock them out.

An officer of No 41 Commando went forward to try to locate the enemy positions, but was cut off and taken prisoner. He was made to sit down beside an enemy observation post consisting of about six men with an officer manning a telephone. They were high up on the side of a hill, hidden by bushes, but after about two hours, they withdrew, taking the Marine officer with them. He was being guarded by a Hun sergeant-major who had his own revolver in one hand, and the revolver which he had taken from the officer in the other.

As they were moving back, they came to a rocky patch and the officer decided to make a bolt for it. Whether the fact that he was a ballet dancer before the war had anything to do with it I do not know, but he managed to cover about twenty-five yards downhill before he was hit in the leg, and after a perfunctory search, the Germans moved on. The officer managed to get back to our lines during the night, and was evacuated to hospital.

The next morning, I was returning from a reconnaissance in the pass with Philip Dunne and Baldwin when I met Randolph, who told me that the Boche had infiltrated a heavy machine-gun team round the shoulder of the hill which overlooked Vietri, and consequently, he had been sent by the brigadier to collect one of the American 4-inch mortar detachments to help to shoot them up.

I hurried back to Headquarters and found Jack on the roof directing the fire of his 3-inch mortars, and some brens, at this enemy patrol. They lookd very sinister as they climbed round the cliff in full view of us and high above, and it was obvious that unless we knocked them out at once, they were going to make our position untenable. Lieutenant Brunswick's mortars were getting the range, and soon the pale grey mortar bursts could be seen crunching right amongst the unhappy Germans. The American mortars were also getting the range, and Bob and Jack, who were looking through field glasses at the time, had the satisfying experience of seeing a Hun blown into the air and crash to the earth, a sprawling mass of arms and legs. About three of them escaped round the shoulder of the hill, but all the others were either killed or wounded and captured. Their officer, an Austrian, was hit in the leg and he was later brought in to me for questioning.

After four days the commandos were relieved and taken out of the line for a rest, and we found them billets in houses on the cliff road between Vietri and Salerno. Although this position was only about a mile from the front line, so steep was the cliff that artillery fire could not hit us, as anything fired in our direction passed close overhead to explode down in the sea beneath us. The Navy had intended to use the port of Salerno as soon as it was cleared, in order to bring ashore heavy stores which it was difficult to unload over the beaches; but the Germans were shelling the port with batteries of multiple mortars which used to pitch as many as 48 bombs at a time into the harbour, and these used to go whistling over our heads at frequent intervals during the day. It was a comforting feeling knowing that the angle of the slope was steeper than the trajectory of the shells. While we were here, General McCreery paid us a visit, and told us we should have to hang on a good deal longer as the position was still difficult on the main American-held beaches.

After twenty-four hours' rest, the commandos were rushed back again into the pass, to take up their old positions, as the infantry which had relieved them was wanted elsewhere. No 41's position was between steep hills, but owing to the smallness of their numbers, they were only able to occupy the lower slopes, and they soon reported that enemy patrols were infiltrating on the upper slopes of the hills on their left. The Germans were attacking everywhere more strongly, and as our casualties had been increasing, we asked for a company of infantry to hold the top of the hill on the left above 41's position.

We were told that one would come up in the afternoon, but it was not until 5 p.m. that the company commander appeared, accompanied by his colonel. They did a reconnaissance and returned to say that it was impossible to do anything before the following morning! Unless something was done at once, dawn would probably see the Germans in Vietri, so we had to order a troop of 2 Commando from the top of the hill on the opposite side of the valley to come all the way down and, before they had had time to recover their breath, to go straight up to the top of the hill on the other side. They had to fight their way up, as the previous delays had enabled the enemy to get some men on to the hill first, but 2 Commando established itself securely and so probably saved Vietri. The next day we moved the whole of the Commando on to this hill and they moved forward about a mile until they were holding the village of Dragone, and were in touch with 41 Commando lower down the valley.

Lieutenant-Colonel Lumsden was wounded in the foot when a mortar bomb hit the house in which his headquarters was established, and was evacuated to the beaches, while Major J. R. Edwards took command of the Commando. They were being hard pressed all the time, and were having difficulty in stopping the enemy creeping between their troop positions in the scrub. The enemy was up to every sort of trick, frequently calling out in English, and wearing our battle-dress and steel helmets. One man approached one of their positions dressed in British uniform, dragging a Hun who appeared to be wounded, and talking loudly all the time in excellent English. Suddenly, the 'wounded' man leapt to his feet, and they both started hurling stick grenades at our position.

At six o'clock the following morning I was called to the wireless and told that 2 Commando wanted me. It was Jack's voice speaking:

'I think something's happening up here. We've been mortared for over an hour, and I am out of touch with my two forward troops.'

'Are you in touch with the FOO?' I asked.

'Yes,' he replied, 'I have seen him, and he is just fixing up his wireless.'

'OK. I will remain on set, keep me informed.'

'OK. Off.'

Half an hour later, he came through again, rather faint, and speaking very deliberately:

'Things are now a bit tricky up here. Enemy is coming forward under a rolling mortar barrage, and they've got through our lines at several places. Am still out of touch with my forward troops. The gunner can't speak to his guns. Over.'

I yelled for a spare FOO, who happened to be asleep on a bed in the next room. He came bundling in, and I asked Jack on the wireless if he could give me targets to fire at, and report corrections. He replied:

'Yes, OK, but bring everything you've got on to the vicinity of the church now.'

I asked the gunner to put five rounds of gun-fire on to this target and gave him the map reference. He leapt to his set, and passed the order, and then bobbed his head round the door a minute or so later:

'Fired, sir. You will hear them pass over in a second.'

And we heard the whistle of the shells and the distant crump as they landed. Jack came through again a few minutes later:

'That was fine, but a bit close. Increase the range 200 yards and repeat again please.'

The battle raged until after midday. During this time my brother's headquarters was surrounded, and the tide of battle passed right over Brian Lees's dressing station which was in the cellar of a house. He continued quietly looking after the wounded, which now included some German casualties, with the fight seething all round him. Jack collected his reserve troop under Morny Wellington, and got Teddy Edwards to scrape up as many marines as he could, and he and Morny led a counter-attack supported by our artillery. The welcome message came through on the wireless: 'They are putting down a hell of a lot of smoke, and I think they are retiring,' and soon we learnt that the Boche had legged it down the hill. A very nasty threat to the northern flank of the whole landing had been repelled, but 2 Commando in their gallant action had suffered severe losses in officers and men. Amongst them were their second-in-command, Dick Laurie, and three troop leaders, Dick Broome, Frank Mason, and Arthur Brunswick.

After this battle, the Commandos were given a night and a day's rest in buildings in Salerno town; but the place was still under fire from the surrounding hills, and the men snatched as much sleep as they could, realising that they might be called on again at any time to help the hard-pressed infantry. Some of them managed to fit in a visit to the beach to bathe, but they had to choose their time as they were liable to coincide with a mortar concentration on the seafront. The Germans also had a battery of 88-mm guns which had an unpleasant habit of bursting just outside our billets, and as there were no shutters left in any of the windows, and the field telephone was fixed to the window-sill, telephoning at times became uncomfortable.

There was a bright moon at night, and visibility was as much as several hundred yards. The British were so thin on the hills, that the Germans used to penetrate with small patrols into Salerno town and shoot up people moving in the streets. One used to hear their schmeisers rattling away, and we kept sentries on our billets in the shadows of the porches, and up at the windows.

At 5 o'clock in the afternoon, the brigadier had to hurry away to a conference, and shortly afterwards both Commandos were put at instant notice to move. Lorries arrived at the billets to take them down to a rendezvous on the front of 46 Division, which reported a serious threat down one of their valleys. After discussions with the various commanders on the spot, 2 Commando, now reduced to about two hundred and fifty men, were ordered to advance and clear a thickly wooded valley interspersed with vines built on steep terraces. Their orders were to clear the enemy out of the valley until they reached the village of Pigoletti, and then to withdraw back again to the rendezvous where a hot meal would be ready for them. They set off in moonlight, in five columns abreast and, in order to co-ordinate the advance, each troop yelled 'Commando' every five minutes or so. It must have been an awe-inspiring experience for the enemy – the noise of the advance as the men trudged and climbed through the vines, the shouts of the troops, and the incessant rattle of tommy-guns.

The Boche was completely overrun, and by the time the Commando reached its objective it had taken no fewer than 150 prisoners, far more than the whole of 46th Division had taken to date. It then withdrew to the rendezvous in accordance with its orders, but even before it got back, Jack was informed by wireless that they were to turn about and advance once more, this time remaining on the objective and digging in.

No 41 Commando were ordered to join in this advance, and four tanks were produced to go up with them. The mountain track however was so bad, and the bridges over the streams so frail, that none of the tanks managed to complete the course. Opposite the village of Pigoletti was a wooded knoll known as 'The Pimple', and on this the Germans had established a strong position. In the first night advance, 2 Commando had succeeded in reaching it, but when they returned the second time the Germans had reoccupied it; and it was here, leading his troops very gallantly in an assault on this dominating feature, that Morny Wellington was killed. He had fought like a lion through all those bitter days, and had proved himself a fine and resolute leader.

The commandos gave the Boche no rest during that day and mortared him continuously in the thick undergrowth in which he had dug his funkholes. The fighting was at such close range that the enemy could be clearly seen bolting for his dugouts when our mortar concentrations landed, and this was the opportunity for 2 Commando's bren gunners, some of whom were established at the windows of an upper room in a house in Pigoletti village. This room had been an onion store, and the floor was littered with onions, which the men had crushed with their boots as they replenished the guns at the windows with ammunition. They were all weeping copiously and when I first went in I could not understand why they were so cheerful and yet so tearful; but I was soon weeping myself.

The division ordered us to carry out yet another attack that night, and 41 Commando was detailed. An artillery barrage had been arranged for 2 a.m. and, during this concentration, the Commando was to form up on its start line. Unfortunately, when the barrage started, it was at once clear that something was wrong; a large proportion of the shells were falling amongst our own men, and caused many casualties. In fairness to the gunners it must be said that when the attack was mounted, they pointed out that only one of their batteries had registered in this area and they asked for time to register the others, but were told that this could not be afforded. One patrol of No 41 reached the enemy ridge, but the attack itself came to a standstill.

After a further day of fighting, the Germans had had enough and pulled out and left the hills in our hands. The two Commandos were withdrawn, this time for good, and the Salerno battle was over. The British and American forces went forward through the pass which the Rangers and the Commandos had held for so long and, shortly afterwards, entered Naples.

It had been a long and critical battle and, in the eleven days' fighting, the Commandos had had only two nights' rest. They were not organised or equipped to take part in long defensive engagements, and their casualties had been very severe. Unfortunately, these could not be replaced by drafts from reinforcement units, as was the case with the infantry, and it was to be many months before Nos 2 and 41 Commandos were up to strength again. But they had given a splendid account of themselves, had made a great contribution to the success of the landing, and had earned a battle honour which figures as one of the most glorious of the war.

CHAPTER TEN

The Garigliano Raid

When we came out of the line at Salerno, the commandos were given rest areas in a large apple orchard near the beaches. X Corps staff had kindly lifted the mines on a stretch of the beach near our camp so that the men could bathe, and everyone took the opportunity to do so after the long period in action. A good deal of washing went on at the wells near the farmhouses, where the men were to be seen stark naked scrubbing and soaping their shorts and shirts. The area was still within range of the enemy's medium artillery, and every now and again salvos of shells would land in the orchard or on the beach.

After two days, General Sir Richard McCreery, the commander of X Corps, came to see the Commandos to have a word with them before their departure for Sicily, where they were going to reform. The two units were drawn up in the orchard and, considering they had only just come out of the line, I was very proud of their turn-out and bearing. The General spoke to them for over twenty minutes, and took the trouble to explain to them the whole course of the battle from the time of the landing. As one only sees one's own particular part of the fighting, this broad picture was extremely interesting, and the men much appreciated the fact that the General took the trouble to come and see them and explain it all to them.

General McCreery was tall and thin, and walked with a limp which was the result of a wound in the First World War. He had a shy, slightly hesitating manner in personal conversation, but when talking to troops he was direct and clear and frank. He thanked them for their hard fighting and for the sacrifices they had made. 'In the hard times, you always *looked* like soldiers,' he said, 'and you retained your discipline and self-respect; make no mistake – the effect this had on the morale of others was considerable.' I was glad he mentioned this point, as it bore out what we were always trying to instil into the commandos.

Brigadier Laycock had received instructions from London to fly home as soon as he could be spared, to confer with Lord Louis Mountbatten on the matter of the Commando reorganisation which was being discussed in Whitehall; so he and Philip Dunne had flown off the previous day from the air strip on the beach. I was left in charge of the two Commandos, and the following day we embarked in LCIs for Sicily. As we sailed past the coast which had been the scene of such bitter fighting, little groups of men could be seen on the decks pointing to the shore and discussing the battle. The first few days of comfort after action is something only to be understood by those who have experienced it, and it was good to see the men stretch out in the sunshine on the decks, cracking jokes with each other, and finally dropping off to sleep.

Now followed a month of rest and reorganisation in Sicily. 41 Commando went into a bivouac area in a vineyard close to the coast a few miles north of Catania, while 2 Commando were billeted in the old Italian barracks in the town itself. Brigade Headquarters was established in two villas on the coast at Aci Castello. The little bay was enclosed on one side by an old castle, and on the other by three pointed rocks which jutted up out of the sea and were said to be the ones that Polyphemus hurled at Ulysses from the slopes of Etna. Above and behind us towered the majestic peak of the old volcano.

The men seized the opportunity to do a bit of shopping in Catania, to which the inhabitants had flocked back now that the fighting in Sicily was over. A little silk could still be bought, and certain cafes were placed in bounds for the benefit of the soldiers. There were cinemas to go to, YMCA and Army clubs, and as much sea bathing as they wanted. Several of the troop leaders took their troops to the top of Etna, which was a strenuous climb, but the sight of the sun rising out of the sea at dawn repaid one's exertions.

My brother and I did a bit of sailing in a curiously rigged boat which we hired from some fishermen, and Jack was well forward with negotiations for the loan of a racing yacht from the Yacht Club at Catania, but unfortunately these were not concluded by the time he had to leave. He introduced me to an excellent little man called Franco Lombardi, who was a lawyer in his father's firm which was one of the biggest and most respected in the island. We enjoyed the hospitality of many of his friends, amongst whom I remember the Nicolesis who owned a delightful villa on the slopes of Mount Etna and produced one of the best white wines of the island from the vineyards which surrounded their house.

To look at the more wealthy houses of Sicily from the outside, you would think they were merely rather large farmhouses. There was no attempt at gardens or lawn, and the surroundings and exterior seemed not to differ from those of the poorest dwellings; but on entering, you found spacious rooms with exquisite furniture and fine pictures of the various Italian schools. Another charming man we met was Prince Borghesi, the senior member of that large Italian family, who spoke excellent English, and took a keen interest in genealogy. He was particularly proud of his family connections with several of the great families of England. He dined with us at our mess at Aci Castello, and I was to meet him again in the Borghesi Palace in Rome nearly a year later.

The oranges of Sicily were a great joy to all of us, and they were exceedingly plentiful as the export trade had entirely ceased and the markets in the island were flooded with them. Franco arranged to take Jack and me over the orange plantation of one of the biggest exporters, and we spent a most interesting afternoon being shown all over it. I was interested in the complicated irrigation system which is all-important on account of the dry and sun-baked soil. This particular plantation was in a little plain entirely surrounded by barren lava hills, and it made a wonderful picture of lush green grass and orange trees with the fruit already golden on the branches. I should very much like to visit it again when the trees are in blossom.

To return the hospitality which we had received in generous measure from so many Sicilian friends, we gave a dance in the mess one evening on our little balcony which overlooked the bay. The brigade signal troop had fixed up fairy-lights on the balcony and flood-lighting behind large pots of palms in various corners. There was a brilliant moon over the sea, and the setting could hardly have been more romantic. All our friends were invited, and we knew by now that if we wished the presence of a young Sicilian damsel, the only way to get her was to invite her mother, father and all her brothers. We provided chairs round the edge of the balcony, so that the family, in the Sicilian fashion, could keep their eye on their young woman. We had a plentiful supply of delicious ice-cream from a local cafe and, by saving up the spirit ration of everyone in the mess, we were able to provide whisky and gin for our guests. I may add that an entire month's supply went bang that evening, but it was a great success and appeared to be appreciated.

The problem of obtaining reinforcements to replace our severe casualties was of much concern to me. If recruits were to be obtained in the Mediterranean theatre, the authorities would have to agree to our taking volunteers from the Eighth Army, but this they were at first unwilling to do, as their own reinforcement problem was difficult. Recruits were easier to come by in England and the first decision was for both Commandos to return to the UK to be replaced by two fresh ones which were up to strength; but in the end General Alexander stated that he was prepared to make No 2 Commando up, if it remained in the Italian theatre, so it was decided that they should remain.

No 41 Commando was ordered to return to England, to be replaced by No 43 Commando, a new one which the Marines had just formed. They did not have difficulty with recruits, as they had just decided to break up the Royal Marine Division, which, never having been in action, was consequently up to strength. With it, they were forming four new Commandos, and also providing officers and men to man landing craft.

To make 2 Commando up to strength, volunteers were called for not only from the Eighth Army, but also from all the reinforcement camps in North Africa. The latter were full of men who were longing to get to units, but who often vegetated for as much as six months in one camp or another. We had an enormous response to our call, and had we taken everybody who put his name down, we should have had enough men to form three Commandos, let alone one. We found personnel of AA units only too anxious to get into something more active, and though the men we took from these units knew little about our weapons or type of fighting, we found that when they were trained, they were good material.

The surviving officers of 2 Commando were formed into interview boards, and travelled over Italy, Sicily and North Africa selecting recruits. This made a pleasant change for them, and fulfilled an essential function. There was always a long delay between the time that we accepted a man, and his arrival, and sometimes he was lured away by another unit in the meantime. A few changed their minds and decided not to come to us, so that we were never certain exactly how many would turn up, and as there was always a wastage, during the training period, of men who failed to make the grade and had to be returned to their units, we tried to allow for this in the recruiting stage by accepting about twenty per cent more than we wanted.

A frequent subject of discussion amongst officers and men was the question of the future of commandos after the war. It was one which always provoked interest. Many suggestions were made, and an argument on this topic was refreshing in one respect – that those who took part in it had seldom an axe to grind, for few were likely to wish to remain in the commandos after the war.

Unlike the airborne troops, the commandos had never been formed into regular units with a permanent place in the army. A commando unit was merely a temporary war-time unit which consisted of officers and men of different regiments and corps (to which they still belonged, and indeed whose badges they still wore in their green berets), who were serving voluntarily, and *for the time being*, in that unit. In the case of the more recently formed Marine Commandos, there was a difference in that those units are composed of men who all belonged to the same corps, but were volunteers within that corps, that is, the Corps of Royal Marines.

One night about eleven o'clock, I was sitting with some of the officers in our mess at Aci Castello, when a signaller knocked at the door and came in.

'Have you heard the news, sir?'

'What news?' I asked.

'The wireless, sir.'

'Well what about it, Wright?' I asked.

'It's Brigadier Laycock, sir.'

'Explain yourself, man. What's happened to Brigadier Laycock?'

'He's been made Chief of Combined Operations, sir, and promoted major-general. They've just said it on the wireless.'

'Good heavens!' I exclaimed. This was amazing news.

'What's happened to Admiral Mountbatten?' I asked. 'Did they say?'

'Something about Asia, sir. He's got another job out there.'

'Well, I'm damned!' I said. 'Thank you, Wright. Tell the other fellows. Let me know if you hear any more details tomorrow.'

Lord Louis Mountbatten had in fact been appointed Supreme Allied Commander, South-East Asia Command, and our late brigadier succeeded him as Chief of Combined Operations. We were all overjoyed to think he had been selected for so good an appointment, and we felt that with his knowledge and experience as a commando officer, he was ideally fitted for the job. His promotion to major-general at the age of 36 was a great triumph for him and was also a welcome promise that the younger men of outstanding ability would receive the promotion they deserved irrespective of age or length of service. Not only the officers, but also the troops took the keenest interest in this announcement, as the commandos had always been rather a family affair in which we watched each other's fortunes with a personal interest.

There was, of course, much speculation as to who would succeed Brigadier Laycock as commander of the Special Service Brigade. I was expecting to be recalled to England to take command of No 4 Commando, as I had been promised this appointment shortly before we left the British Isles, and it was generally supposed that one of the commanding officers of the commandos either in England or Italy would be promoted to succeed Bob. A week later, however, a signal arrived from London appointing me as the new brigadier. I could hardly believe my eyes as I read the telegram, and surprise and joy ran in alternating currents through my mind.

I flew to Italy at once to take command of the other portion of the brigade, and found them at the town of Molfetta, about twenty miles north of Bari, on the east coast of Italy. These units consisted of No 3 Commando, No 40 (RM) Commando, and the Special Raiding Squadron. They had all recently taken part in a landing at Termoli, where they had earned much praise from Generals Montgomery and Dempsey. After they had completed their landing successfully, the enemy had counter-attacked, and as the elements of XIII Corps which were to relieve them were late in arriving, the commandos had had to fight a difficult action to hold the enemy off; but they inflicted much damage and held Termoli until the Eighth Army eventually reached them.

General Montgomery sent a message to say that he wished to see me on my arrival, so I set off early on the morning of the day following my arrival for his headquarters, which was situated at a place called Lucera. It was now the end of October, and the weather was intensely cold, and the rain came down in torrents. Travelling by jeep was a cold and tiring undertaking, and the roads were crowded with transport and extremely skiddy.

On arrival, General de Guingand took me to General Monty's caravan. The latter remembered me from our last meeting in Sicily and asked a number of questions about our battles at Salerno. He went on to explain his plans for the further advance of his army, and pointed out that he had to keep step with General Clark's Fifth American Army on the other coast. The mountainous country ahead made progress very slow, and to use his own expression, the situation was getting 'very tight'. He said he would want us for real or feint landings on the east coast, and he asked his Chief of Staff to make a note of the units which I now had in my brigade, and of those which were being sent out from home. On leaving his caravan, I noticed his famous bird-cage which went everywhere with him, and which was painted with the Eighth Army sign. It contained quite a variety of birds and was a feature of his headquarters.

When the news got round that Bob Laycock had left the brigade and I was to be the new commander, Brian Franks, the brigade major, came to see me to ask that he might be relieved of his appointment and proceed home, in the hope of obtaining a unit command in England. He was followed by Captain Basil Bennett, the administrative officer, who also wanted to be posted to the home establishment.

Before the war, Franks had been employed by Bennett, who owned the Hyde Park Hotel. Neither of them was a regular officer, and I think they felt that Bob in England would arrange more congenial jobs for them than they were likely to find under me in Italy. Frank's staff captain, whose name I have now forgotten, also asked to be posted. I was not worried by their desire for departure as I knew I could find as good if not better potential staff officers in the units of my brigade, whom by now I had got to know pretty well.

Towards the end of November, when I had had command of the brigade for a month, I received a signal from General Laycock to say that he was in Cairo and was anxious to see me to discuss matters affecting the brigade, and that if Fifteenth Army Group (which was General Alexander's headquarters) could spare me, he would be glad if I could fly over to meet him. There was nothing very much for us to do at the time, so permission was granted and I fixed an air passage. It took eighteen hours to reach Cairo, flying by way of Sicily and North Africa, and we touched down at Cairo West aerodrome at about midnight. I was surprised to find that we were met by a group captain and were taken straight to a room where all our passes were examined minutely and enquiries were made as to our destinations in Cairo. All this fuss and interest was most unusual, for normally when one arrived at an aerodrome no one took the slightest notice and it was often extremely hard to get a lift to the nearest town.

I asked the group captain if I might use the telephone in his office, for I had been told to get in touch with General Laycock at the Mena House Hôtel. He showed me the way to his Orderly Room.

'What number do you want?' he asked.

'Well, I want to book a room at Mena House,' I said.

'Mena House!' he exclaimed. 'You can't book a room *there*!'

'Why not?' I asked innocently and somewhat surprised. 'Are they full up? In any case I want to speak to a friend who is there.'

'You can't phone Mena House – at least, I very much doubt it, especially at this time of night. And who's your friend anyway?' He was obviously getting suspicious, and eyed me narrowly. I was wearing a raincoat, without badges of rank, and my green beret, so he had no idea who I might be.

I was getting impatient.

'What's all the fuss?' I asked irritably. 'I merely want to phone the hotel to speak to my friend.'

'Unless your friend is Winston Churchill, President Roosevelt or Generalissimo Chiang Kai-shek, you won't be very lucky,' was the astonishing reply.

I then began to realise what was afoot. This was the first whisper I had heard that the Big Three were meeting, and then I appreciated why Bob was in Cairo. I told my friend the situation, and he advised me to stay the night in Cairo, and to get in touch with Mena House the following morning.

The Cairo Conference was in session, and all the notables of England and America seemed to be assembled at Mena House, which had been taken over for the conference, as well as most of the rich Egyptians' villas in the neighbourhood. I met a number of friends whom I had not seen for over two years, who were holding appointments on the military and Air Force Staffs which were represented at the conference. General Laycock was busy most of the day, so I did not see him until the evenings, when we had long talks about matters of mutual interest; and he put me in touch with Commando affairs at home and told me of the recent changes of organisation which had occurred. He was anxious to hear news of his old brigade, and I was of course able to tell him all that had happened since he left us on the beaches of Salerno.

Cairo was a town of plenty, and one seemed able to buy almost anything in the shops. Rarities such as watches abounded, though prices were much inflated. It was extraordinary to go to the Gezireh Club and find polo still being played, bathing parties in progress at the swimming pool, and cricket matches in the evening. I met my old friend General W. D. A. Williams, who was also attending the conference. Bill Williams was Director of Freight Movement at the War Office and had, I suppose, one of the most brilliant brains on the General Staff. His apt and entertaining comments on matters large and small made him an excellent companion. We dined together one evening and he came to see me off when I returned by air to Italy after a very pleasant four days' break.

The hammering which No 3 Commando had received in their battles in Sicily and Italy made it necessary for them to be sent home in order to be made up to strength in the UK, and they consequently left the brigade shortly after I took over. The Special Raiding Squadron went with them, and as replacements I received No 9 Commando, the Belgian and Polish Troops of our Inter-Allied Commando and, as related above, No 43 (RM) Commando.

We were asked at this time to reconnoitre the Italian islands of Tremeti and Pianosa which lie in the Adriatic, east of the port of Termoli. The Navy were uncertain whether there were any Germans on these islands, and they wanted us to make sure that the signal stations were not being used to aid enemy shipping using the Adriatic. Small detachments of Nos 40 and 9 Commandos carried out these reconnaissances, but found no enemy.

I was anxious that the Poles and Belgians should obtain some battle experience, and had written to General Sir Miles Dempsey who was commanding XIII Corps to ask if it would be possible for them to operate on his front. He replied that in certain sectors he was virtually held up by mountain masses, and the only form of activity that was possible was offensive patrolling in front of, and behind, the enemy's lines. He said he would be very glad to have the loan of these two Allied troops to assist in this work, and invited me to stay with him for a couple of nights to discuss their employment. I therefore motored up to his headquarters in the high mountains, and examined the project in detail.

The General explained that that portion of his front which overlooked the Sangro River was very lightly held by both sides and seemed to offer excellent opportunities for offensive patrolling. I went up to make a reconnaissance, and contacted the 17th Brigade at a small and dirty little village called Pescopennataro which was nearly 6,000 feet above sea level. In peacetime, it was a favourite skiing resort of the Italians, and from the glass observation verandah of a small hotel one looked down a long slope to the River Sangro in spate at the bottom of the valley, and then up at the massive hills beyond the river.

We were in the front line at Pescopennataro, and the enemy front line was beyond the river on the slopes on the far side. The crossing of the river presented a problem as there were no bridges and the river was deep and very fast flowing. At this altitude, and at this time of the year, conditions were extremely cold and of course the waters of the Sangro were icy. Our men were trained to get across rivers, using toggle ropes, and it seemed to me that the best procedure would be for small patrols to get down to the river during the night, lie up the following day observing, and then cross the following night to patrol behind the enemy lines and get back again before daylight. While I was up there, there was a certain amount of shelling by both sides but, otherwise, little activity.

About a week later, the two troops were sent up there, the Poles going into a village on the top of a pointed hill, a few miles north of

Pescopennataro, and the Belgians to St Pietro further to the south and a bit closer to the Sangro. I went up to visit them after they had been in the line for ten days, and stayed two nights with them. The village the Poles were occupying was very like the drawings of Edmond Dulac in illustrations to fairy stories. St Pietro, however, where the Belgians were, was on the side of a valley and had been utterly destroyed by the Germans before they were driven out. No single house in the village had more than three walls, and few had complete roofs. The Boche had systematically carried out demolitions in order to deny winter quarters to our men, and had even left notices on the walls which read: 'Hullo, Tommy, hope you enjoy your winter billets.'

The climate was cold and crisp in fine weather, but damp when cloud lay on the hills, which was the case on most of the days that the troops had been in position. Visibility was normally limited to 30 yards, but the clouds were liable to lift suddenly for brief periods, when a vista of ten or fifteen miles would suddenly be revealed. All movement had to take place on foot, and the Poles were being supplied by mule train.

Both troops had made themselves at home from the moment they arrived in their sectors; the Poles even commenced patrolling the same night, and the Belgians the night after. During the ten days, they had carried out numerous patrols on the far side of the river and both had had many brushes with the enemy. A small patrol of the Belgian troop one night crossed the river and proceeded to reconnoitre some houses about a mile beyond. The door of one house was seen to be open, and a figure was peering out. The Germans were called upon to surrender, but they replied with a fusillade from every window in the house. The first burst, from a schmeiser, struck one of the Belgian sergeants in the stomach, but the five bullets which hit him landed on his tommy-gun magazine pouch, and although one of the bullets in his own magazine was actually exploded, nothing penetrated the pouch, and he did not receive so much as a scratch. The hun in the doorway was killed, and another wounded, before the Belgian patrol withdrew. During my visit, the sergeant showed me his pouch and magazine which were retained by the troop as an interesting souvenir.

On another occasion, a German patrol penetrated at night as far as Pescopennataro. A Polish sentry in that part of the village saw one man approaching, and kept him covered. The man suddenly yelled out '*Hände hoch*' and at the same time opened fire with his automatic weapon. The sentry was wounded slightly in the arm, but a Polish bren gun, which was already in position, immediately opened up from the flank, while another sentry armed with a tommy-gun also brought fire to bear from the other side.

Five other Poles armed with rifles left their quarters in the neighbouring houses in double quick time and opened up on the Germans. The patrol at once withdrew, and though the Poles could not see clearly, owing to the darkness, it appeared that they were carrying two wounded men. The villagers, however, from the outskirts of St Angelo, through which the Germans passed on their way back, brought information next day that one German was killed and two others wounded.

On another occasion, a Belgian patrol which had penetrated two miles beyond the enemy lines, was returning towards the river, on the German side, when it suddenly met a German patrol from the opposite direction. Both sides opened fire simultaneously and a furious exchange lasting about half a minute ensued. The Germans were heard yelling out in German: 'Imbeciles, don't fire on your own men', being evidently convinced that their own side was firing on a returning patrol. Casualties were certainly inflicted on the German patrol, but in the heat of the engagement it was impossible to estimate how many. One Belgian was wounded, and was brought back by his comrades.

At 5 o'clock in the evening of the second day that I was up there, an Italian civilian came in from the enemy lines with the following story. He said that he had been taken by the Germans three days previously on the far side of the river, and had been closely questioned as to the British disposition. He was then told that a German attack by 20 mountain 'Jäger' troops would be carried out with the intention of cutting out the British field guns near Pescopennataro. The attack was to cross the river at St Angelo at 7 p.m. clearing the village held by the Poles before proceeding to the guns. He was detailed to guide the attacking troops during the approach march. He gave details of the arrival of eight 25-seater buses the previous afternoon, which contained the mountain troops who were to carry out the attack, and he described an officers' reconnaissance which took place on the forward slope of a hill on the German side of the river, in which the plan of the attack was explained to the officers who were to take part.

It was not known whether this information was true or false, but as the man sounded convincing, it was clearly unwise to ignore it. Accordingly, the artillery were ordered to fire concentrations on the St Angelo crossings at 7 p.m. and were told to be prepared for a busy night. The Poles were warned and all other posts and reserves ordered to stand by.

At 8 p.m. the Poles reported that they were being attacked from the east by two parties of enemy each about forty strong. Three-quarters of an hour later came the news that another party of approximately the same strength was attacking from the west. From then on until midnight the Poles were entirely surrounded and had to beat off successive attacks launched against their village from different directions. During this time the artillery was firing concentrations close to the walls of the village as directed by the artillery FOO who was with the Poles. At midnight they announced that activity had died down but that they suspected that the enemy was still in the neighbourhood forming up for a final and bigger attack.

At 3 a.m. came the news that this expected attack had been launched. With the assistance of the gunners the enemy was again driven off, and at 5 a.m. contact ceased and the enemy was thought to be retiring. Patrols sent out by the Poles confirmed this, which was not surprising, for after the handling that they had received that night it was unlikely that the enemy would wish to be caught in daylight.

It was obvious that the Germans had no idea that the Polish garrison was as strong as it was, and their intention of capturing the guns was completely thwarted as they never got past the village. There were less than 80 Poles in the garrison, yet they had driven back a force of at least 160 Germans – possibly 200 – and only suffered the incredibly low casualty figure of three wounded. The enemy losses were in the neighbourhood of 30 killed and wounded, and may have been higher.

Shortly after I left this sector, snow fell deeply and movement was practically impossible without skis. The Germans had removed all those that the Italians had possessed, so we tried very hard to obtain them through army sources, as many of the Poles were completely at home on skis; but they were not produced in time.

About a week before I paid my visit to the Belgian and Polish troops, I had received a call from General McCreery for one Commando to carry out an operation on the west coast of Italy. He was still commanding X Corps, which was held up on the Garigliano River some 20 miles north of Naples. I selected No 9 Commando for this task, and sent them off to Naples, and they found a billeting area at Baia in the Gulf of Pozzuoli, north of Naples. As soon, therefore, as I had visited the Belgian and Polish troops, I went over to Naples to discover how the planning was going for their project.

Lieutenant-Colonel R. Tod, who was in command of No 9 Commando, put me up in his mess which was in a house on the sea shore; the front door opened on to the beach, and the sea was only four yards away. The next day he and I attended a conference at 56th Division's Headquarters, which had been called to coordinate the naval, artillery and infantry cooperation in the commando landing.

The raid was planned in order to focus the enemy's attention on the coast and the lower reach of the Garigliano River. This was necessary because in order to enable X Corps to advance over the river, forces had to be withdrawn from the river-line and massed opposite those points at which the crossings were to be made. It was thought that a commando raid at the mouth of the river might conceal from the enemy the withdrawal of forces from this part of the line.

The country is so low-lying on each bank of the river that high bunds have been built to prevent flooding; but even so, the ground is water-logged in winter. The whole area was overlooked by the hills on the north-east, which were in enemy hands. Consequently our line did not extend up to the south bank of the river; instead, it ran about a mile away from it, and the enemy held both sides of the river. Our infantry used to patrol up to the river at night, and frequently had clashes with enemy posts on it and with small bodies of Germans which patrolled between their posts. On the far bank, not only were there enemy positions at the mouth of the river, but also strong-points had been established at an isolated hill on the coast about one and a half miles north of the river-mouth, and at an old Roman amphitheatre which was a mile and a half up the river and a quarter of a mile beyond it. This amphitheatre was on the Appian Way, which crossed the river by a bridge which had now been demolished.

The plan was for the Commando to land from landing craft on the beach on the far side of the river, and split up into three parties known as Force X, Force Y and Force Z. Force X was to move to the mouth of the river and destroy the enemy post on the north bank, and then assist in the formation of a bridgehead through which the other forces would retire when they had completed their tasks. Force Y was to turn northwards on landing and attack the German position on the isolated hill. They were then to retire to the bridgehead and cross the river in boats which were to be provided by a detachment of Sappers. Force Z was to advance to the amphitheatre and wipe out the enemy positions there. Having done so, it too was to return to the bridgehead and get back across the river.

To assist the Commando in its task, the 201st Guards Brigade which was holding the line south of the river was to do a night advance to the river bank and eliminate any enemy who were on the south side. The Scots Guards were thus to attack enemy posts near the mouth of the river, and assist the Commando back across the river, while the Coldstream were to attack towards the broken bridge and eliminate any enemy on their side of the river who might try to interfere with the commando force which was attacking the amphitheatre on the far bank.

There was a detailed artillery programme to assist the Commando, and a FOO was to land with them to call for fire and direct it. All major points were settled at the conference, and apart from one or two minor details which were gone into in the succeeding days, all was ready for the battle. The date for the raid was fixed for 29th December.

While the Colonel and I had been working on the plans for the operation, we heard that our old friends the American Rangers had been withdrawn from the line and had gone into camp on a beach between Baia and Pozzuoli, so we decided to call on them on Christmas morning. We visited them by DUKW, and arrived just after midday to find them already at their meal – we had forgotten that the US army feeds early – and they insisted that we shared their 'Turkey Dinner'. Bill Darby was there, and Captain Sim, his old adjutant (who possesses the longest waxed moustache I have ever seen), and Colonels Dammer and Murray, in fact all my old friends.

They told of the fighting up at Venafro, where they were in the high mountains, and described how it took 24 hours sometimes to get a wounded man down to a field dressing station. They were in excellent spirits as always, but were faced with our old problem of having to train the new recruits they had just acquired to replace their heavy casualties. I tasted pumpkin pie for the first time that day. Later, several of their officers came back to No 9 Commando's officers' mess, and had a scratch supper, and Mike Long, one of the Commando's subalterns, played them some tunes on the pipes.

On the morning of 29th December the Commando embarked in the landing ships HMS *Royal Ulsterman* and HMS *Princess Beatrix*, and sailed from Pozzuoli Bay at six o'clock in the evening. I motored off to the headquarters of 201st Guards Brigade where I was to remain during the raid.

The Commando was due to land on the beach north of the river at 11 p.m., so the Guards put in their attack towards the south bank about 9 p.m. and got up to the river as planned, the Scots Guards down by its mouth, and the Coldstream in the area of the cross-tracks by the broken bridge. The former were heavily shelled and had to hang on and 'take it', as they were to assist the Commando back across the river at the conclusion of the raid, and I am sorry to say they suffered a number of casualties. The Coldstream met hand-to-hand fighting in the houses near the cross-tracks, but did their job and kept the enemy busy all night on their side of the river.

By 11.30 p.m. there was no sign of the Commando on the far bank, and we supposed that the Navy must be having difficulty in finding the beach. At midnight there was still no sign of them, and General Templer got on to me on the telephone. I said that I expected that the LCA flotilla was trying to find the right beach, as I had had plenty of experience of late landings; I advised the General not to worry unduly, but suggested that he ask the Naval Authorities at Naples to signal the landing ships to enquire whether the LCAs had been released to time, and whether they were back yet from the beach. This he did, and got the reply that they had been released all right but that they were not back yet, so this more or less confirmed my surmise.

The Commando landed at 12.35 a.m., one and a half hours late. The flotilla had first of all tried to land them two miles south of the river-mouth, but the Colonel had observed the navigation lights which had been put up south of the river to assist the flotilla, and he also saw the smoke-shells bursting away to the north, which were fired especially to help the craft to judge the direction of the correct beach; so he went alongside the craft in which Major Francis Clark, the second-in-command of the Commando, was embarked, and told him to take over the navigation and move up the coast with the first wave and find a suitable landing place. Major Clark accordingly led the LCAs up the coast till he passed the river-mouth which he could just see in the darkness, and landed some 700 yards north of it. The second wave followed and landed shortly afterwards.

The lateness of the landing caused a good deal of anxiety because the hours of darkness in which the Commando had to operate had been reduced by an hour and a half, and this left a bare minimum of time for them to complete their tasks and get back across the river before dawn broke. Were they to be caught in daylight trying to cross the river, they might have a very sticky time.

As soon as the landing was completed, the Commando split up into the three forces in accordance with the plan. It was soon found that one boat-load was missing. This contained half of Force X, which was to proceed to the mouth of the river. The reason for its non-arrival was not known at the time, but was in fact due to the breaking down of the steering-gear of the craft. It was eventually towed back to Pozzuoli by a motor-boat and the men on board missed the battle.

The Colonel dispatched Force Y to its objective, the isolated hill to the north, but he retained Force Z for a time in the vicinity of the beach until it was ascertained how strong the enemy were at the river-mouth, as with a depleted Force X it might not have been possible to deal with this position. Much depended on its being wiped out, as the whole Commando was to cross the river in this vicinity on its way home. In due course Force X reported that the enemy post was lightly held, and the Colonel ordered Force Z to proceed to its objective, the amphitheatre.

The enemy post at the river-mouth was wiped out and one prisoner was taken alive. There were many mines in this area and Force X sustained five casualties at this time. Meanwhile Force Y was proceeding towards the hill. On the way several deep ditches were encountered and wire and minefields had to be crossed. Two mines were exploded, each causing one casualty. These obstacles delayed the advance, and it was not until 3.20 a.m. that the force reached its objective which it assaulted. The enemy posts were found to be chiefly on the lower slopes of the hill, and they were overrun. A tank was found in a cave, and its crew were killed and the tank-tracks demolished with explosive charges. Two officers were wounded, and two men, one of them seriously.

Captain Jack McNeil, who was in command of Force Y, now commenced his withdrawal, and wishing to avoid further casualties from mines on the way back, utilised his prisoners to point out the minefields; they led the force back by a more easterly route than they had taken on the advance, and the party suddenly found itself in close proximity to Force Z, which had evidently just commenced its assault, for Jack McNeil heard them playing 'The Pibroch of Donald Dubh' which Captain Ralph Cameron, the commander of Force X, used for the charge. As there was danger of the two forces engaging each other in the dark, Jack McNeil ordered his piper to play 'The Green Hills of Tyrol' which he used normally on the march, and the two forces thus identified each other.

During all this time there was a great deal of artillery fire from both sides. The enemy were shelling the northern bank of the river and bringing down the concentrations on the area of the broken bridge and the river-mouth, while they thickened up this fire with mortar bursts; our artillery was firing up and down the Via Appia, particularly in the vicinity of the ampitheatre. There was a tremendous noise, and the night was torn by the flash of the shell-bursts. By this time there was a lot of dust and smoke thrown up by the shelling, which lay over the northern bank and made visibility even more difficult.

Force Z, it will be remembered, had a late start. It found that almost all the route it had to cover was under water due to flooding, and like Force Y's route, was intersected by ditches and obstructed by wire and minefields. The latter however were marked by notices and strands of wire, so that they could be avoided, though this increased the time of the journey. By 2.40 a.m. Captain Cameron realised he could not complete his assault and withdraw across the river before daylight, so he spoke to the Colonel on the wireless. The Colonel told him to go on with his task but added that if it seemed more feasible to cross the river in the area of the broken bridge, instead of withdrawing to the river-mouth as planned, Cameron could do so, and a special smoke programme would be arranged with the artillery to help to cover him as he withdrew.

The force formed up for the assault south-west of the bridge at about 5 a.m. and attacked after an artillery concentration which came down within fifty yards of the troops. They were fired at from a wood which lay just to their flank, but a party was despatched to deal with it, and the assault went in. Little opposition was encountered from the amphitheatre itself, but the enemy resisted strongly from the houses on the road. A pill-box near the bridge was captured, two of its occupants being killed and the remaining four captured. Mortar fire came down heavily during the fighting, and an infantry gun which the enemy were firing from another pill-box was captured and destroyed.

At about 5.30 a.m. the withdrawal commenced, and as Captain Cameron had been informed that the area south of the bridge was by now clear of the enemy, he decided to cross the river in this area. A section under Captain Mike Long withdrew first, covered by the fire of the remainder of the force. Mike Long himself swam over the first 15-yard gap in the broken bridge with a rope tied round his waist. Owing to the speed of the current it was impossible to cross by reconnaissance boat until a rope had been fixed. The second 15-yard gap was spanned by a toggle-rope bridge which the men constructed. It was now 6.30 a.m. and broad daylight, and a lot of mortar bursts were coming down. The artillery put down a smoke-screen which greatly helped to conceal the crossing, though the enemy increased his mortar fire as soon as it started.

The crossing was completed by 7.55 a.m., and all weapons and equipment were brought across, as well as twelve prisoners, though there were several casualties and one man was drowned. The area south of the bridge was not found to be entirely clear of enemy, but those that were left were timid and mostly hid in the houses and did not interfere with the withdrawal. The Coldstream Guards greatly assisted the force by fire.

During this time Force X and Force Y were crossing the river down at its mouth. Only three reconnaissance boats remained afloat as all the others had been holed by shell and mortar fire; so these were used to ferry back the wounded and some dead. In the meantime some DUKWs had been moved up the coast to a point on the south side of the river whence they were in touch with the Commando by wireless. The Colonel ordered them to move up to the river-mouth, and six managed to negotiate the sand-bar and beach themselves. The first two were sent off with the remainder of the wounded, while the others ferried Force X and Force Y back down the coast. Intermittent mortar fire was continuing while this was going on, and daylight was getting steadily brighter. Tempers were a little short, chiefly due to delays in getting the DUKWs into the river owing to the sand-bar. The sorely tried Colonel called out to the first DUKW as it went off with its load :

'Now don't go off and leave us to it; we want you back to take another load.' To which the equally tried driver of the DUKW replied :

'If I say I'll come back, I'll bloody well come back !' and he was as good as his word. By 7.20 a.m. the last DUKW left the river-mouth, and ten minutes later a fearful artillery concentration came down just where they had been, but all were safely away.

The raid had been a great success, and in spite of the late landing, which introduced serious difficulties, the Commando had performed its task with a dash and determination which provoked much praise from the commanders of both 56th Division and X Corps. It had suffered 30 casualties, nine of whom had been killed. The wounded included six officers. Sixteeen of the enemy were known to have been killed, and 26 prisoners were taken and brought back.

The raid unfortunately had a sequel which I am sorry to have to record. Although the Commando managed to bring back five of its nine dead, it was ordered a few nights later to send out a party to find two more of its dead which were reported by the Guards to be lying on the river bank. I protested against this as I considered it the height of folly to risk lives bringing in dead bodies, but I was overruled. The Colonel took a party back three or four nights later and they searched the whole area but found no one. All that happened was that one of their best sergeants had his leg blown off by a mine.

CHAPTER ELEVEN

The Anzio Landing

I was standing at the top of the stairs in the elegant seventeenth-century building which served as my headquarters in Molfetta, receiving the guests for our dance on New Year's Eve 1943, when I spied the not unfamiliar figure of Randolph Churchill mounting the staircase accompanied by my brother Jack, and a tall slim Cameron Highlander whom I did not know. Randolph quickly introduced his friend as Brigadier Fitzroy Maclean MP, the head of the British Mission to Tito. Randolph had just been dining with Jack in Bari, and my brother brought them both along to the dance, as they said they were anxious to talk to me about future commando operations.

While Jack was getting them both a drink, I continued to greet our guests. Two of my commando units had received severe casualties at the battles of Salerno and Termoli, and many of our wounded officers had been tended in the base hospitals which had been set up in south-eastern Italy. It was on these officers that we relied to produce dance partners from the nursing sisters that they had got to know.

Soon the revels began, assisted by an Italian dance-band borrowed from the Hôtel Imperiale in Bari, and I suggested to Maclean and Randolph Churchill that the three of us might retire to my adjoining bedroom to talk. Randolph immediately bagged the only chair, and Maclean and I pushed the mosquito-net out of the way and sat on my bed. I had some Canadian whisky which I poured out in tooth-glasses, and we got down to business.

Although I had not previously met him, I knew Fitzroy Maclean's outstanding record with the Special Air Service in the Western Desert, and I had read that Winston Churchill had recently appointed him to take charge of the British Mission to Tito's Partisan Headquarters. I could not help connecting his visit in my mind with the possibility of an invitation to take some part in operations in the Dalmatian Islands, because I had long regarded the Yugoslav offshore islands as an ideal hunting ground for my commandos, all of whom were specially trained in amphibious operations, and had already taken part in assault landings in Sicily, at Salerno, at Termoli and at the mouth of the

Garigliano River, and were about to take part in the Anzio landings. I was not therefore greatly surprised when Maclean broached this subject.

He explained that Tito's partisans were heavily engaged inside Yugoslavia with the German forces of occupation, and though greatly handicapped by lack of food, weapons, medical supplies and clothing, were inflicting much damage on the enemy and forcing him to maintain a large number of divisions in their country in his attempt to subjugate it. The British advances in southern Italy, however, and the recent Italian surrender, had prompted the Germans to extend their activities to the Dalmatian Islands, which hitherto had not been occupied by them.

The British had been using these islands as a base through which to send supplies to Tito's armies, and also for advanced operations by light naval forces to harass the German coastwise traffic down the Adriatic Sea to Greece. Now it appeared that the enemy was systematically overrunning the islands, and the partisans based on them were withdrawing, because they were not strong enough to resist the Germans.

Maclean was convinced that it would be disastrous for the partisan cause if the Allies were to surrender the islands completely, and pointed out that there was one island, called Vis, which was separated from the others by ten and more miles of sea, and which possessed two good harbours which could be used both for supplying Tito's forces and to provide a base for naval light forces. To persuade the partisans to hold it, however, it would be essential for a token force of British troops to go there immediately, to inspire sufficient confidence for them to put the island in a state of defence, until more British forces and equipment could be spared. Maclean wanted to know if I could provide any Commandos to go over to Vis, as General Sir Harold Alexander was unable to release any unit from the Army of Italy, owing to the fierce fighting that was in progress on both the Fifth and Eighth Armies' fronts.

I had already received orders to move three of my Commandos to the west of Italy for forthcoming operations, so that the only unit I could think of using was my fourth and last Commando, No 2 Army Commando; but this unit was still much under strength as a result of its losses at Salerno, and was busy training its new recruits. However, I fully saw the force of Maclean's arguments. I got hold of my brother Jack, the commanding officer of No 2 Commando, and asked him whether he could possibly spare, say, a hundred men as a token force to go over to Vis almost immediately. The snag was not only the lack of trained commandos in his unit, but the need to keep trained NCOs and men as instructors for the recruits. But Jack was not the man to let slip the chance of action in what promised to be a highly worthwhile and typical commando role. We agreed to meet the commitment, and I told Maclean that I was ready to send this token force immediately, to be followed by further instalments as the recruits were trained. He was delighted, and said he would go and see General Alexander the following day, as his headquarters was only a few miles away at San Spirito. We then rejoined the party next door.

I had to leave the next morning to establish my headquarters on the other side of Italy, and I had to arrange for Nos 40 and 43 Royal Marine Commandos to be accommodated somewhere in the vicinity. No 9 Army Commando was already established at Baia in the Gulf of Pozzuoli, north of Naples. This shift to the western coast of Italy was due to the virtual stalemate on the front of the Eighth Army, and the decision to try to break through on the Fifth Army's front to capture Rome.

The problem which faced the Allies in Italy was how to break through the German Gustav Line. This line ran from the west coast to the Abruzzi, using rivers and mountains as defensive obstacles and constituted by far the toughest challenge that the British and American armies had met since their assault landings at Salerno and Taranto three months previously. A key feature in this German line was the enormous hill mass of Monte Cassino, on top of which was situated the famous Benedictine Monastery, and which towered above Highway 6, the high road leading to Rome. General Alexander had decided to put in a heavy attack against the western portion of the Winter Line using the British X Corps and the American II Corps, and a week after this attack had commenced, an assault landing of two divisions was to be made in the rear of the German line at Anzio. I suspected that the move of my brigade to the west coast was the prelude to our becoming involved in these plans.

The Naples area was the focal point on the lines of communication of the American Fifth Army, and the port was being used to capacity, though it was not yet cleared of all the obstructions which the Germans had left behind them when they retired. This resulted in the area being much overcrowded, and I had some difficulty in getting a billeting area for 40 and 43 RM Commandos and my Brigade Headquarters, but we eventually settled down in Castellamare and its neighbourhood, on the south of the Bay of Naples, and only a few miles from Pompeii.

We were rather a long way from the HQ of the Fifth (American) Army under which my brigade was now under command, because that HQ was situated at Caserta, some ten miles north of Naples and forty miles from our new location at Castellamare. I realised that this was a disadvantage which might involve us in long journeys at short notice for operational reasons, but such was the congestion of units in the area that this had to be accepted. Our actual accommodation was satisfactory, the headquarters situated in a reasonably large school, and the two units within a few miles and also in public buildings. Vesuvius presided over the scene from some seven miles to the north – at this time emitting quite a lot of smoke, but at least not actually erupting.

I had only just got the accommodation of my Commandos sorted out when I was sent for by General Mark Clark, the commander of the Fifth (American) Army to come to his headquarters about fifteen miles north of Naples, and to bring a small planning staff, and be prepared to stay for a week or more. Just before I left Castellamare for this new assignment I heard from General Alexander's Fifteenth Army Group that No 2 Commando, my brother's Commando, was to come forthwith under the command of Force 133, a formation of Special Operations Executive, and that the despatch of the unit to Vis was authorised.

Caserta Palace, where Clark had established his headquarters, was (and is) an enormous edifice built by the Bourbon kings of the Two Sicilies in the middle of the eighteenth century. It represents the swan-song of the Italian baroque, and is an exercise in majesty rather than grace. It has a grand stairway in the centre of four inner courts, and a sumptuous chapel and theatre both with marble interiors. But its water gardens were its most remarkable feature, including an impressive water staircase which fell from a distant hill on which a hunting lodge had been built, down a long straight course, to the gardens and canals surrounding the palace itself far below.

The ample staff of the Fifth (American) Army was accommodated in caravans, wooden huts and tents which had been erected in the gardens, and the vast salons in the palace were mostly used for conferences. My small staff were allotted two rooms on the fifth floor of a servants' wing separated by various courtyards from the main building. There were no lifts, and when one had climbed to the top of the narrow stairway, one had to pass gingerly round the edge of a room which had a bomb-hole through its centre, about twelve feet in diameter, before reaching the two rooms allotted to us. The first was occupied by the staff officers that I had brought for planning purposes: Major Patrick Henderson, my brigade major, Captain Clifford James, my signals officer, and Lieutenant Ian Morrison, my liaison officer. The inner room was used by our batmen and one or two clerks. We were all a bit cramped, but we laid our camp beds down and were reasonably comfortable. We messed in one of the many American messes in the neighbouring buildings.

The morning after I arrived, General Al Gruenther, the Chief of Staff, took me to General Clark's caravan. Clark was a very tall man with a long neck and prominent Adam's apple. He was neat and tidy in his uniform and had an easy flow of language, but I felt he was without much personality, or impact. He told me that General Alexander had recently visited his headquarters and had suggested that while the assault landing of two divisions was taking place on the beaches at Anzio, it might be a good thing to insinuate a force of commandos by road into Rome itself to create havoc and confusion.

'What do you think of the idea?' asked Clark.

'It's a job after our own heart,' I replied.

'That's fine,' he said, and, turning to Gruenther: 'Al, there isn't much time, so take Brigadier Churchill along to G3* and tell them to give him all the help he wants in the planning.'

We studied the charts of the coast and the maps very thoroughly, and I examined the air photographs. Although a landing at the mouth of the Tiber offered the shortest advance to Rome by either of two good roads, the beaches were heavily protected with concrete pill-boxes and machine guns, and there were many roadblocks between the coast and Rome. It was the obvious place for such a landing to take place, and the Germans had disposed themselves in the area accordingly. But what finally ruled it out for our purposes was the absence of a suitable beach on which to land transport, and we simply had to get transport ashore.

Finally, the Navy agreed that the beach which offered the best chances was near a place called Palo, some twenty miles north of the Tiber, and practically the same distance from Rome. Here, a good road, the Via Aurelia, ran within a mile of the coast, and there appeared to be few defences. For naval reasons the landing could not take place before 2 a.m., but with jeeps the force should be able to reach Rome before dawn. Considering the size of the capital I judged that nothing less than two Commandos would be sufficient for the job, for a town swallows up troops very easily, and once the initial shock of our arrival had worn off (and the Germans react very quickly to

* G3 is what the Operations Branch is called in an American HQ.

situations of this sort), we should have to barricade ourselves in to a strongpoint which we would have to defend for an indefinite period.

When I asked the Fifth Army staff for sufficient vehicles to transport a force of approximately 800 men, they threw up their hands in horror. Did we not know that there was an acute shortage of transport in Italy? Did we not realise that every available truck had already been gleaned to make possible the forthcoming landing at Anzio? We finally ascertained that the total number of jeeps that could be made available was twenty-two, though I managed to screw out of them a similar number of trailers.

This limited the strength of the force that could be lifted to approximately 250 men, and I could not see how so small a force could possibly do any appreciable damage. However, I told Gruenther that I was prepared to take the job on, if General Clark reckoned that the project was still worth while. But what I did not know was that while I was doing my planning, that branch of the Fifth Army staff which was concerned with the organisation of Rome once the Allied armies had captured it, had strongly objected to Gruenther that any such attack should be made; they averred that if we entered the capital and created such havoc as we could, it would be just the excuse that the Germans were waiting for to destroy the town before pulling out, and they argued that the harm that we could do in the town would be as nothing compared with what the Germans could do to vital installations such as the railway stations, the post offices and the bridges, not to mention the historic treasures of this Eternal City. They pointed out that provided the Allies did nothing to provoke the Germans in this matter, the chances were that the enemy would leave these installations intact – to the inestimable advantage to the Allies in the subsequent campaign. These arguments proved decisive, and the project was abandoned.

There were times during the Italian Campaign when I felt rather like a juggler with too many balls in the air. While I was planning at Caserta for the Anzio Landing, I was ordered to send No 40 (RM) Commando up to the 56th Division to take part under the orders of that formation in the forthcoming battle to force the crossing of the Garigliano River; and at the same time I was ordered to recall the Belgian and Polish Troops from the upper Sangro, and put them under command of the 5th and 56th Divisions respectively, to take part in the same battle. Simultaneously, No 2 Commando (as has been said) had been put under command of Force 133 and was preparing to cross the Adriatic to garrison the island of Vis; and No 9 Commando and No 43 (RM) Commando were still under my command, though without, at present, any operation in prospect.

There was a large briefing meeting arranged at X Corps Headquarters for participants in the Garigliano River Operation, to which all generals, brigadiers and commanding officers concerned were summoned. I attended with Lieutenant-Colonel J. C. Manners, the CO of 40 (RM) Commando, and the troop leaders of the Belgian and Polish Troops. The meeting was held in a huge marquee, and I remember General Mark Clark landing in a Piper Cub plane on a very short landing strip beside the marquee, having flown up from Caserta. He made the opening address, explaining the operation as seen from his standpoint as Fifth Army commander and describing the part to be played by the 2nd American Corps in simultaneously attacking across the Rapido River on our right. He did not enter into any detail, and his remarks could really be regarded as a pep-talk. He then departed, and Lieutenant-General Sir Richard McCreery, the commander of X (British) Corps, dealt in detail with the plan for the crossing of the Garigliano. I was sitting with a group of British brigade commanders, and we were appalled at the way the plan euphorically envisaged the capture of successive objectives miles beyond the start-line, and all over the most difficult mountainous country in Italy.

'They'll be lucky,' one brigadier whispered to me, 'if we manage to take and hold the *first* objective, let alone any of the others!'

On returning to Caserta, I knew that my brother was making a reconnaissance of Vis Island, so I sent him a signal asking him to come over to Caserta to tell me about the situation on the island, as I couldn't get away from my planning responsibilities.

The final conference on Operation Shingle was called for 9 p.m. on 15th January 1944 at Caserta Palace, and I decided to take my staff captain with me. Pat Henderson had only recently rejoined my staff, having been suffering from an attack of jaundice, and as he had had a lot of work connected with the abortive planning for the descent on Rome, I told him to go to bed and get a good night's sleep.

General John P. Lucas, the commander of the American VI Corps, presided at the conference, as he had been nominated as the commander of the Anzio operation; but Generals Clark and Gruenther, and the divisional commanders involved – Generals Penney (British) and Truscott (American) were also present, as well as a host of heads of Services, brigade commanders, COs and senior staff officers.

The plan to land two divisions on the beaches on either side of the small port of Anzio was carefully explained. The British 1st Division, under Penney, was on the left, and the American 3rd Division under Truscott, was on the right. Between the divisions, a force of three battalions of American Rangers were to land at the harbour of Anzio and take control of the port so that combat-loaded trucks could be driven off the landing craft and proceed straight to their units. Meanwhile an American parachute battalion was to land ahead of the American division.

Late in the conference, however, a major alteration in the plan was announced, to the effect that the American parachutists, who were to have been dropped a few miles inland to seize an outer perimeter for the beach-head as well as a particular hill which overlooked the American landing beach, were not now to be available. General Truscott at once raised an objection, saying that it was vital to the success of his plan that the hill should be in Allied hands. I was sitting next to my old friend Colonel William O. Darby, the commander of the American Ranger formation. He nudged me and whispered: 'Here's where you come in, I guess!'

In a moment, General Al Gruenther, the Chief of Staff, turned to me:

'Brigadier Churchill,' he said, 'can you take this on?'

'Yes,' I replied, 'we can take it on, and will be glad to, but I must point out that we have only four days before embarkation, so we shall need all the help you can give us to plan the naval side, and I would be grateful if General Lucas and his staff could give me half an hour as soon as this conference is over, for we have very little time to arrange the details.'

'OK,' he said, and then turning to the commander of VI Corps: 'Will that do you, Lucas? They'll only have 800 men, and no transport.'

'Gee!' said General Lucas, 'I'll be glad to have anyone who can even heave a rock!'

It was because we were such late starters that we could not take any transport, as all available shipping space for vehicles was already allotted. It was eventually decided to land us over the British beach, from which we were to carry out a seven-mile march across country (and across the enemy's front) to reach the hill which was our objective. Having no transport, we would have to exist on what we could carry on our backs, and I worked out that this could not be for much more than 36 hours, for though in emergency one can go without food for a good deal longer, one cannot go without ammunition in war. The hill lay outside what was to be the initial beach-head, so that we might be in for a sticky time if the main forces did not join up with us fairly quickly.

Further, I had my eye on the future, for our Salerno experience had taught us that we might be needed for much longer than it took to perform the original task. It is all very well to be promised the loan of transport from other units; provided all goes well, the loan will materialise; but if things go wrong, such promises go by the board. I therefore got Lucas to give me an assurance that either our transport would be brought forward from Naples to join us as soon as our first task was completed, or, if that was impossible owing to lack of shipping space, we should be sent back to Naples.

When my conference with VI Corps was over, it was well after midnight, so I went to bed. But early the next morning I got my staff officers together and gave them verbally my plan for the operation, so that they could then get written orders drafted for my two commando units; and, of course, a warning signal was sent to them both to stand by for a new assignment.

I was surprised to find the effect that this sudden new task had on my brigade major. He looked at me uncomprehendingly, wide-eyed, and said:

'But you can't do it, sir. The units just can't be got ready in time. We've only got three days. I don't see *how* we can take this on.'

'Don't you worry, Pat,' I said, 'you get the orders out, which can be regarded as confirmatory, because I'm going to give both COs a verbal briefing this morning. We can do it all right – this is the sort of thing we exist for. I'll be back late this evening, and when I've seen the orders, we can send them out by dispatch rider first thing tomorrow.'

Clifford James was already working on the signal plan, and my staff captain and Morrison were ready to help Pat with the text of the operation order. I had sent for Lieutenant-Colonels R. J. F. Tod and R. W. B. Simonds, the commanding officers of No 9 and No 43 (RM) Commandos respectively, and they came in about noon, covered in dust, having motored in open jeeps from their billets some forty miles away. In the interval before they arrived, I motored down to Naples to see Bill Darby of the American Rangers, as when we got to our objective outside the Anzio beach-head, they would be our nearest neighbours. I had had confirmation from No 2 Commando on the other side of Italy that my brother Jack would be arriving in the mid afternoon, and I arranged for a jeep to meet him at the aerodrome and bring him to Caserta Palace.

The Rangers had received their commando training at our Commando depot and school at Achnacarry in Scotland, and we all knew them well. Bill was a wonderful commanding officer, forceful and straightforward with a great sense of humour. He knew a lot about assault landings by this time, having led his Rangers in the landings in North Africa, Sicily and Salerno. We were both a little alarmed at the light-hearted way in which some of the planning had been conducted and the easy assumption that the VI Corps would be in Rome in a week or two.

'They seem to think it will all be free love and nickel beer when we get ashore,' he said, 'but I'm not so optimistic!' He was a great realist, and we quickly arranged certain code words and made other bipartite arrangements for our mutual assistance in the beach-head.

I then returned to Caserta and briefed my commanding officers. They took things pretty calmly, and I had every confidence that all would go smoothly both in the embarkation and, after the eighteen-hour voyage, the landing, which was to take place soon after midnight.

Jack arrived in the late afternoon and we went off to the Officers' Club in Naples for dinner and a full discussion. It was certainly a pleasant change to sit at a table with a clean tablecloth under chandeliers and be waited on by Italian waiters, and we were even serenaded by an Italian lady who sang 'Lili Marlene', among other songs, in a fine contralto voice, no doubt exactly as she had done only three months earlier to the officers of the German Göring Division and the Luftwaffe!

Jack had spent five days on his reconnaissance of Vis and the neighbouring islands, accompanied by Brigadier H. G. P. Miles, the head of Force 133, and Captain R. W. Keep, the adjutant of No 2 Commando. They had been taken over in a motor launch of the Royal Navy, after having been delayed in Italy for three days owing to violent winds and high seas.

He told me that the partisans, who were disposed in defensive positions on the island, and who numbered perhaps nine hundred or a thousand men, were friendly and welcoming, and were under the command of two idividuals, one, an ex-petty officer of the Royal Yugoslav Navy called Cerni, and the other, an ex-schoolmaster from Zagreb called Milic. Which of the two was the senior was obscure but basically Cerni commanded the partisan schooners and other seagoing boats, and Milic was in charge of the soldiers. The latter was understood to have commanded a Yugoslav battalion in the International Brigade in Spain.

With them at Partisan Headquarters was a commissar, a giant of a man with blond hair and the face of a Greek god. He was known as 'Perot' to the British, and perhaps this was the wartime sobriquet that he assumed, for I later learned that his real name was Petar Radovic. We all liked him, and we were distressed to hear later that owing to some difficulty which arose between him and the partisan cause, a revolver was put on the table beside him and he was told to shoot himself. He did.

My brother told me that he reckoned the morale of the partisans was good, though they were very short of rifles, automatic weapons, mortars and ammunition, and they had no artillery at all. They had been withdrawing successively from the other Dalmatian Islands as the Germans landed on them, and the possibility existed that if their strength and armament was not quickly augmented, they would either withdraw from, or be driven off the island of Vis. Jack also told me that our light naval forces were operating from the island, attacking the German coastal traffic which used the sealanes between the islands to supply their troops on the mainland of Yugoslavia and further south in Greece.

Our forces had previously been operating from the other islands as well, but now they were reduced to using the island of Vis as their only base. He was obviously thrilled at the opportunity to take his Commando over there to stiffen up the partisan defences, and he told me he thought it would be possible to adopt an offensive attitude and attack the Germans on neighbouring islands, though this would have to be on a small scale to begin with, until his Commando was fully up to strength.

We returned to Caserta about 10 p.m. and I received a shattering blow: I was told that Pat Henderson had shot himself.

I still find it hard to dwell on the circumstances of this tragedy, and on the painful hours that followed it. I could only assume that he had not fully recovered from his jaundice – although the doctors had passed him as fit – for it is well established that the after-effects of this disease often include bouts of depression. I still blame myself for not recognising that Pat was in fact ill when he reacted as he did on hearing of our new mission.

I was concerned that the news of this suicide might engender a lack of confidence in the commando plan when my units got to hear of it, but there was little that I could do about this, though I spoke to both commanding officers on the phone. I had a personal feeling of loss, as Pat was a high-principled, gallant* and valuable staff officer whom, in the six months that I had known him, I had come to regard as a friend.

Obviously, an inquest had to be held, and this alerted the American security staff, because suicides are sometimes connected with leakages of secret information. A lot of questions had to be answered, and I shall always be grateful to my other staff officers who, at this fateful moment of time, relieved me as much as possible from the inevitable consequential steps that had to be taken. I suppose it was fortunate that we all had so much to do getting ready at such short notice for the forthcoming operation.

We embarked at Castellamare on the *Derbyshire* which, by coincidence, was the ship which had brought my brigade headquarters out from England for the Sicily landing seven months before; and we found many of our old friends still on board including the captain, the first officer, and the OC Troops. They, like us, had had many adventures in the meantime, and naturally, we spent what spare time there was swapping yarns. As before, the whole ship's company put themselves out to look after us and make us comfortable, though our time on board was so short: we embarked on the morning of 20th January 1944, and the landing took place in the early hours of the 22nd. During the passage, final conferences were held and last-minute preparations made.

Shortly after the big ships got to their release positions, and while we were waiting to be lowered away in our landing craft, there was a considerable stir on the bridge when a dark object was seen floating on our port bow. This was soon identified as a mine, which was slowly drifting towards our side. A motor-launch was quickly hailed to go alongside the mine and keep it from striking any of the many large ships that were at the anchorage – a nasty job, as the ML's captain pointed out to me when I met him by chance in Italy many months later.

We landed on a sandy beach in darkness without even getting our feet wet. There was no opposition, but we had to be very careful crossing the beach as it was heavily mined. My headquarters and the two Commandos formed up clear of the beach, but it was almost impossible to tell exactly where we were, as there were no features in the landscape, and the beach and the coastal road ran parallel to each other for miles and miles.

* He had been awarded the Military Cross at Salerno for knocking out a tank at considerable personal risk.

However, I had as usual brought air photographs of the locality with me, so I took these out of my waterproof bag and studied them, in the early dawn. By comparing the trees near the road with those shown in the photographs, I was able to get my bearings. Some shelling had now developed, and an 88-mm gun started dropping shells in the middle of No 43 (RM) Commando and my headquarters. A close one wounded Fusilier Laws, my batman, in the leg. He was lying down beside me at the time while I was standing on the road talking to Ian Morrison, the acting brigade major. Shortly afterwards, two Messerschmitts machine-gunned the area, and between them and the shelling we sustained four casualties.

The lack of opposition was a surprise to everyone, but I had the feeling that the enemy might have some counterstroke up his sleeve, so we advanced from the beach rather warily. No 9 were ahead in column of troops proceeding south-eastwards down a cart track which was muddy and uneven, and they had considerable difficulty with the handcarts which they were using to transport their machine guns, mortars and reserve ammunition. They passed through the Scots Guards, who were holding the perimeter of the beach-head, and continued on in order to get behind our objective so that they could attack it from the rear. Six German prisoners, the crew of a 10-cm gun encountered on the track, were captured and passed to the rear, while a number of armoured cars and motorcyclists were reported moving on the road running north from Anzio. Some more shelling occurred, and at 10.30 a.m. No 9 got to the road and killed a German despatch rider on a motorcycle whose wallet contained a number of interesting documents. Two more were killed in the next hour.

No 43 Commando were behind No 9, having penetrated beyond the perimeter, and they then branched off to the right and made for the objective, approaching it from the flank. Brigade Headquarters was following them, and I remember seeing Clifford James struggling between the shafts of his signal handcart while ten signallers pushed from the sides and behind. No 43 reported that they had secured their first objective, a level-crossing, and ten minutes later No 9 ambushed and captured a German patrol of eight men. Soon, movement was reported on the final objective, the hill overlooking the beaches, and the two Commandos launched their attacks simultaneously from the north-east and from the west. Our mortars were bursting on the top and on the slopes of the hill, and from the level-crossing, to which I had now moved my headquarters, I could see the attack going in. 43 Commando had several brushes with the enemy between the railway and the hill, and took six prisoners. The objective was secured by 2.45 p.m. and the hill was promptly put in a state of defence, both Commandos and headquarters digging in deeply.

We were now stuck out on our own in front of the beach-heads secured by the British and American divisions, and as night was approaching I ordered the Commandos to send out patrols in all directions. I myself motored forward in a jeep with an escort of two men through Aprilia as far as Campoleone and saw no signs of the enemy, but as I was by then ten miles north of the perimeter, I judged it wise to return to our hill position. The wireless was not working very well and it was not until midnight that I got through to Colonel Darby's Rangers, who were our nearest friends; and Lieutenant-Colonel Murray of the 3rd Rangers paid me a very welcome visit at four o'clock in the morning.

Next morning early I met Darby* on the road near my position, and he gave me a lift in his jeep to his headquarters, and then took me on to see General Lucas. The Rangers had had a sharp fight in the harbour of Anzio and there were a lot of German dead lying about on the sea-front. A number of staff-cars and motorcycles had been burned-out in the streets, and the Rangers had captured some of the undamaged German transport and were using it for their own purposes. Lucas told me that as soon as the Allied divisions advanced and included our hill in the beach-head, we would be withdrawn and embarked at Anzio for return to Naples. This in fact happened late that same evening.

Lucas has been much criticised for not advancing more quickly to the Alban Hills and getting astride Highways 6 and 7 so as to cut the German supply routes to their positions in the Gustav Line. Certainly, the landing took Kesselring by surprise, and when we landed there was next to no opposition. But even as I motored up in my jeep to Campoleone on the day after we landed and saw no signs of the enemy, I felt it in my bones that in a very short time they would scrape some sort of a force together and fling it at our beach-head. The Germans are very good soldiers and they very seldom panic. We now know that by the end of the second day they had managed to send *seven battalions* to the Anzio front, and that they continued to reinforce their positions until at the end of the third day they had *26,000 front line troops* facing the Allied beach-head, drawn from the north of Italy, from Germany, from their forces opposing the Eighth Army in eastern Italy, and even one and a half divisions from Yugoslavia.

* This was the last time that I saw Bill Darby. He was killed in action in Northern Italy three days before the Germans surrendered in 1945.

I have always felt sure that if Lucas had rushed forward to the Alban Hills, the Germans would have driven into his rear with a scythe-like sweep and his forces would have been cut off from their base and port, and would all have been destroyed or made prisoners. Critics seem to forget that Lucas only had two divisions at his disposal; and to suppose that so small a force could have made an advance of 25 miles, and still kept its lines of communication secure to Anzio, is to dwell in cloud-cuckoo land.

The Allies had to build the Anzio force into more than *seven divisions* before they were able to break out of the bridge-head and advance on Rome. Anzio was mounted with far too few divisions in the first place, and for this Winston Churchill and Field Marshal Alexander are primarily to blame – Churchill because he insisted on the operation when there were not enough troops, landing ships and craft available, and Alexander because he let Churchill have his way.

CHAPTER TWELVE

The Capture of Mount Ornito

On reaching our old base at Castellamare, my first concern was to know how the other units of my brigade were getting on. It will be remembered that No 40 (RM) Commando and the Belgian and Polish Troops were under X Corps on the Garigliano. I learned that the former were being employed as infantry in the hills beyond the river, where casualties from mines as well as from mortar and machine gun fire had been heavy. Altogether, 40 Commando was with the 56th Division for a month, and their casualties amounted to 12 killed, 3 missing and 65 wounded.

The Polish and Belgian Troops were with the 56th and the 46th Divisions respectively, being used mostly to carry out patrols and for reliefs in the line, and I was glad to know that their casualties were light.

It was while we were at Castellamare that I received an unofficial and exceptional accretion to my staff in the person of Admiral Sir Walter Cowan,* a retired 74-year-old naval officer who, by special agreement of the Admiralty, had been allowed to rejoin the Navy at the outbreak of war, in the rank of commander. Through his long-standing friendship with Admiral Sir Roger Keyes, the Director of Combined Operations, he had been allowed to serve with the commandos in 1940, when I had first met him. Now, three years later, having fought in the Western Desert, and been captured at Tobruk, and having been exchanged for an Italian general and repatriated to England, he was once more back in harness. He returned to the Mediterranean and Admiral Sir John Cunningham, the Commander-in-Chief, asked me if I would accept him as a liaison officer at my brigade HQ, and I readily agreed. He was to remain with me for six months, and very fond we all became of this gallant and inspiring warrior.

By this time I knew that No 2 Commando, or most of it, must have arrived on Vis Island. I therefore sent for their administrative officer, Captain R. Mitchell, who had recently visited the island and was now back at Molfetta on the east coast in charge of the Commando's rear

* Admiral Sir Walter Cowan, Bt, KCB, DSO, MVO.

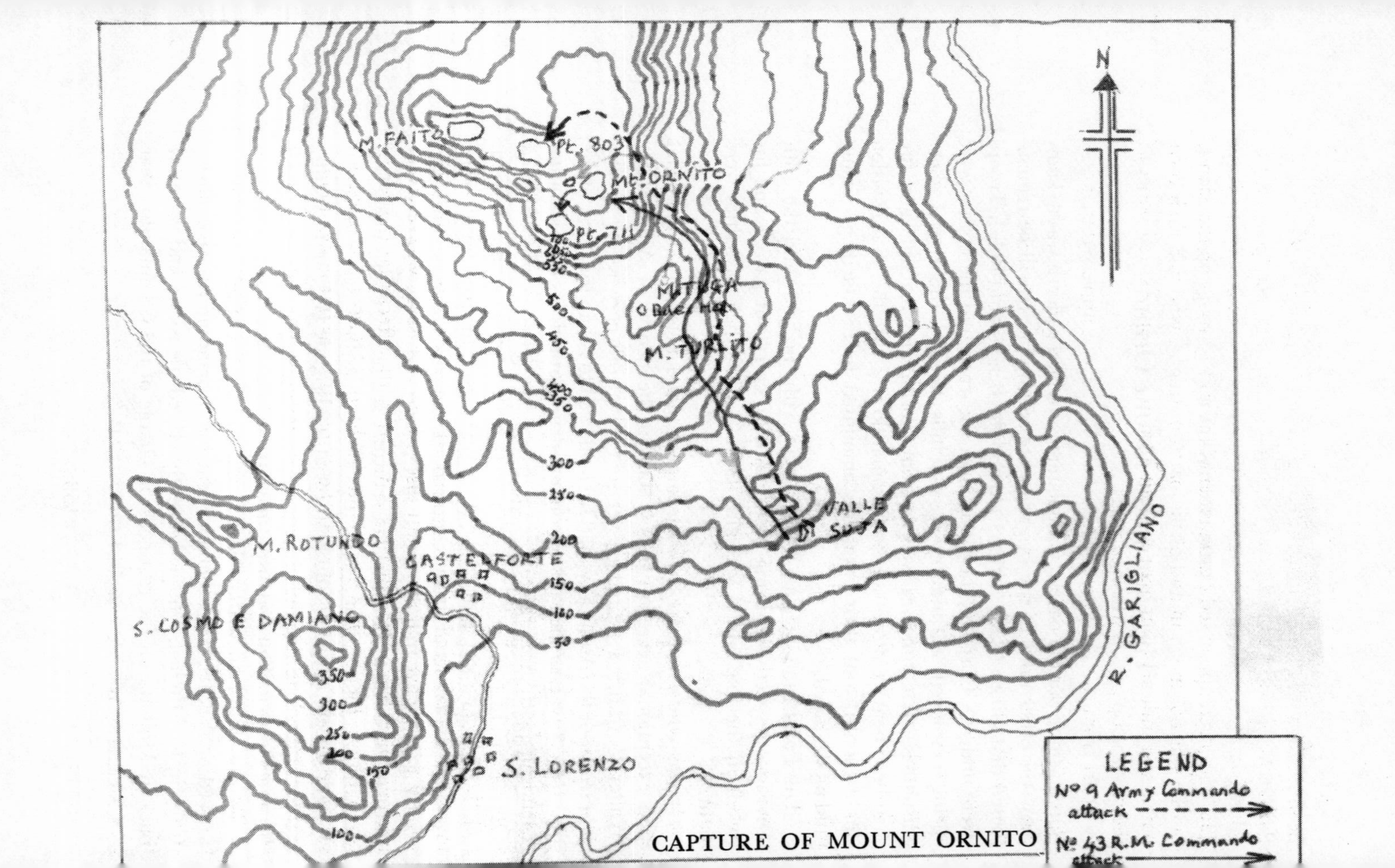

CAPTURE OF MOUNT ORNITO

headquarters. Ronnie Mitchell told me that invasion of the island by the Germans was imminent, as the enemy had now occupied all the other islands in the vicinity, and their aircraft reconnoitred Vis daily. Jack had been appointed commander of the Allied troops on the island, but he was not in command of the partisan troops, who had their own naval and military commanders; but cordial relations existed between them and cooperation was excellent.

Apart from the shortage of troops and artillery, it appeared that one of the chief difficulties was lack of vehicles on the island. There was only one road which was passable for vehicles, and this ran from the port of Komiza, at the west end of Vis, up a steep shoulder of a mountain and then along an extensive central plain, until it descended again to the port and lagoon of Vis, at the eastern end of the island. This road was in need of major repairs.

To make up for the deficiency in manpower, Jack was keen to mine certain parts of the coastline, but he was short of mines and of experts to supervise the laying of them.

On hearing this, I told Ronnie to arrange for the despatch of additional jeeps and trailers from the brigade resources, and I drew in various vehicles from No 9 and No 43 (RM) Commandos to swell the numbers. We had a brigade dump of engineer stores which included mines and barbed wire, which was under the charge of my Royal Engineer Staff Officer, Captain J. Pirrie. I got hold of him and asked if he would like to take over to Vis as much of these stores as could be shipped, and to remain on the island to supervise the static defence layout under my brother's orders, and to give assistance in the road repairs that were necessary. This was of course a great opportunity for a young Sapper officer, and he was thrilled with the idea.

I then set about obtaining permission for more of my Commandos to go over to the island to increase the garrison and reinforce No 2, but while I was engaged on these staff discussions, a message was received late one night from Headquarters X Corps to the effect that the corps commander, Lieutenant-General Sir Richard McCreery, wanted to see me early the next morning. His headquarters was in the mountains beyond Sessa Aurunca and 65 miles from where I was at Castellamare, so I set off in my jeep with my new brigade major.

McCreery told me that his corps was held up on the far side of the Garigliano River in very hilly country, and in spite of the landing at Anzio, the Germans were showing no signs of pulling out of the Gustav Line. Although he didn't say so, I knew his two divisions were exhausted as the result of a long period of fighting in one of the wettest and coldest winters that Italy had known for many years. McCreery wanted to put my brigade (or that part of it that was still under my command – Nos 9 and 43 (RM) Commandos, the two that had just come back from Anzio), and the Belgian Troop, under command of the 56th Division, in a counter-attack role, while his own divisions rested on the defensive. My units were to move immediately to a bivouac area east of Sessa, and would be moved north of the Garigliano River the following day to take up a reserve position.

As no warning order had been issued by X Corps, and as the Commandos were some 65 miles distant, it was clear that they could not arrive before early dawn on the following day. I sent them an order to stand by to move, and told the commanding officers to meet me at a rendezvous near Sessa. I then motored to the 56th Division HQ, which was in a huge stone building on high ground in the middle of Sessa, and overlooking the Garigliano. There I was shown maps and air photographs of the divisional position on the far side of the river.

I got into my camp bed in a tent about 10 p.m. hoping to get a few hours sleep before meeting my Commandos at the bivouac area; but I had no sooner got to sleep than I was woken by General McCreery's chief of staff who had come to tell me that the corps commander wanted to see me again early the next morning, and that a change of plan was likely.

My units arrived at half past two in the morning, and it was early dawn before they were able to turn in. I motored off to X Corps with Tod and Simonds, my two COs, arriving at 8 a.m. to be told by McCreery that my brigade was now to come under command of the 46th Division, and that it was to carry out an attack on certain hill features to the north of a mountain called Monte Tuga. So my COs and I set off again, and after a drive on roads cluttered with every sort of military traffic, we found the 46th Divisional headquarters situated in the bend of a road on a fairly steep slope, in amongst olive trees. There were three or four caravans, and a good many tents. I had fought with the 46th Division at Salerno, and knew Major-General R. Hawkesworth, the divisional commander, and many of his staff.

'Ginger' Hawkesworth was a stocky officer with fair gingery hair and a clipped military moustache. He wore a khaki beret, a crumpled gas-cape, and he always walked with a thumb-stick. He and all his staff and, of course, his three brigades, had had a hard time fighting in the mountains ever since the Salerno landing. Monte Camino and Monte Maggiore had taken their toll in December, and now on the bare rocky hills on the far side of the Garigliano, the 46th Division was just about holding on, up against the forbidding heights of Monte Ornito and Monte Faito. In rain and snow, with only rock-built sangars for warmth and dryness, the men had all but reached the limits of endurance.

When I arrived Bill Eking, Hawkesworth's chief staff officer and an old friend of mine, took me to the General's caravan. Knocking on the door he called out: 'Brigadier Churchill is here, sir.'

'Well, take him away,' came the angry reply. 'I don't want to see him now. Come back in two hours' time.'

So on this unpromising note I retired with my COs to Eking's office tent, where he gave us some tea, and with the help of maps described the division's present positions, and the recent fighting.

In due course Eking and I returned to Hawkesworth's caravan. He said that he wanted me to attack and capture four hill features that were directly on his front, two of them about three quarters of a mile distant (as the crow flies) from his division's front line, and the other two about another mile further on. One of the first two was Monte Ornito, 2,000 feet high, and one of the second two was Monte Faito, nearly 2,500 feet in altitude. In those hills, a distance of a mile as the crow flies would certainly be at least twice that distance on the ground.

I was interested to know where the enemy's defensive fire was directed, and also whether he had shown any particular tendencies or reactions, since such information should be taken into account in making a plan; but I was told I would have to learn the answers to these questions from the battalions which were holding the front line. As it was over a week since the hills had been captured, I was surprised that more was not known at divisional headquarters. Hawkesworth pressed me to tell him my plan as I was about to leave his HQ, but I said that until I had seen the ground, and spoken to the forward company commanders, I couldn't be certain what it would be. I did, however, say that while I was happy about the first three objectives, I felt that, with my unit strengths, which were half the strength of one of his battalions, and supposing we met normal opposition in the mountains, we might find Monte Faito beyond our capabilities. I asked him if we might regard it as an objective to which we might exploit our success – if indeed we achieved success on the first three objectives.

'No, no!' he said, 'Monte Faito is your final objective. I'll not have it regarded as an exploitation task. You capture Monte Ornito first, and then you go on and take Faito.'

'Uh! Huh!' I thought, 'he hasn't learnt anything from the Garigliano battle;' but I kept my thoughts to myself. 46th Division still hadn't taken their second objectives in *that* plan.

I left the 46th Divisional HQ at about ten in the morning and reached the Garigliano River an hour later. There was a track made by the sappers running down to the river, called the Sun Track – I never discovered why. It was in view to the enemy in the hills on the other side, and it was constantly under shell-fire. You waited until a 'stonk' had landed, and then made a dash for the pontoon bridge and crossed to the other side. Once across, one soon came under the lee of the hills.

We motored on for about a mile, and then had to leave our jeeps and start climbing. A guide had been provided by the 6th Battalion of the York and Lancaster Regiment which was holding the forward positions on Monte Tuga. There were a lot of soldiers about, carrying supplies and ammunition up to the troops in the front line, and we passed casualty clearing stations, forward dumps of shells and mortar bombs, and headquarters of the battalions that were holding the line. I was rather surprised that these HQs were so far back from the line. We spoke to those COs who were available, and picked their brains as much as we could about local conditions.

The climb became steeper and steeper, and if we had had more time, we would have followed the tracks and zig-zagged up the hills; but it was quicker to take the direct route straight up the side and often we were climbing on all fours. It was five o'clock in the afternoon by the time we reached the top, and found that there was a gentle but stony valley running parallel to the front line, the latter being on the rocky ridge of Monte Tuga just beyond the valley. The companies holding the line had their headquarters in the valley, and I asked the first company commander I met to allow us to go forward to his defended localities to see the enemy's positions. He agreed and came up with us, and we had to do some crawling amongst the quite large boulders between his platoon and section posts, as we were in view of the enemy. There was one of our artillery observation posts in the company's area, and from this we got a very good view of the valley which lay between the two front lines and was, in fact, 'no-man's-land'.

The company commander pointed out Monte Ornito and a crest called Point 714, which were respectively the right and left of our first objectives. The third objective, a mile beyond, could not be seen, as it was behind and concealed by Monte Ornito; but the fourth and last objective, Monte Faito, *two* miles away, was only too clear – a huge mountain nearly three thousand feet high. We spent over an hour looking at the ground, and when we came away I said to the company commander:

'Thank you for showing us round; sorry to have taken up so much of your time.'

'Oh, don't mention it,' he said. 'We're only so glad it's you and not us who are going to do the attack!'

Tod and Simonds and I scrambled down the hills, and it was dark by the time we reached the lying-up area in the foothills. My brigade staff, while I was away, had arranged the move of my units, though owing to the distance to be covered, they did not arrive until four o'clock in the morning. All stores had to be brought up by mule, and the roughness of the tracks and the lack of knowledge of the ground, plus the darkness, meant that the final consignments of ammunition, rations and engineer stores were not delivered until after dawn had broken: so for a second night running my men had had no sleep.

At 8 a.m. I phoned Hawkesworth and said that I wanted to postpone the attack for 24 hours in order to give units an opportunity to organise themselves during the day, and to obtain some sleep prior to climbing the hills on the morrow and attacking that night:

'I'll only agree, Churchill,' he said, 'provided you guarantee to put in an absolutely first-class attack tomorrow night.'

In the circumstances, I thought this rather a stupid remark, but I let it pass, having got the postponement I wanted and which was essential.

I had intended that the COs should utilise the daylight hours pointing out the objectives to their troop leaders and artillery observation officers, but a thick mist prevented any visibility, and the day was spent instead in tactical reorganisation. During the morning the enemy shelled the valley causing casualties in two of my units – five killed and nine wounded in No 9 Commando, and two wounded in the Belgian Troop.

My plan was to put 43 (RM) Commando at Monte Ornito, and No 9 Commando at Point 711. We had artillery support from the whole of the divisional artillery, plus an extra field regiment and a medium regiment; but because I learnt that it was the custom on both sides to precede attacks by heavy artillery preparation, I had decided, with the agreement of my COs, to do a silent night attack, thereby, I hoped, gaining surprise and enabling the units to get well forward before the enemy detected what we were up to.

The men got a good night's sleep which was undisturbed by enemy shell-fire. The two Commandos and the Belgian Troop made an early start and climbed up the hills to their assembly positions, arriving about noon. Brigade Headquarters and the Belgian Troop were established in the upper valley alongside the company headquarters of the 6th York and Lancasters, and while the Commandos were settling in, I went forward with the commander of the infantry brigade, and the CO of the York and Lancasters to look at the ground again and to show them what our movements would be.

In the course of our reconnaissance the CO revealed that an enemy post about two platoons strong was established on a sub-feature between Monte Tuga and Point 711, and that the enemy's defensive fire had been precipitated by patrols the previous night and it had come down rather heavily in the valley between Monte Tuga and our first two objectives, and also along the crest of Monte Tuga. Obviously, the plan would have to be changed, and the valley in front of the objectives avoided at all costs.

I sent for Tod and Simonds and explained why I had decided to change the plan, and then gave them my new one. It was to carry out the attack from the right flank, No 43 (RM) Commando moving round the eastern (or right) slopes of Monte Tuga and attacking the eastern slopes of Monte Ornito, exploiting on to Point 711; while No 9 Commando was to move in rear of No 43, also round the eastern slopes of Monte Tuga, then round the eastern slopes of Monte Ornito to attack and capture Point 803 from the north-east; and to exploit on to Monte Faito. The Belgian Troop was to remain in brigade reserve in the valley under Monte Tuga. The attack was still to be a silent night attack. I took Tod and Simonds on a final reconnaissance at three o'clock in the afternoon, and pointed out the objectives and the new routes to be followed. While I was thus engaged, the Germans shelled the valley where my headquarters and the Belgians were established, and wounded five of the latter.

The ground over which the commandos were to attack consisted of rugged hills devoid of cover and strewn with rocks and boulders. The slopes of the hills were exceedingly steep and movement, even in daylight, was difficult owing to the looseness of the stones and screes. Monte Tuga is exactly two thousand feet high, and the commandos had climbed it from the lying-up area of the night before, which was only three hundred feet above sea level. Digging was practically impossible, and the only way to obtain protection from shell and mortar splinters, as well as from small arms fire, was to build sangars, or little round walls of stones, as one used to do on the hills on the North-West

Frontier of India. Mules could only be brought half-way up to Monte Tuga, and thence onward Italian porters carried up the loads to small advanced dumps consisting chiefly of water, ammunition and blankets, in the vicinity of Brigade Headquarters.

This attack was going to be the second operation for No 43 (RM) Commando, and it looked to me as if it was going to be a good deal stiffer than Anzio had been. Simonds, a responsible senior commanding officer who before the war had been one of the Parade Adjutants of the Royal Marine Divisions – picked appointments which generally pressaged preferment in the corps – was a reserved but cooperative officer who was much respected by his men. The whole unit had been put through a Commando Course at Achnacarry when it was switched from being the 2nd Royal Marine Battalion to becoming the 43 (RM) Commando. There was a subtle difference between a unit which had completed a commando course (as 43 had), and a unit which consisted of men, each of whom was an individual volunteer for the commandos, and who had been accepted and posted to a commando unit once he had successfully completed the Achnacarry course.

Of the Marine Commandos, only No 40 was of the latter category. They were the first Royal Marine Commando to be formed, and had their baptism of fire in the Dieppe Raid – a very tough initiation. Since then they had fought in the Sicily and Salerno landings, and at Termoli. They were a tried and hardened unit, with a splendid commanding officer in Pops Manners, already the possessor of a DSO which he had won at Termoli. Of course, all the Army Commandos were of the second category, and in my brigade I had two of them, No 9, commanded by Ronnie Tod, and No 2, commanded by my brother.

No 9 Commando had performed one operation since they had been with me, the raid across the Lower Gargiliano in unit strength the previous December. In this they had shown dash and resilience; had carried out the objects of the raid, and had taken a number of prisoners. Tod was a good and popular leader, and he had a highly efficient and dedicated second-in-command in Major Frank Clark, and a first-class adjutant in Captain Mike Allen. He maintained rather informal relations with his officers, and at times it seemed that the unit was run by a soviet, but because of his character and powers of leadership, he got away with it, though among my staff his unit was sometimes referred to as the 'Tod Organisation'.*

I had established my advanced or tactical headquarters in the valley

* Hitler's *Todt Organisation* was the engineer-construction agency which had built the *Siegfried Line*.

level with one of the infantry company headquarters. I had found a small stone pigsty nine feet square and about four feet high, with a muddy floor. You had to bend double to get into it, and then sit down. Inside, I was in one corner, with my maps on my knees, the brigade major was next to me, a signaller with the wireless set in another corner, the gunner lieutenant-colonel, with his set to talk to his forward observation officers moving with the two Commandos was in another corner, and Admiral Cowan. The latter was so small and unassuming one hardly noticed him; but he performed a very useful service in collecting twigs and attending the fire on the floor of the pigsty by which we kept off the bitter cold of a February night in the high Apennines. It got a bit smoky at times, and it was hard to read my map by the hurricane lamp, but the smoke eventually percolated through the hole in the roof.

The zero hour for the move of No 43 (RM) Commando from its assembly position lower down and behind Monte Tuga was half past six in the evening, and No 9 Commando was due to start an hour later. This timing had been chosen to ensure that when the leading Commando first came round the broad base of Monte Tuga and skirted the eastern end of the valley, darkness would have already fallen and the long approach to Monte Ornito would be unobserved by the enemy.

I walked down to the assembly area and chatted to some of the men of No 43, and then watched them move forward in column of troops. They were wearing denim uniform and stockinet caps, and round their webbing equipment each man had wound his commando toggle-rope – that invaluable adjunct which could be put to a wide variety of uses. The nature of the country over which the attack was to take place was so steep and rough that it had been decided to leave the heavy weapons behind, but the men had the light mortars and their bombs with them, and at the end of the column came the stretcher bearers and the medical orderlies under the Commando Medical Officer. I then went on to see No 9, who were wearing serge battledress and green berets, and were similarly equipped.

After they had started, I went to talk to Captain George Danloy and the Belgian Troop, and was on my way back to my headquarters when the brigade major came up and said that the division had sent us up an American Intelligence Officer called Captain Dietrich G. Stechert, who would be able to interrogate any prisoners that we took, as he spoke fluent German. I shook hands with him, and asked him to try and find out the strengths in which the enemy was holding the hills, and where his reserves were. By now it was getting distinctly cold, and he noticed me shiver. He immediately handed me his American uniform greatcoat, saying he would not be needing it during the battle. The string vest and khaki pullover that I wore under my tunic were hardly sufficient protection in the open, and I was grateful for the loan.

About the same time that No 9 moved forward, we heard the divisional artillery of the 56th Division on our left firing a diversionary shoot, as arranged, to mislead the enemy as to our plan, and at the same time the York and Lancaster posts on Monte Tuga fired small arms on to enemy targets on the left flank. Nothing more happened for just over an hour, and though the waiting was hard to bear, I was glad to know that our men were evidently approaching their first objective without detection. But then suddenly intermittent rifle fire was heard from the direction of Monte Ornito, which continued for twenty-five minutes, and then enemy artillery and mortar fire came down heavily, and I knew that No 43 must be attacking.

Several salvos of shells burst in the valley in the vicinity of Brigade Heaquarters and then wireless contact with the marines was broken. James my signal officer sent out a junction set to the crest of Monte Tuga to try to re-establish communication, and then a report was received from No 43 that they were in contact with the enemy on the lower slopes of Ornito, and with an enemy post down in the valley on the right flank.

Not long afterwards three prisoners taken by No 9 Commando were brought in and were identified as belonging to the 2nd Battalion of the German 276th Infantry Regiment, and they reported that there were two machine guns on the top of Ornito, and a machine gun post on Point 711. The whereabouts of an artillery observation post was also indicated, and my gunner liaison officer set about destroying it with his guns. At an hour before midnight No 9 Commando reported, 'OK, but progress slow', and half an hour later, 'OK so far'. I sent a message to both units, 'Well done, keep going.'

Around midnight three intercepts showed that No 9 had been delayed by mortar fire, and soon afterwards No 43 was heard asking No 9 for a situation report as they thought they might be crossing their front. At this time the Brigade Headquarters area was shelled again, and I asked the gunner representative to put down a concentration on certain enemy heavy mortars which the corps flash-spotters had located north of Monte Faito. This incident repeated itself half an hour later. From this time onwards until half past seven in the morning, the two Commandos were out of wireless contact with Brigade Headquarters and efforts by the Brigade Signal Troop to remedy the situation were unavailing.

At half past two in the morning there was a sharp burst of shelling which lasted about three minutes in the vicinity of headquarters, and green, orange and white Very lights were reported from the area of the battle by observers on Monte Tuga at various times during the next three hours, and certain reports from the artillery observation officers with the Commandos were received, one of which reported fifteen casualties from mortar fire in the rear troop of 43 Commando; and another which stated that the gunner observer with the Marines had been hit. About twenty prisoners had been escorted in to Brigade Headquarters, and these were very efficiently interrogated by Lieutenant Stechert, from whom it was learned that the 2nd Battalion of the 276th Infantry Regiment was holding Monte Faito and Monte Ornito, while a battalion of the 71st Regiment was holding Point 711. It was also learned that a reserve company from the enemy positions away below Tuga on the right flank had been moved to the village of Cerasola a mile beyond Ornito, and this was important news because it probably meant the enemy was hard pressed in the positions we were attacking; it might also indicate the direction from which a counter-attack might be expected.

It was not until 7.30 a.m. that I next got in touch with the Commandos, when the colonel of 9 Commando spoke on the wireless set belonging to Major Pearce, the artillery FOO attached to his Commando. It was difficult to hear owing to interference, but I understood him to say that his Commando had penetrated as far as Point 803, just short of Mount Faito, but had been caught in heavy shell and mortar fire in the early hours of the morning and had suffered considerable casualties. The unit had had to fall back to Monte Ornito, which was firmly held, and so far as he knew, 43 Commando had gone to Point 711.

The wounded were slowly coming in, and I saw Captains Kither and Long, both of whom had been hit, and shortly afterwards Lieutenant Wilson who was brought in with a nasty wound in the head. The officers told me that Colonel Tod was wounded, that his second-in-command, Major Francis Clark, was wounded and missing, with Lieutenant MacDougal Porter the intelligence officer, and that the regimental sergeant major, RSM Beardmore, had been killed.

Beardmore's was a particularly unfortunate case. Having been wounded by shellfire, he was being carried on a stretcher to the rear when the stretcher bearers ran into a burst of machine gun fire and he was killed. I got on to Division by telephone and gave them the situation as I understood it, and then went forward with Captain Roger

Wakefield, my second staff officer, to see the Commandos and ascertain the exact situation. As I was leaving, Admiral Cowan asked if he might come along too. He was wearing his green commando beret, but as there was a lot of shellfire I suggested that he put on his steel helmet. He replied characteristically that he didn't carry one, so I borrowed one from a signaller and handed it to him. When we were well forward I looked round and saw that he was carrying it in his hand!

When I got to the Commandos I found them on the steep slopes of Mount Ornito, digging in (where there was enough earth) or building little stone walls to provide some protection from splinters. They looked pretty tired, and were reorganising their sub-units and weapons because of their casualties. Colonel Tod had been hit by shell-splinters in both legs and arms, and though they were light wounds, he had lost a lot of blood and I ordered him back, telling Captain Mike Allen, his adjutant, to take command of the unit. All except one of their troop leaders had been killed or wounded, and they had lost their second-in-command and the intelligence officer.

No 43 Commando had fortunately had better luck and their casualties were light. About half of this Commando was established on Ornito, and the remainder were over to the left on Point 711. I saw Colonel Bill Simonds and discussed the position with him, and arranged for a patrol to go out and reconnoitre the ground in front of Ornito during the morning to make sure that the enemy did not creep back. Then I returned to my headquarters to get in touch with Division again.

Mount Ornito was the eastern bastion of a mountain range and from its slopes one looked down over foothills to the River Garigliano in a deep valley some five or six miles distant. Many of these hills were still in enemy hands, and he therefore had excellent observation of our movements on the slopes. His artillery shelled our positions intermittently all day, and made the slow process of evacuating casualties over the rough and steep slopes even more difficult. I went back with Roger Wakefield, and the Admiral accompanied and assisted Colonel Tod down the slopes. As they went along, they noticed one individual who flung himself down every time a shell whistled overhead. The Admiral remarked dryly, 'That fellow seems to hold life very dear; you are too hurt, and I am too old, to duck!'

During the day a close watch had been kept on a hill lying below and beyond Ornito, for it was here that the German reserve company (of which we had been warned by our American Interrogation Officer) was thought to have taken up its position. Sure enough, during the afternoon the Commandos noticed forward movement from this hill, and rightly guessed that this was the beginning of a counter-attack. Colonel Howard got his artillery on to them a number of times, and all posts were warned to be ready for the attack. It came in just as it was getting dark, and received a very hot welcome. The enemy succeeded in getting within hand-grenade range at one or two points, but were driven off with heavy losses.

We had received orders to carry out a small attack that night to clear a feature that lay in front of Ornito and Point 711, and I detailed the Belgian Troop for this task. They had had a near squeak earlier in the day, when a large shell had landed in their midst without exploding. It made a very odd noise as it came over, and it could clearly be seen for the last second or so of its flight, looking 'like an empty champagne bottle' as Captain George Danloy, the Belgian commander, graphically described it.

The Belgian attack met no opposition and the hill was secured, and not long after midnight the Commandos were relieved by the 5th Hampshires of the 46th Division. Early next morning the corps commander arrived up at our position. He must have made a very early start, and we were impressed with the alacrity with which he had come up to see the new position, particularly as it was such a punishing ascent. We never saw anything of Hawkesworth, the divisional commander.

The Commandos were moved down the mountains to a rest area in a ruined village, where we spent two nights, and then returned to our original billets in the Naples area. The attack had cost No 9 Commando over a quarter of its strength in casualties, which included 50 per cent of its officers. 43 Commando and the Belgian Troop had come off more lightly and had only suffered 55 casualties between them. I spent the next few days visiting the many hospitals near Naples to see our wounded, but it was difficult to find them as they had been distributed widely, and many of them were evacuated to Sicily.

General McCreery sent me a letter a week afterwards in which he said:

> . . . the fact that the Bosch has reacted so strongly shows clearly that the objectives you captured were of real importance. I want to congratulate your Brigade on the good work done during 2/3 Feb. by both Commandos. The country was extremely difficult, and the courage, enterprise and endurance shown by many parties, after officer casualties had made control difficult, were in the best traditions of the Commandos . . . I am more than satisfied with the results achieved.
>
> Good luck to you all.

One footnote only need be added to the Ornito battle. Monte Faito, at the foot of which No 9 Commando received such severe casualties from the German defensive artillery fire, and which Hawkesworth had insisted should be designated as the final objective, was in fact never captured by Hawkesworth's 46th Division. It was only evacuated by the Germans when General Juin's French Expeditionary Corps advanced through the Auruncian mountains in the early days of May – over three months later – taking part in General Alexander's great battle for Rome.

CHAPTER THIRTEEN

Vis Island

One of the characteristics of a commando brigade is that its units are seldom together for any length of time, and more often than not at least one unit is detached and fighting under some other formation's temporary command. When Nos 9 and 43 Commandos came back from the attack and capture of Mount Ornito, the other two units of the brigade were still away, No 40 Commando on the further bank of the Garigliano River, and No 2 Commando partly on a Dalmatian island and partly on the eastern coast of Italy where it was completing the training of its recruits.

I did my best to get around and visit each unit in its particular location, and to discuss with its CO any problems or difficulties that he might be experiencing. The ever-present problem was the replacement of casualties, and this had to be arranged by the staff of my brigade HQ because the formation under which the unit was operating had no responsibility in this matter.

There was also the question of the morale of the unit. The commandos were a very closely-knit force and were used to working with each other and under their known and accustomed superior formation. If, for instance, in their detached assignment they were unlucky enough to sustain heavy casualties, there might be a tendency on their part to think that they were being used unfairly, and being made to undertake unpleasant and dangerous tasks which should more properly have been undertaken at least equally by the units of the formation under which they were then serving. Provided I was able to get around and keep in close touch with the Commando concerned, as well as with their temporary masters, I was generally able to cope with this sort of situation, and the unit itself felt that it was not being abandoned by its own hierarchy.

Another consequence of the dispersion of my brigade unit was the difficulty we experienced in repairing or replacing weapons, vehicles or equipment which became damaged by enemy action. The smallness of my staff, and the remoteness of my brigade arms and vehicle depots in relation to the locality in which the Commando was operating made such replacements particularly difficult.

Finally, there was obviously a disadvantage to all concerned, both my brigade headquarters and the various individual commando units under my command, in being deprived of our entity while detachments to other formations was necessary. It was much easier to operate if the brigade was entire; but obviously one had to accept existing circumstances and do one's best to cope with them.

The authorities were getting a bit anxious about Vis island as the German threat of invasion was a serious one which was confirmed by Ultra intercepts, and it was obvious that if it took place it would be touch and go whether we could manage to hold on. The experience of the German invasion of Crete and of the islands of Cos and Leros had taught that when they decided to carry out an island invasion they did it pretty thoroughly, using air support on a large scale and employing airborne troops as well as an assault from the sea. It was decided therefore that No 43 (RM) Commando should be sent over to Vis immediately, and that I should go too with my headquarters to take command of the garrison. We were also arranging for Nos 9 and 40 (RM) Commandos to follow in the near future, when a call came from Anzio to reinforce the beach-head which was still being hard pressed. As Italy was the main theatre of war, its needs had to take precedence, and the two Commandos had to be despatched to Anzio. They were to spend a month in the beach-head and they did not revert to my command until the middle of April.

The island of Vis or Lissa (the old Austrian name) is about eighteen miles long by eight miles wide. It is extremely hilly and the highest peak, Mount Hum, rises straight out of the sea at the western end of the island to a height of 1900 feet. It possesses two small harbours, one at Komiza on the west, nestling under the slopes of Hum, and the other at Vis near the north-eastern corner of the island and situated at the end of a long lagoon. Like all the Dalmatian islands, its slopes are for the most part bare and rocky, and where vegetation occurs it consists of small bushes which grow in amongst the rocks to the height of a man's waist. Trees are very scarce, and on Vis they were only to be found in a small area on the south-east of the island. The shores are rocky, and small inlets abound, but sandy bays are practically non-exitent, and when they are found they are never more than fifty yards long.

The group of Dalmatian islands which lie between the Yugoslavian ports of Split and Dubrovnik consist of seven islands of which Vis is one. The others, reading from north to south, are Solta (pronounced Sholta), Brac (Brartch), Hvar (Hwhar), Korcula (Korchula), Lagosta and Mljet (Millet). Vis itself lies furthest to the west of these six, being

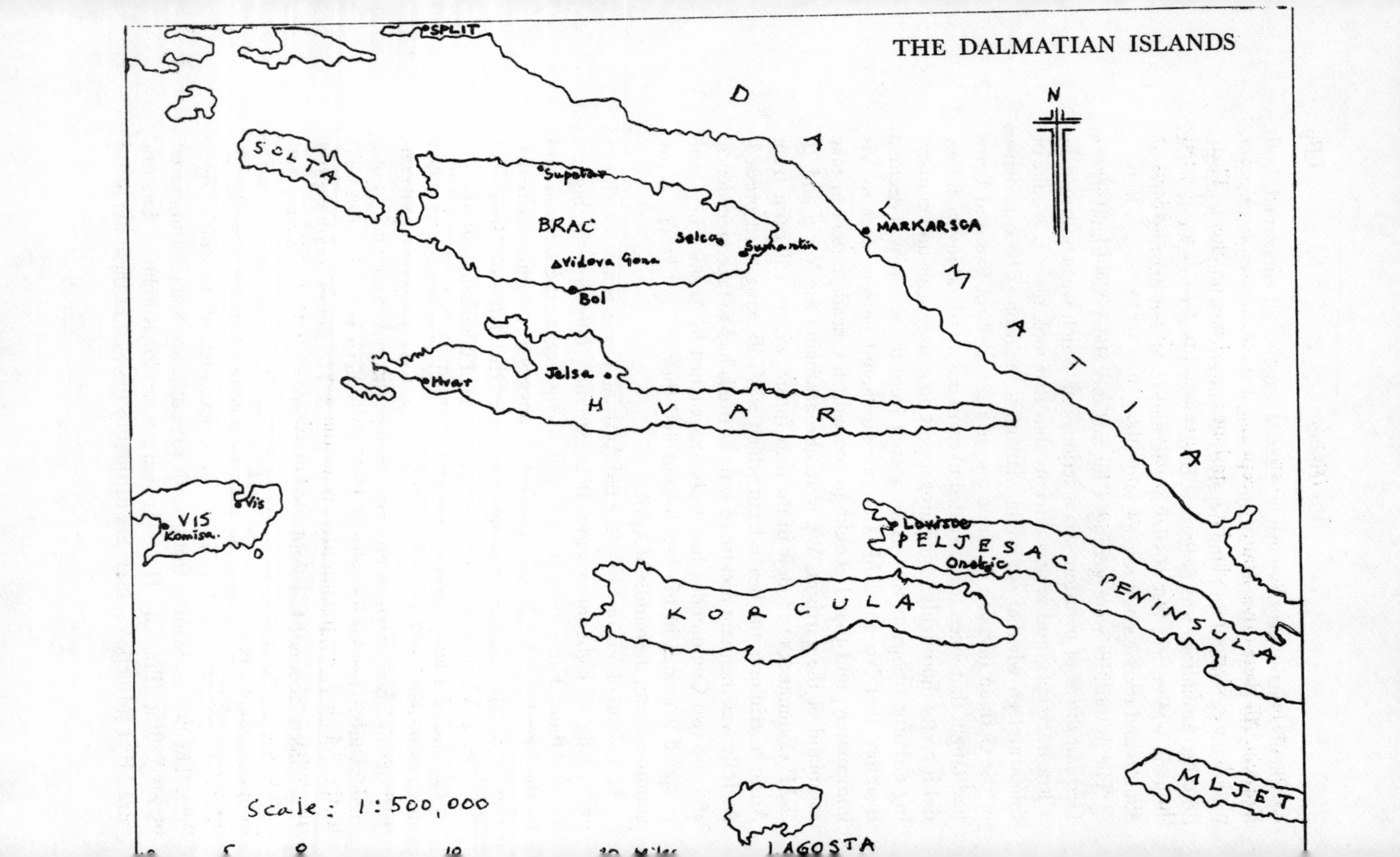
THE DALMATIAN ISLANDS
N
SPLIT
D A L M A T I A
MARKARSCA
SOLTA
Supetar
BRAC
Selca
Sumartin
Vidova Gora
Bol
Jelsa
Hvar
H V A R
VIS
Vis
Komisa
Lovisce
PELJESAC
Orebic
PELJESAC PENINSULA
K O R C U L A
MLJET
LAGOSTA
Scale: 1:500,000
5
0
10
Miles

about 17 miles south-west of Hvar and 23 miles west-by-north of Korcula. All these other islands except Lagosta had by now been occupied by the Germans, who had stationed garrisons on them. Their purpose in taking them was probably three-fold : to provide a protected shipping channel inside the islands by which their coastal garrisons in Yugoslavia, Albania and Greece could be supplied; to use the islands as an outpost position for the protection of the coast against invasion; and to deny the islands to us.

I crossed over to Vis on 1st March 1944, and arranged for my headquarters to come forward in the course of a few days. I was anxious to see the island as quickly as possible and familiarise myself with the situation, before it arrived. We made the journey in a naval motor-launch, sailing from Manfredonia on the east coast of Italy. The distance was about 130 miles and took just under eight hours. Admiral Sir Walter Cowan came with me, and also Captain Roger Wakefield. We timed our arrival so as to reach the vicinity of the island after dark, as enemy aircraft and surface craft were active and there was less chance of meeting them after sundown.

My first view of the island which was to be my home for the next five and a half months was therefore by night, and all I could see as we drew near was the huge mass of Mount Hum (pronounced Hoom) above the bay in which the little port of Komiza was situated. As we approached the land we reduced speed, and were suddenly challenged by light by another craft. The signaller lost no time in giving the reply, for E-boat clashes were frequent, and the crews of the MGBs and MTBs were pretty quick on the trigger. As the outline of the houses clarified and I made out the breakwater ahead, a rifle shot rang out which was apparently the partisan method of challenging approaching craft. Again the bridge gave the answering light signal, and we passed round the head of the mole and came alongside. There were several other naval craft tied up, and I could discern the masts and rigging of one or two schooners.

My brother was on the quay to meet me, and after introducing him to the Admiral, we made our way to the flat which he occupied on the water-front. I was glad to see Guardsman Stretton, his batman, again, and he took charge of our luggage. The flat was in a modern building which had been built just before the war, and was the only up-to-date building on the island. There were two storeys, on each of which were two self-contained flats. Jack had taken over the lower of the two storeys, and the naval staff occupied the upper one. The house belonged to the Mardesic family, the only wealthy people on

Vis, who owned the anchovy industry which they carried on at Komiza. All export of their products had ceased during the war, so that there were certain stocks of tinned anchovies still available, and we used to eat them with biscuits as cocktail savouries. They were the best anchovies I ever tasted, and I believe were considered in the trade as among the best in the world.

The next day Jack motored me over the island in a jeep, and pointed out the main features and introduced me to a number of officers. He had fixed an appointment for me to meet Commander Cerni (pronounced Cherni) and Colonel Millic, the Partisan commanders of their naval and military forces respectively. Cerni was a short little man in the early forties with sharp features, a clean-shaven swarthy face and dark brushed-back hair. He had been a petty officer in the Royal Yugoslav Navy before the war, and had attended certain courses in England. He spoke excellent English, and consequently we had many dealings with him on matters other than naval as he was able to act as an intermediary.

Millic, on the other hand, was much less a man of the world. He was darker and better-looking than Cerni, with longish hair that was not always quite in place, and a gentle manner. He had obtained a philosophy degree at Zagreb University, and was teaching that subject in a secondary school when war broke out. His ambition had been to become a University professor. During the Spanish Civil War he had fought in Spain on the Republican side, and he was an idealist in whose eyes burn the light of the dévot.

The partisans had provided me with a guard of honour of thirty men who were formed up in three close ranks on a rocky hillside just outside the house which was their headquarters. Their uniforms were of grey-green serge and their equipment, chiefly consisting of leather belt and straps, had certainly never tasted polish. They wore caps in the style of a Glengarry with the cloth badge of a red star in front, and were armed with German and Italian rifles and tommy-guns which had been captured from their enemies on the mainland of Yugoslavia. Jack had warned me that the correct procedure after inspecting the ranks was to call out '*Smrt Facismo*' which means 'Death to Fascism', and every soldier replied in unison, '*Slobodna Narodu*' meaning 'Freedom for the People'. This was the slogan adopted by the National Army of Liberation of Yugoslavia, and all written orders or notices ended with these words.

The one road that was motorable ran from Komiza, on the west, to Vis, on the north-east, by way of the southern part of the island. Its

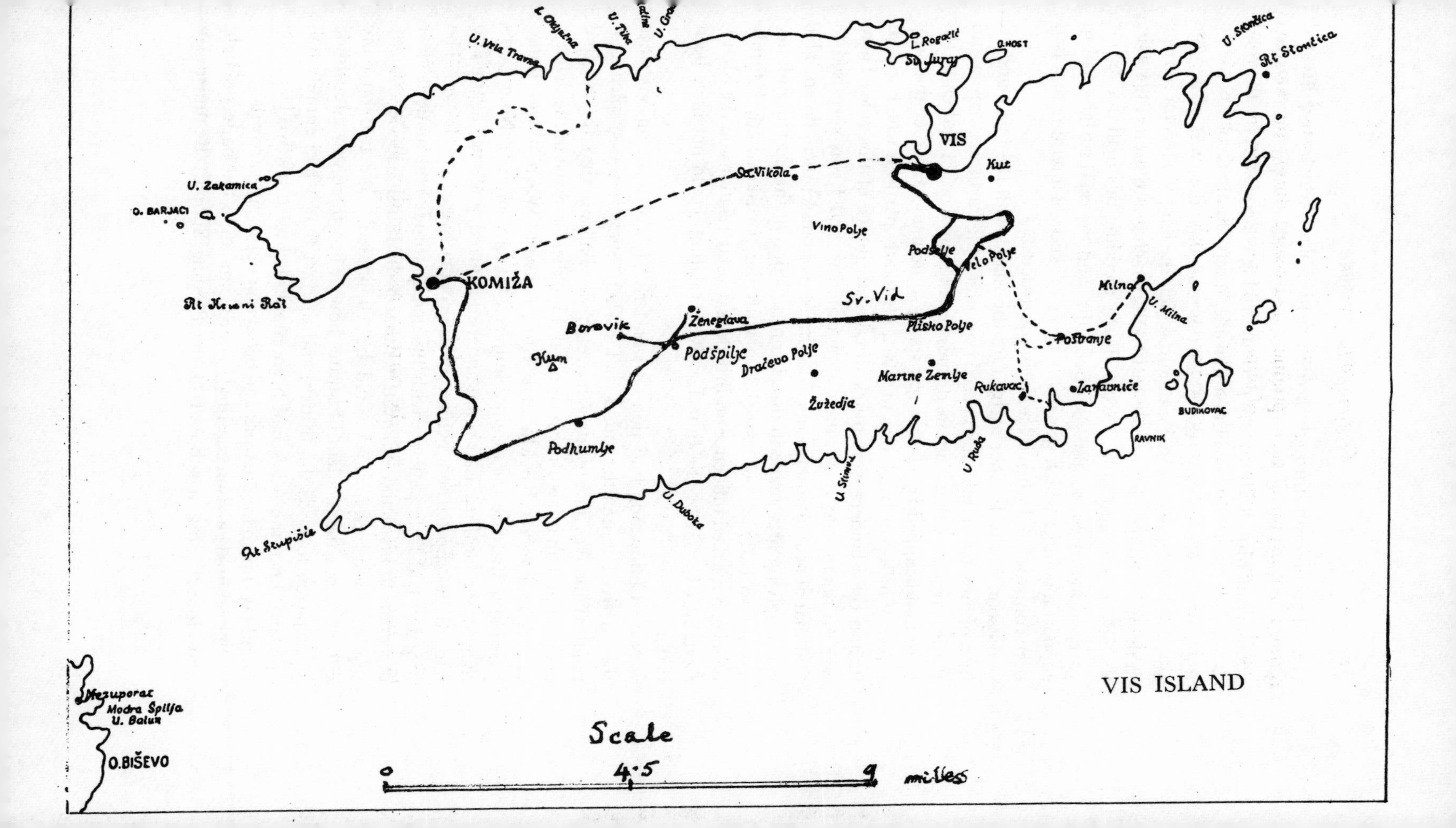
U. Vela Travna
U. Tiha
L. Rogačić
Sv. Juraj
VIS
Kut
U. Stončica
Rt Stončica
U. Zakamica
O. BARJACI
Sv. Nikola
Vino Polje
Podselje
Velo Polje
KOMIŽA
Milna
U. Milna
Sv. Vid
Ženeglava
Borovik
Plisko Polje
Podšpilje
Dračevo Polje
Poštranje
Kum
Marine Zemlje
Rukavac
Zaravniče
Žužedja
BUDIKOVAC
RAVNIK
Podhumlje
U. Ruda
U. Stiniva
U. Duboka
Rt Stupišće
Mezuporac
Modra Špilja
U. Balun
O. BIŠEVO
Scale
0
4·5
9
miles

VIS ISLAND

central portion runs through three successive plains which are cultivated with the vine, but on leaving Komiza it ascends sharply up the steep shoulder of Mount Hum, and careful driving is necessary, for the road is built on the precipitous mountainside, many hundreds of feet above the sea. After traversing the plain the road tops the crest of a ridge and suddenly reveals a panorama in which the long Vis lagoon mirrors in its sheltered blue waters the rocky hills which guard it on either side. Squads of men and women were always mending this road, for as our garrison increased, so also did the traffic, and the road surface had to support a volume which was many times in excess of anything that had been contemplated when it had been constructed.

As soon as my brother arrived on the island with the first hundred men of his Commando, he realised how much the Partisan garrison and the few peasants that remained (mostly old men, women and children) were handicapped by lack of transport, so he made an order that any driver of a jeep or truck was to give a lift to any partisan who required it, and the islanders were quick to take advantage of this rule. There was no doubt that they much appreciated it, and I was surprised to find that almost invariably one was thanked as one set them down. This rule of giving lifts, made in direct contradiction of the normal military custom so early in our association with the partisans had, I firmly believe, a marked influence on British–Yugoslav relations on the island. Certain it is that by the time I arrived, relations could not have been better.

No 2 Commando had done a wonderful job of work on Vis since they arrived a month and a half earlier. Such is the suspicion of political motives in any new move in the Balkans that the original decision to send a few British commando soldiers to assist in the defence of Vis had to receive Marshal Tito's consent. When it was found possible to increase the original hundred by some more of No 2 Commando, the local partisan commanders demurred, and once again Tito had to be approached before the objections were withdrawn. The Marshal had little patience with this local attitude and made it clear in signals to his island subordinates that if the British experienced any trouble, those responsible would be 'eliminated'! We had no more difficulty, but the incident illustrates how at first there was an attitude of suspicion towards the British, and the fact that it had entirely disappeared once the Allies had been established for a few weeks on the island says much for the work and behaviour of the early arrivals.

The original garrison consisted of one Commando, one battery of light anti-aircraft guns, a sub-unit of the Raiding Support Regiment, an

RAMC Surgical Team, two units of American Operational Groups, and certain officers and men to deal with supplies. The partisan forces consisted of three brigades (approximately 3,000 men), two batteries of captured Italian howitzers and four 105 cm guns which were used singly in a coast defence role. This was the sum total of the garrison apart from the naval component, which consisted of a small staff and half a dozen MTBs.

The first task was to ensure that the slender forces available were disposed to the best advantage for the defence of the island. To this end Jack tramped over the whole island to make himself familiar with every feature, and made several tours of the island in naval craft and schooners, inspecting all the inlets in order to estimate which were the most likely landing places for an invasion. In all matters he maintained the closest liaison with the partisans, whom he found ready to cooperate to the fullest extent. It was obvious that the defence of the island would be greatly facilitated by early warning of invasion, and to this end he relied on three factors: first, naval patrols which took place nightly in the waters around Vis and the neighbouring occupied islands; secondly, on partisan schooners which stationed themselves off the island and were ordered to fire light signals if the enemy approached; and thirdly on a coast watching system which was entrusted to the partisan forces.

The island was divided up into three sectors, a north-eastern, a southern and a north-western; and one partisan brigade was responsible for the defence of each. These brigades disposed roughly two-thirds of their strength in one or two-men posts on every headland and slope of the coast, so that no single area of sea was unobserved by day or by night. These posts were most cunningly camouflaged and were permanently manned, and there is no doubt that on account of the strict discipline of the partisan army, the sense of duty of the individual soldier and the natural keenness of his eyesight, the island was probably better watched than any other coastline in this war. Certainly when I thought back to our own eastern and southern coasts in 1940 I could not help realising how much better off we were in Vis.

There were two areas of coast which were major danger-spots for seaborne invasion. They were, respectively, the inlets north-west of the Vis lagoon, and the portion of coast immediately opposite Ravnik island, off the south-eastern corner of Vis. The coast at both these areas was favourable for landing in moderate weather, and the former offered an approach to the high ground west and south of Vis harbour (as a preliminary step to capturing the town), while the latter gave access to a branch of the main Komiza–Vis road which the enemy would probably try to cut at an early moment. It was always my view that invasion would embrace simultaneous landings at these two points in an attempt to over-run the eastern end of the island. There were of course other points which might be chosen, and which offered certain advantages to an invader, but these were the most dangerous, for either or both offered a means by which he could bring supplies and further reinforcements to his first flights.

To guard against these threats, Jack decided to turn the headland of Sv Juraj (St George) into a strong-point to guard the entrance to the Vis lagoon and frustrate attempts at landing in the inlets to the westwards. He put a whole commando troop into the old English fort at this point, and stiffened up their armament with three Bofors guns and one of the Italian 105-mm gun-howitzers. The commando troop was specially equipped with three six-pounder anti-tank guns, additional Vickers guns and some litle Italian anti-tank guns. The garrison had orders to hold the fort to the last. The partisans established a similar strong-point on the headland opposite, so that the entrance to Vis harbour was guarded from both the western and eastern shores. In addition, the American Operational Groups and another commando troop were stationed in reserve in Vis town itself, with reinforcement and counter-attack tasks.

For the defence of the other vital area in the south-east, it was decided to hold and fortify the island of Ravnik. By so doing, the sea approaches were threatened in flank, and even if enemy landing craft succeeded in getting past the island, the disembarkation of troops on the shores of the main island could still be interfered with by fire from Ravnik. To thicken up the fire of the garrison on Ravnik, three Bofors guns were located on the coast of Vis opposite the small island, to help to break up the enemy invasion, while still sea-borne, in the channels on each side of Ravnik. The garrison of this little island, which included commando and RSR troops armed with six-pounder anti-tank guns and Brownings, was likewise ordered to remain to the last.

The construction of living accommodation and defences on Ravnik was a major undertaking, for the island consisted of one large rock, so that it was necessary to blast deep shelters for use as billets, and to blast emplacements for the guns. The island was ringed round with barbed wire, the picquets for which had also to be blasted into the ground, and the entire coast was mined. The garrison was maintained by boat from the adjacent port of Rukavac, while 14 days' reserve food and water was stored on the island.

›on showing Fort
‹on, the building on
ıt top left; Hoste
he small island above
ntly left of the church

harbour, Vis, with
Motor Gun-boat
le quay. Mount Hum
ackground

left) Admiral Sir Walter

right) Fitzroy Maclean
ndolph Churchill in
ı Korcula

(*Top left*) The author's
Borovik on Vis

(*Top right*) Heavy anti-a
guns defending Vis Isla

Millic presenting prizes
NCOs' course. The auth
on the left

Some of the German
prisoners captured in th
Solta raid

Attack by parachutists and gliders was very much a possibility, and steps had to be taken to guard against this threat too. The most likely landing area appeared to be the two valleys called Dracevo Polje and Velo Polje through which the main road ran. These two valleys were separated by an isolated hill called Sv Vid, so this was fortified and defended by another commando troop armed with heavy mortars and machine guns. The troop kept sentries permanently on the guns by day and night, while the rest of the unit lived in buildings in the valley. Partly because these buildings had been a farm, and partly because Captain 'Sid' Walker, the troop leader, was a farmer in pre-war days, this billet was always known as 'Ducksplash Farm'.

The remaining two troops of the Commando were billeted in Komiza, where Jack lived and had his headquarters, but in the event of invasion he decided to move at once to the partisan headquarters which was in the village of Borovik, in a valley just east of Mount Hum. He therefore arranged with the partisans for certain rooms in houses there to be kept permanently vacant for his staff, and got his signal officer to put in the necessary telephone and wireless communications in advance.

Apart from the five Italian guns which had been sited singly at various points on the coast, the artillery defence consisted of three batteries of partisan-manned 100-mm guns which had taken up positions so that they could all bring down fire on any part of the coast. The gunners had been trained by a cadre of British officers and NCOs under Major Geoffrey Kupp who maintained a small artillery school on the island which later received the pretentious title of 'The Balkan School of Artillery'. This continued to train partisans in different types of artillery and had undoubtedly greatly assisted Tito's forces on the mainland.

In spite of the manifold activities which occupied Colonel Jack as commander of the garrison, he found time, within a week of arriving on the island, to commence the planning of a series of raids on the neighbouring German-occupied islands. It was obvious that owing to the smallness of the garrison of Vis and the imminent danger of invasion, only a few troops could be employed away from the island for such raids, but the small enterprises which were now planned and executed were an excellent illustration of the military axiom that the best means of defence is attack. These early raids were directed against the islands of Hvar and Brac, and the first two were led by Colonel Jack himself.

It was known that the enemy had split up his island garrisons into small posts round the coast, each of which had communication to larger reserves located further inland. Normally reliable information was available from partisan sources of the location of these posts, their approximate strength, and the type of arms with which they were defended. By a careful study of maps and air photographs, a suitable cove was selected for the raiding party to land, either from naval craft or a Yugoslav schooner, and a route selected by which to approach the enemy post. This was usually situated in a house, with sentries posted on the approaches.

In one of these raids the commandos landed on Hvar from a schooner on an exceptionally dark night, and had some difficulty in getting from the ships to the shore as the cove was rocky and the water deep. The unloading of the weapons was a tricky operation as it was difficult to avoid dropping equipment owing to the swell and the slipperiness of the rocks. Torches could not be used, and when a magazine or tommy-gun clattered on the rocks it seemed that the landing was bound to be detected by the enemy. Then came the approach march, in pitch darkness over boulders and up steep slopes, to the objective. To maintain direction officers led the column, using a compass to aid in direction finding. When the enemy post was only about two hundred yards distant, the column split so that at least two separate parties threatened it from different directions. Slowly the Colonel approached the house which could dimly be discerned.

Suddenly a vehement and guttural 'Haaaaalt!' rang out from a sentry secreted somewhere in the shadows and then, almost immediately, a burst of fire followed from a schmeiser. The flashes from the muzzle gave his position away, and as the raiding party opened fire, he ran back to the house shouting to his comrades. At once lights began to appear at the windows.

The raiding party closed on the post and while they kept the windows under fire, Captain Jack Bare of No 2 Commando rushed in through the door with one of his sergeants. The sentry inside was killed, and some Germans in an adjacent room were wounded. Captain Bare mounted the stairs and searched the upper rooms, but was mortally wounded while doing so. The Colonel followed with more men, and after fighting at pistol-point, those Germans who were left alive put up their hands.

By this time the firing had raised the alarm, and another enemy post some quarter of a mile distant started firing Very lights and a stream of tracer from a machine gun which passed overhead. The time for evacuation had come, for in a few minutes the German reinforcements would arrive, and if they detected the point of re-embarkation on the coast, the commandos would run the risk of being attacked during the slow process of transferring prisoners and wounded to the boats. Accordingly a rearguard was formed and the party returned to its cove, carrying Captain Bare with them on a stretcher, and leading the enemy prisoners, several of whom were wounded. Jack Bare died on the return journey.

The swell had increased, and re-embarkation was even more difficult than the disembarkation. The Yugoslav skippers of the schooners showed infinite patience and seamanship of a high order in repeatedly nosing the bows of their craft in against the rocks to enable the men in twos and threes to transfer to the decks. The operation was accomplished successfully and without interference from the enemy who had failed to follow the raiders, and the return voyage to Vis was undisturbed, thanks to the protection of the MTBs and MGBs which convoyed the schooners across.

Shortly after this raid, a young subaltern named Barton of No 2 Commando carried out a very successful operation on the island of Brac. Having landed at night from a schooner, he contacted the local partisans who lived in caves near the coast. They informed him of the location and strength of the German garrison, and also mentioned that the Garrison Commander lived in the village of Nerejisce, in the centre of the island, where also there was a garrison of 200 German troops. Lieutenant Barton decided to attempt to kill or capture the Commandant. He learnt that the latter stayed in his billet a great deal and was little seen by the populace. He usually dined with four or five other officers at 7 p.m. but these officers left him after dinner and did not sleep in the same house.

The village had been prepared for defence and positions had been dug and manned. There was a curfew at 6 p.m. until 6 a.m. each night and between these hours the roads were watched and the defence perimeter was patrolled constantly, so that the partisans said that entrance to the town, unseen, during these hours was next to impossible. Two partisans who knew the town were put at Barton's disposal, and one of them was sent at once to ascertain the layout of the house in which the Commandant lived. This man returned the next day with the news that there was no sentry but that the house was inhabited by three German batmen besides the Commandant and the civilians who normally lived there.

Barton decided to make his attempt the following night, and taking his two partisans with him he approached the town from the north-west as soon as it was dark, but had to give up the attempt that night as he was challenged by a sentry and had to withdraw. This failure did not surprise him as he had spent the afternoon watching the village from a nearby hill and had realised that the lie of the country made it comparatively easy to protect. He had however noticed that at sundown all the shepherds on the surrounding hills collected their flocks and drove them straight past the sentries on the road into the town. Barton decided to try again, this time mingling with the shepherds and hoping that, in the dusk and the crowd, he would manage to slip past without being noticed. The partisans approved of the plan, and contacted a shepherd with whom a meeting-place on the hills was arranged for the following evening.

He left his hide-out the next day at noon with his two partisan guides, and met the shepherd about two miles outside Nerejisce. He took his sten gun to pieces and concealed it in a bundle of twigs and brushwood which was entrusted to a woman with a mule, who was to take it to a prearranged rendezvous in a barn in the village. Shortly afterwards the partisans walked in, and at dusk the shepherd and Barton followed with the flocks, mingling with other shepherds on their way. This part of the affair amused the shepherd greatly, and he nearly gave the show away just after passing the German sentries when he turned and slapped Barton on the back and shouted 'Bravo'.

Everything after that went smoothly, and Barton went straight to the barn and met the two guides and reclaimed his sten which he re-assembled. They then waited for about half an hour, during which time a dog nearly gave them away by standing outside the door and barking and sniffing. It was now quite dark, and they took about twenty minutes to cross the village and reach the Commandant's billet.

The door of the billet was locked, so Barton knocked and a woman opened it. One partisan remained outside to guard the street and the other entered with Barton who ran at once down a corridor to the kitchen intending to kill the batman first before looking for the Commandant; but he found no one but civilians, one of whom was a woman who started shrieking. The partisan made the others hold her down, and explained that Barton was a British officer, who had an account to settle with the German Commandant, and that he would do them no harm. They replied that the Commandant was dining out, but that one of them would take the officer to the house where he was. Barton agreed, but first went and searched his bedroom, where he found and pocketed his automatic, compass, binoculars and Mauser rifle.

As he was looking through his papers, he heard a movement in the room next door, which was the dining room, so he ran to the door and threw it open. There was a candle burning on the table and at first it seemed that the room was empty, but then Barton's eye was attracted by something shining near the wall which he quickly saw to be an iron cross on a man's tunic, and he gave it a burst with his sten. The man fell to the floor and Barton gave him another burst. He had no time to search his pockets, or see his rank, as the partisan was pulling him out of the room, the civilians in the kitchen were in an uproar, a dog was barking, and the village was waking up outside. They ran out of the house collecting the partisan at the street door, jumped a wall into a field and, led by one of the partisans, sprinted for open country.

The retreat was somewhat hasty and undignified, but it worked perfectly for they were through the perimeter and well clear of the village before the sentries realised what was going on. There was a great commotion in the town, and some firing, but this did not affect the small party, who made straight back to their hide-out.

Later, full evidence was obtained that the Commandant had been killed, his rank and name was furnished (he was a *Hauptmann*) and the place of his burial. The attack was the signal for an outbreak of sabotage and ambushes on Brac by the partisans, and the Germans were put in a great state of nervousness.

There is no doubt that these early raids not only raised the morale of the defenders of Vis island, but also made the Germans think that our strength must be greater than it really was. We heard, through partisan sources, that they had issued orders as a result of these raids, warning their garrisons of the constant threat of small seaborne attacks; and they began to give up the small isolated posts which they had maintained, sprinkled round the coasts of their islands, and instead went in for bigger posts which maintained watchers during the day who withdrew into the posts at night. This deprived us of the favourable little targets against which we had had a number of successes, and we had to adjust our future offensive plans accordingly.

The partisans with whom we now found ourselves in such close contact provided us with much food for thought and enquiry. We had most of us heard of Tito and Mihajlovic, but few knew the ins and outs of the national resistance movement in Yugoslavia, nor what sort of fighters the partisans were. It was part of my business to get to the bottom of this subject since I was obviously to be bound up with them for some time to come.

When invasion first came to Yugoslavia in April 1941, the army was totally unprepared for the magnitude of the event, and the Government by no means held the confidence of the nation. The majority regarded the calamity with a dazed amazement, which was quickly succeeded by a feeling that they had been betrayed by their King and Government, and if they were to save themselves, it would have to be by their own efforts.

Resistance to the invader was therefore offered by the peasants in Serbia in a haphazard and uncoordinated manner while those Serbs living in Croatia also took to the hills and opposed the Germans as best they could. It was these peasants who later formed the nucleus of the partisan army, and were directed and led by Tito. Soon afterwards a second body of resistance made its appearance, consisting largely of the remnants of the Yugoslav army but also of townsfolk, priests and peasants who grouped themselves under the leadership of Colonel Draza Mihajlovic.

This new group was certainly better organised than the peasant movement which as yet had no form at all, and it succeeded in driving the enemy out of Western Serbia. The supporters of this group were known as Cetniks, and they gained the recognition of the British Government for the part they played in resisting the Gemans and carrying on the fight against the common enemy; but unfortunately they soon changed their policy and ceased to offer opposition to the enemy. This change of attitude was not comprehended for a long time in Britain, and led to a good deal of misunderstanding with Tito and his partisans. To explain it, mention must be made of the Ustase, the Croat terrorist party led by Ante Pavelic. These terrorists had carried out innumerable excesses against the Serbs and had been responsible for wholesale massacres. The Cetniks were Serbs, and Mihajlovic directed them more and more towards a policy of non-interference with the Germans, in order to avoid reprisals against Serbs by the Germans and their collaborators, the Ustase; at the same time he turned their offensive activity against the partisans, being influenced by anti-communist feelings, as were most of his followers, since they were drawn from that section of the people whose political colour before the war had been anything but red; and gradually their organisation became directed by political considerations which soon embraced such tenets as the Greater Serbia movement, and the return of the monarchy. This led to the re-establishment of contact with the emigré government in London, and in January 1942 Mihajlovic was appointed Minister of War.

To the common peasants who had taken to the hills spontaneously to carry on the fight against the invader, these political moves were irrelevant. But as Mihajlovic's disaffection from the common cause grew, so also did the influence of the leaders of the pre-war Communist

Party of Yugoslavia among the peasants. This party had been outlawed by the state and had consequently gone underground several years before. Tito and its other leaders were wholeheartedly anti-German and anti-Italian, and their besetting urge and aim was to get rid of the invader from the soil of their native land. Parallel with this aim was the foundation of a Free Yugoslavia, after the country was liberated, based on equal representation of all nationalities found within the borders of the state – Serbs, Slovenes, Montenegrins and Macedonians.

These twin ideals made a powerful appeal to the fighting peasants, who willingly submitted themselves to the direction of leaders who organised with such remarkable alacrity an army and a civil administration for those areas which had already been liberated. This was achieved in spite of the difficulties which existed by reason of the presence of the Germans and Italians, and the fact that all industry and means of communication were in the hands of the enemy. No doubt those leaders of the partisans who had been members of the Communist Party brought experience of the conduct of an underground movement which was valuable. The partisan movement did not, however, identify itself as such with the Communist Party, and steadfastly avoided the introduction of political aims, no doubt realising that such issues might tend to split the movement into factions, and thus hinder the prime object of defeating and expelling the invader from Yugoslavia. The attitude adopted to all political questions was the same, that after the liberation of the country and the setting up of a truly representative government, the people must decide for themselves all such matters.

Of the partisans with whom we rubbed shoulders, the majority seemed to be of the peasant class. Their officers were mostly drawn from peasants also, though there was a sprinkling of schoolmasters, lawyers, journalists and industrial workers. All had gained their promotion by prowess in action. They were of all nationalities found within the Yugoslav state, and certainly there seemed no evidence of difficulty in all these nationals serving side by side. When we first arrived, their salutes were of the closed-fist type, though this noticeably declined the longer we remained on the island.

Their army was of course badly off for clothing and equipment, though the collapse of Italy had provided them with a vast amount of war material which they were quick to seize. Curiously enough, one of the grudges that they bore against the British was that we did not give them the several days' warning we could have done of the collapse of Italy for, had we done so, they could have reaped a greater harvest in disarming the Italian Divisions on their coast. Their soldiers were dressed in the most motley collection of uniforms imaginable – British battledress, German and Italian uniforms, and home-made suits, the basis of which was usually the American army blanket. Their arms were drawn from the same diverse sources, but in spite of this they evidently paid attention to uniformity as much as possible, and would, I think, even have liked to foster smartness by the use of polish, had such a commodity been available. They spent some time in drill parades, and utilised a form of goosestep on ceremonial occasions; it was less blatant and wooden than the German one, and took the form of stamping the feet while marching, with perhaps a slightly exaggerated flexing of the knees. Their method of paying compliments on the march was, I thought, more effective, and smarter, than the British army method: they would stamp their feet as they turned their head and eyes to the right or left, and after proceeding a pace or two, stamp their feet again and turn their heads to the front. They always sang enthusiastically on the march, their songs being all modern war songs, the words of which recounted their battles in Yugoslavia, or the strength and success of their reborn national solidarity.

Singing appeared to be one of the few pastimes that they indulged in. Any meeting they attended, any luncheon held to celebrate anything, was always punctuated by the singing of these partisan songs, nearly always unaccompanied. Any member present, man or woman, would start a song, and the rest would at once take it up and sing with the utmost gusto. I suppose the complete absence of such entertainments as the cinema, the theatre, organised concerts and the wireless, had thrown them back more and more on this type of relaxation. Many of the songs were sung to Russian tunes – modern Red Army marching songs – with Yugoslav themes in the Yugoslav language. Several were mournful, and dealt with the hardships of their country and their folk. I remember one which described the prowess in battle of two friends, one of whom is finally killed in action. As they are weeping at his graveside, the dead man implores them to sob no more, for (he says) one of their tears is heavier than all the earth upon him.

Perhaps the most unusual feature which struck the observer was the place that women held in the partisan movement. There can be no doubt that because the women played an integral part in it, they exercised the strongest influence over the men. With women participating in the army as combatants, medical staff, couriers, and the commissariat, there could be no excuse for any man to hang back. In the army a woman was given equal status to a man and, provided she was physically capable of enduring the rigours of a campaign, she might, if she so desired, serve in the ranks, as a non-commissioned officer or as an officer, depending on her ability and aptitude. There was a considerable number of women serving as simple soldiers, and a certain number as NCOs and officers.

Obviously such a system demands a remarkable discipline, but that is exactly what the partisan movement possessed; its discipline can best be described as puritanical. Where men and women have to share billets, whether they be in rooms, trenches, forests or fields, and often have even to share blankets, nothing but a puritanical discipline could serve. Loose sexual behaviour was punished with the utmost severity and was considered effete and unworthy. The death sentence was used regularly for looting and violence. Drunkenness was also drastically dealt with, but cases were rare, though Yugoslavs have always been great wine-drinkers.

There were no women's services as such. There were many women in the medical service, where they acted as first-aid dressers, stretcher-bearers and orderlies in the field, and as orderlies and nurses in hospitals. In the operations in the islands in which the commandos cooperated with the partisans, it was no rare occurrence to see the women stretcher-bearers rushing into a mortar concentration to tend to the wounded. After any battle there was always a percentage of women among the wounded. Practically no children were born in Yugoslavia during the war. With no areas which could be regarded as permanently liberated, there was no stable life, and with the men and most of the younger women at the front, there simply was not the opportunity to raise families. That this loss of a generation would be a serious disadvantage to the nation was realised, but accepted as part of the price to be paid for the war.

From what has been already said of the problems arising out of the defence of Vis, it will have been apparent that the naval forces operating from the island played a prominent and integral part. Not only did we rely on the Navy to give us warning of an invasion, but also we looked to that service to do all in its power to break up the enemy convoys before they reached the island's shores; even then their work was by no means finished, for we would rely on them to prevent any reinforcements reaching the enemy forces that had succeeded in landing. In addition to their role in the defence of the island, the Navy alone made possible our raids on the German-occupied islands.

When all this is realised, it will be seen how necessary it was for us to maintain the very closest liaison with the naval staff. This staff was headed by Lieutenant-Commander Morgan Giles RN, who had come to the island as Senior Naval Officer at the same time as Colonel Jack. Previously he had been concerned with the supply of food and other commodities to the partisans in Yugoslavia by sea, and though he worked in an office in Italy, he had visited the island from time to time. His second-in-command was Lieutenant K. J. Webb DSC, RNR (known to everyone by the inevitable nickname of 'Spider'), who for nearly four months had lived in the islands of Hvar and Vis, together with a few others, coordinating the arrival of supplies for the partisans from Italy, and their onward transmission to Yugoslavia. Both of these officers therefore already knew a good deal about the Dalmatian Islands, and were accustomed to working with the Partisan Naval Staff. Morgan Giles could easily have been mistaken for a Scandinavian, being tall and broad-shouldered with fair hair and wide-set eyes. He cooperated first with my brother and then with me from January until August 1944, and no military force in the long history of naval and military cooperation can ever have been better served than we were. Morgan attended all meetings that we held, whether for offensive or defensive purposes, since everything depended upon naval cooperation, and any credit for the successes that were achieved must be shared in equal measure by the Navy.

Cooperation with the commandos, however, was only a part of their work, for they used Vis as an advanced base from which to strike at the enemy's naval forces and merchant shipping in Dalmatian waters, and the remarkable achievements of the MTBs, MGBs and MLs will be told in a later chapter. I will only say here that we watched their work with a keen and friendly interest, and rejoiced with them in their successes. It was a pleasure to be able frequently to assist them with boarding parties when they went out on their nocturnal forays.

CHAPTER FOURTEEN

Raids on Solta and Hvar Islands

In the middle of February No 43 (RM) Commando arrived on the island, shortly after our mountain battle of Ornito. They were a most welcome addition to the small garrison, and it was decided to locate them in the vicinity of the village of Podselje, between the two danger-spots of Vis and Ravnik. They could thus be used to reinforce the defenders at either or both areas, and could also be used in the broken territory in the eastern tip of the island, if the enemy decided to attempt landings in that sector. Housing accommodation was now very scarce, and all the troops had to go into bivouacs on the hillsides. One or two houses in the village itself were taken over as offices, but practically all the personnel were under canvas or groundsheets.

Lieutenant-Colonel Bill Simonds, their colonel, became the chief planner of offensive raids, with Ted Fynn, the second-in-command of No 2 Commando, to help him, while No 43 Commando's second-in-command, Major Neil Munro, took over the day-to-day administration of the Commando. This was the position on the island when I arrived on 1st March, and I did not interfere with it for it was working well and seemed a good basis on which to build. Soon after my headquarters took over the command of the island, we received reinforcements in AA artillery, Royal Engineers and administrative services, so that the work involved in supplying and administering a steadily increasing garrison became considerable and placed a great strain on my small Brigade Headquarters. Captain Ronnie Mitchell, however, who had been No 2 Commando's Administrative Officer, was promoted to become DAQMG on my staff, and he and Captain Ian Morrison, my staff captain, coped manfully with our multifarious problems.

Even before I arrived Colonel Jack had been turning over in his mind a project to carry out a rather bigger attack on the enemy than anything that had been attempted to date. To this end he had set Bill Simonds and Ted Fynn to work to examine the defences and dispositions of the Germans on the island of Solta, to work out a plan for a landing on the island with the object of killing or capturing as many of the island garrison as seemed feasible. He had also sent several officers to the island to remain in hiding in caves with the local partisans, for anything up to a week, to observe the habits and strengths of the Germans. After my arrival we went ahead with this project, and commenced planning on three-service basis.

Captain Ianto Jenkins, one of No 2 Commando's troop leaders, who had carried out a number of reconnaissances on enemy-occupied islands already, went over to Solta by schooner with Lieutenant Macminamin (also of 2 Commando) to carry out a rather more detailed survey of the enemy's positions. They took with them two commando soldiers and special wireless sets to enable them to keep in touch with us. On arrival at the island about midnight, they went ashore and safely contacted the partisans who were living in a cave at its eastern end. Each day they went out to the hills from which they could get a good view of the village of Grohote, where the headquarters of the German garrison was located, and watched the movements of the various patrols that searched the island, and observed the defence posts which were manned during daylight. They discovered that at night the entire garrison retired into Grohote, where it remained until daylight the next morning. One night they decided to make a close reconnaissance of the village in order to inspect certain defences which the Germans had dug in its vicinity. They took with them two partisan guides, and penetrated to the northern coast, paying attention to the tracks and gradients that they traversed, as these would be used subsequently for the raid.

Having seen all they wanted to, they were about to return by the route by which they had come when the partisans intervened to say that it would be much quicker and less arduous if they took a new route which passed very close to the village. The two officers thought this would be a little risky, but the partisans assured them that there was no possibility of their meeting anyone, as by this time all enemy patrols would have returned to the village; so they set off. There was a bright moon at the time, and the party were using a rough road that ran along the side of a hill with a valley below planted with vines.

Suddenly they heard a German patrol close behind them on the same road and moving a good deal faster than they were. The patrol was about ten men strong, with a NCO in charge who saw our party at the same time as Jenkins and Macminamin heard them. The Germans opened fire at once, but aiming must have been difficult, and the shots went wide. Our party split into two, Jenkins, one of the soldiers and the two partisans running up the slope of the hill, while Macminamin and the other soldier broke downhill towards the vineyard. There was a lot more firing and a good deal of shouting on the part of the Germans.

When Macminamin got back after daylight to the hide-out, he found that none of Jenkins' party had returned; but by night fall the partisans and the other soldier had come in, the latter with a badly twisted knee. They said that they had encountered a wall shortly after leaving the road which was over seven feet high, and the Germans had fired at them while they were climbing it. Jenkins did not succeed in getting over, and had presumably been taken prisoner. The partisans therefore contacted the villagers the day after, and heard that a British officer had been captured by the Germans and had been evacuated to Split by boat that day. They said he had apparently been severely wounded in the stomach.

Macminamin returned in due course to Vis by schooner and told us the full story, and in addition to our grief at losing Ianto Jenkins, who was an excellent troop leader and a very old member of No 2 Commando, we had the anxiety of not knowing whether the Germans would deduce from the ambushing of the patrol that we were contemplating a raid. It was certainly no new thing for them to find that we were patrolling on their islands, but though we knew that wild horses would not make Ianto disclose anything, we did not know whether he had been able to dispose of some sketches that he had made that day of the cove at which we proposed to make our landing. If the Germans had got hold of them they were bound to know what we were up to.

The only thing to do was to send an officer back to Solta after a lapse of two or three days to see what the German reactions were, and to talk to the partisans, and as 'Minimax' (as we called him) knew the ropes so well, back he went. He returned in a day or two to say that the Germans had not altered their dispositions in any way, nor had they showed any marked interest in the cove, and their only reaction was to arrest a number of villagers to question them. This reassured us and we went ahead with the planning.

The forces to be used in the raid were No 2 Commando augmented by the heavy weapons troop of No 43 Commando, and the two units of the American OGs. To increase the fire power of these forces, it was decided to take one of the small Italian anti-tank guns manned by AA gunners whom Major Thomas, our anti-aircraft battery commander, had trained. This officer was a great enthusiast for raiding, and was always particularly keen to take on something less static than his normal role. He and we were hoping to take a Bofors gun on this raid, and he made a reconnaissance of Solta to see if it would be possible to manhandle it up the slopes of the cove at which we were going to land; but it was found that they were too rough and broken to make this possible.

We had just decided to rule this out when the authorities in Italy heard in some roundabout way of our intention and became exceedingly stuffy, forbidding us in frantic wires to do any such thing. They were terrified that we should fail to bring the gun back! As one of the chief problems on these raids was to produce some weapon which was powerful enough to knock holes in the houses which the enemy used as pillboxes, a Bofors would have been invaluable.

The plan was to make the voyage to the island by night in naval landing craft, protected by MGBs, MTBs and MLs, and to land under cover of darkness. The Commando plus the American detachment was then to advance and surround the village of Grohote and wait for dawn, when the RAF from Italy were to come in and bomb the village. Immediately after the bombing the troops were to assault the village, and clean up the garrison on the island. When this was completed, the forces were to return to Vis. We were anxious to make the return journey as soon as the job was done, but the Navy were still very concerned about having their craft at sea, loaded with troops, during daylight, owing to the danger of enemy air attack, and insisted that the re-embarkation should not commence until after dark.

A hitch occurred on the night before D-Day when Squadron Leader Le Hardy, who was the RAF controller on the island, returned from Italy (where he had gone to fix the details of the air support required) to say that the bombing effort that was to be provided was only to consist of six fighters carrying bombs, and that they would not arrive until two hours after dawn. Obviously such a small weight of bombs would be totally ineffective against the garrison in the village, and a delay of two hours in daylight before the aircraft arrived made their cooperation not only pointless but useless, as we could not hope to remain unseen for so long. As Italy was under one hour's flying time from the island, we could not understand why so long a delay had been imposed.

I therefore reluctantly cancelled the sailing of the raiding forces, and informed the authorities in Italy accordingly, for I was not prepared to commit my troops under such conditions. Happily, this had the desired effect, and a new air programme was arranged in which we were promised *two squadrons* of light bombers, and their arrival over the target was timed for *one* hour after dawn. This made the plan feasible again, and as soon as the details were firm, we fixed 17th March as the new D-Day.

Colonel Jack was to be in command of the raid, and the Navy took the forces over without mishap; we had sent 'Minimax' over once again to Solta, with the task of signalling the craft into the cove with a torch, to make sure that we did not meet a German force on landing; for the absence of a beach made disembarkation on to the rocks a slow job, and one that would have been quite impracticable under fire. He was there when the ships arrived and his light-signals showed that the enemy were not present, and greatly aided navigation in the small and rocky cove. The disembarkation was accomplished successfully, and the Commando and Americans started off on their trek, over boulders and walls, and across vineyards, to the preselected positions around Grohote, while the mortar teams and Tommy Thomas's AA gunners manhandled their heavy equipment up the hills, to the area from which they were to give support to the Commando on the following morning.

A cross-country journey at night on a Dalmatian island has to be experienced to appreciate the difficulty and discomfort of it. The slopes of the hills are always steep, but this would not be so tiresome if it were not for the never-ending stone walls that bar one's progress. These walls are not built to separate fields (as might be thought), but are, in fact, long lines of stone-dumps, which have been made by the peasants to clear the hillsides of stones so that they can find some earth on which to plant their vines. The slopes are so extensively covered with stones that these walls occur every thirty yards. They, however, are not the only obstacles, for the vines that are planted, when the stones have been cleared away, are set on terraces on the sides of the hills and these terraces, piled one above the other, present a series of steps each at least four feet high. So it will be seen that, even in daylight, a journey over these obstacles would be tiring, but at night, when one is heavily laden, it becomes exhausting in the extreme. Owing to the darkness one is never sure of one's footing, and tumbles are frequent and painful, and tend to be noisy.

While it was hoped that the enemy would not discover the presence of the raiding forces until the bombers arrived, it was realised that this hope could not be relied upon, as even if the lookouts in the village did not hear the troops getting into position, the early morning patrols were likely to discover them. It had therefore been arranged that the mortars were to open as heavy a fire as possible on the village, assisted by Thomas's anti-tank gun, while the automatic weapons of the various troops, and their snipers, would endeavour to drive back any bodies of enemy who tried to leave the town. Colonel Jack had also taken with him a loud-hailer, which he had borrowed from the Navy. This is a kind of loud-speaker which is used in ships to hail each other at sea; and a means was devised, before the raid, of breaking up the equipment and batteries into man-loads, so that they could be carried on the men's backs and assembled at the destination. Jack had in his Commando various men who spoke German perfectly, and one of these had been detailed to be ready to speak into the loud-hailer when the appropriate moment arrived.

As it turned out, the raiding parties succeeded in surrounding the village without hindrance, but shortly before dawn, the enemy became aware that something was amiss, and fired tracer from automatic weapons in the direction of some of the investing forces, though as usual at night, this fire was aimed too high and passed overhead. Then dawn broke, and aimed fire was opened from houses, windows, and the slit trenches that the enemy had dug in and on the edges of the village. The commandos replied to it, though it was difficult to pick out targets; but as the bombers were not due to arrive for an hour, Colonel Jack decided to start up his loud-hailer and harangue the garrison.

'Deutsche Soldaten! Deutsche Soldaten!' shouted the instrument: 'You are entirely surrounded. The British and American forces are here. You will shortly be bombed. You will then be assaulted and killed. If you wish to avoid this fate, you must come out of the village with upraised hands and waving something white.'

Before and after each address, the mortaring was resumed, and one or two rather timid creatures did in fact give themselves up; but on the whole the instrument seemed to have little effect, and the enemy's fire began to increase. They soon located the loud-hailer, and proceeded to lob mortar shells unpleasantly close to it, one shell actually bursting in the branches of a tree just above it. Colonel Jack, who was lying with the German speaker beside the instrument, ordered the rest of his headquarters to move away, but continued to direct the shouting; and in due course the welcome noise of the bombers was heard overhead.

'Here they are!' yelled the infernal machine triumphantly. 'Here come the bombs!' and as each wave went in, bomb-bursts could be seen throwing up huge columns of smoke and dust which hung over the village; and each wave was greeted by delighted shrieks from the megaphone.

The moment the bombing was over, the assault took place, and the commandos closed in from all directions with fixed bayonets. The haranguing went on, and so did the supporting mortar fire until our troops were right in the village, and it had to stop. Street fighting ensued,

(*Left*) Lieut-Commander Tim Bligh, DSO, DSC, RN (right) with captured German Ensign. (*Right*) Lieut-Commander Morgan Giles, DSO, OBE, GM, Senior Naval Officer, Vis, and later Rear Admiral Sir Morgan Morgan-Giles

(*Below left*) Commander Tom Fuller, DSC and 2 bars, Royal Canadian Navy. (*Bottom left*) Lieutenant Wimpey Maitland, DSC and bar, Lieut-Commander Tommy Ladner, DSC, Lieut-Commander Cornelius Burke, DSC and 2 bars; Royal Canadian Navy. (*Below right*) Lieut-Commander Merlin Minshall, RNVR, taken at Hvar Island in October 1943

The author conducts Tito to inspect No 2 (Army) Commando on Vis, June 1944

Allied Commanders on Vis after luncheon given by Tito, June 1944. Borovic. *L to R standing:* Russian interpreter, Air Commodore Carter, Lieut-Colonel Street, Major Maud, 40 Commando, General Arso Jovanovic, Chief of Staff; Major Cox, 64 HAA Regt; Commander Josip Cerni, Partisan Navy, Lieut-Colonel Tod, 9 Commando, Lieut-Commander Morgan Giles, SNO Vis, Lieut-Colonel Elliot, OC III Fd Regt, Lieut-Colonel Simonds, OC 43 Commando, Flight-Lieutenant Le Hardy RAF, Lieut-Colonel T. Fynn, 2 Commando. *Sitting:* General Korniev, Head of Russian Mission; Brigadier T. B. L. Churchill, Commander Allied troops on Vis; Admiral Sir Walter Cowan; Marshal J. B. Tito; Admiral Morgan. Flag Officer, Taranto, and Colonel Save Orevic

and while it was proceeding the commandos captured the German officer who was in command. His troops were evidently shaken by the bombing, and the swiftness of the assault which followed immediately afterwards, so the commandos put the German commander 'on the air', to tell his men to give in as the game was up. He obligingly complied, and in half an hour it was all over, the entire garrison being either killed or captured.

The commandos and Americans had good reason to be pleased with their work, for over a hundred prisoners were taken and brought back to Vis, while not a single German was left alive on Solta island. A clean sweep had been made of the entire garrison, and the Allied losses were exceedingly light. The success was due more than anything else to the fact that the assault was made *immediately* after the bombing, for past experience had taught us that the German is such a wooden individual that the effect of shock lasts a very short time and he recovers his fighting qualities remarkably quickly. I was sure that much of the value of the incredibly heavy artillery bombardments which our infantry on the main fronts had to assist them before an attack was made, was often wasted because the subsequent advance was not made quickly enough.

Arrangements had been made for a fast launch to take the wounded back to Vis as soon as the battle was over, so that they could get proper treatment as quickly as possible; and the rest of the force returned to the cove to wait for the naval craft to take them back. As the fight had been over so quickly, there was a good seven hours to wait, but in the end the Navy decided to re-embark the men about two hours before dusk, as very few enemy aircraft had come over the island during the battle, and it seemed unlikely that they would be caught on the return journey. The evacuation did in fact proceed smoothly and though the men were very tired when they got back, their spirits could not have been higher. They were given a good hot meal, after which they all turned in for a thoroughly well-earned rest.

In these early days on Vis our sense of isolation and remoteness from Italy and the rest of the Allied forces had a marked influence on our thoughts and actions. The garrison was made up of young people, officers and men of the army and Navy, who realised the responsibility that had been placed on their shoulders and were proud that the circumstances made them dependent on themselves. There was no need to emphasise the enemy threat nor our own isolation; daily we looked across the water to Brac, Hvar, Korcula and the Peljesac Peninsula, and could see through binoculars the enemy on those islands. His efforts to concentrate shipping in the coves was a constant reminder of his intention to invade us, and his frequent reconnaissances of our island by aircraft only made this intention plainer. No one was in any doubt that if invasion came, it would be conducted with a strength and ruthlessness which would shake our slender resources to the roots, and that the first 48 hours would be a confused and bitter episode of bombing, parachute landings and sea battles, of false information, sudden alarms and hand-to-hand fighting. We worked ceaselessly to make our defences strong and to provide remedies and alternatives for the many situations which might develop, and at the same time continued to seek for opportunities to hinder the enemy's plans by offensive action by sea, land and air.

Looking back on those days now, I find two factors inextricably bound up with the memories and impressions that I yet retain. One is the influence of the beauty of the natural scene which formed the back-cloth for our sombre and materialistic drama, and the other is the significance which we all felt of the old British military and naval associations with this island, which brooded over us and seemed to twine our story into theirs.

Beauty was everywhere, in the outline of grey stones against the blue-green sea, the sudden vistas of steep hillsides falling headlong into tranquil bays, in the distant views of snow-capped ranges on the mainland rising out of mists to stand out clear against the sky. The red earth of the vine-terraces made a symmetrical pattern in the tumble of rocks and boulders . . . Pink cyclamen, blue gentian and purple orchids grew wild on every slope. The air was rich and clear; the sea in the coves was transparent; the very sunlight seemed to have been filtered or refined. In these surroundings the business of war was made to appear the more incongruous and sordid; the beauty of nature, far from relieving our feelings, made our task the harder – so it seemed to me. Beauty is not a fit setting for war.

The historical background, on the other hand, I found an active help and inspiration. Evidence of it was easy to find. The fort which guarded the entrance to Vis harbour was an old English one, and still over the gate could be seen the carved Union Jack and the words: 'George the Third by the Grace of God King of England Scotland and Ireland and of the British Dominions beyond the Seas.'

Two other forts crowned heights in the neighbourhood of Vis harbour, known as Fort Wellington and Fort Bentinck. Down near the water's edge and just outside the town was the little English cemetery in which could be seen stones commemorating those who fell in naval actions off the island – particularly in the famous frigate action in which Captain William Hoste routed a greatly superior Franco–Venetian force in 1811. The island off the mouth of Vis harbour was still called Hoste island, and in the old days was fortified also.

The forts had been built by the British during their occupation of the island from 1812 to 1815, but when Vis, or Lissa as the island was then called, was handed over to the Austrians, the forts were destroyed. Only Fort George was rebuilt; the others still remained in the ruined state in which they were left by the British in 1815. But when we in 1944 once more returned to defend the island and garrisoned Fort George with British soldiers again, it was pleasant to see the Union Jack waving over the battlements.

When we came to sustain casualties in our battles on the neighbouring islands, we buried our dead in this same British cemetery until the smallness of it made it necessary for us to construct a new one elsewhere on the island. When Vis cemetery was closed finally, it contained officers and men of No 2 Commando, Nos 43 and 40 (RM) Commandos, HQ No 2 Special Service Brigade, the Raiding Support Regiment and of course officers and men of the Navy, all of whom had fallen in action in 1944.

One day Captain Ray Keep, the adjutant of No 2 Commando, came to see me and said that he had heard in the course of conversation with Colonel Millic and Commander Cerni that a partisan course for senior NCOs which had been in progress on the island, was about to terminate, and he thought they would appreciate it if I was to offer some prizes for the first three students. Accordingly I offered to present three automatic Colt pistols and the suggestion was accepted with genuine appreciation. Colts were rare in the partisan army and they were highly considered.

On the day of the passing out parade I met Millic and Cerni at their headquarters and we walked over the slope of a hill, till we came to a wide vine terrace which had been cleared. There drawn up on parade were the sixty odd students with the partisan island band in attendance. After saluting and the playing of the partison anthem and 'Tipperary', which at this time they always rendered instead of 'God Save the King', we proceeded to inspect the ranks.

A particular effort had been made, and on the whole the men were quite smart. They seemed to vary in age between about 18 and 30, and one woman was included in the course. She was a particularly tough-looking Slav type with legs like the roots of a tree and large red hands. Like the others, she was equipped with a tommy-gun and had three hand-grenades at her belt. When we first arrived on the island we used to notice that many of them used to hang the grenade on to a hook on the belt by means of the ring of the split pin which rendered the grenade safe. This highly dangerous method was later given up, I am glad to say, at our suggestion.

After speeches by the two partisan leaders and by myself (which Cerni translated) the prizes were distributed, and then the senior NCO stepped forward and made a speech of thanks in which he said that they would benefit by the course and they all looked forward eagerly to putting the lessons which they had learnt into practice against the enemy. The parade then marched past doing their curious but effective ceremonial 'stomp' step and singing a battle-song at the top of their voices.

When it was all over I started to say my farewells but soon learnt that the affair was far from over, and that there was an informal lunch to follow at which they very much hoped I would be present. So I remained, and while the men piled into the house in which the function was to be held, I was brought a small liqueur glass filled with Rakija, a liquid which is much drunk in Yugoslavia and which tasted as if it was neat alcohol. Drinking these liqueurs in the sun on the terrace of the house, we chatted pleasantly while various partisans took snaps until we were summoned to lunch.

In the room, which was decorated with branches of trees and pictures of Tito, Stalin, Churchill and Roosevelt, the tables were arranged in four parallel rows with one table across the top at which Millic, Cerni, two or three other partisan officers and commissars and I sat. It was a bit of an endurance contest for we were served with seven courses and a good deal of island white wine. Between courses the students would sing their partisan songs with a fervour and lack of self-consciousness which was impressive. We were served by partisan girls in battledress who had also prepared and cooked the meal. Considering that we numbered over eighty at the tables, the service was remarkably good and efficient. The commissars are always particularly voluble on these occasions, and I used to find their interminable speeches on similar occasions rather tedious, but I was interested to notice that the partisans would pay the closest attention to them and never indicated that they had had enough.

When the meal was finished and the speeches ended a number of students left their chairs and disappeared through the door, and with astonishing speed a stage was erected at the end of the room. I was informed that the students were now to entertain us with a series of short plays. With memories of the sketches which terminated the Staff College Course at Camberley I supposed that we should now have some mild chaffing of the instructors and some of the more serious-minded students, but this was not at all the drift of the proceedings. All of them were allegorical and dealt in a most serious manner with the partisan movement and the fight against the Nazi invasion. I will give one instance to illustrate the type of sketch that they produced.

A partisan walked on to the stage dressed as a young Nazi and after strutting around for a bit, planted a small twig in the ground. He then walked to the wings where he remained standing stiffly at attention. In due course other partisans came on to the stage dressed as peasants and farmers, and pointed out the little tree to each other amidst much shaking of heads and wry faces. All this was done as a mime. One by one the peasants attempted to pull up the weed but in spite of superhuman efforts it resisted their attempts. Then the peasants began to pull at it together, and more and more joined the enterprise. Finally the tree yielded and was pulled up root and branch. As it was pulled out of the soil, so the Nazi crashed lifeless to the floor.

Although the partisans had been very short of arms and ammunition and clothing at certain periods of their resistance, they had enjoyed one great advantage in the making of war. This had been an unrivalled intelligence system which provided them with a quite extraordinary volume of information concerning the enemy. This advantage often offset the disadvantages of inferiority in numbers and equipment, and was due to the almost universal hatred of the Nazis, the Ustase and the Cetniks. Elderly men and women, too old to fight in the ranks of the partisans, would nevertheless undertake long journeys on foot to pass information about the enemy, and young girls and boys would be used in the same way. Women were found to be particularly useful for this purpose for they were able to pass through the German lines more easily than the men.

Whenever a partisan band arrived in a new locality, they would at once be met by inhabitants from the nearby towns and villages who had climbed into the mountains and forests to contact the partisans and pass on the situation in their neighbourhood and give details of the strength and equipment of the enemy. This was an understood proceeding and occurred spontaneously. The people were prepared to take great risks of incurring the suspicion of the Nazis, and in this I think they differed greatly from the majority of the populations in occupied countries further to the west.

On our island we benefited in the same way by this great flow of intelligence that came in to us through partisan sources. Inhabitants from the neighbouring islands would meet partisan schooners at night at prearranged rendezvous to notify any changes that had taken place; a constant watch would be kept night after night at those coves to which the partisans brought their schooners, and as one appeared they would creep down and meet it, probably receiving a small supply of food and blankets from the stocks which were being sent in increasing quantities by the British and Americans.

The intelligence officers of the various units on the island attended daily a meeting with the partisan chief intelligence officer, and an exchange of information would take place. We would pass on what we knew from information gained by our patrols on the occupied islands or had heard through our military channels, and they would tell us the latest news brought in by their schooners. In this way we would hear that there was a concentration of shipping in this port, that a new formation had recently moved down to the coast at that point, that the German sailors in the bars in Split or Sibenik were saying this or that, and so on. We would further receive sketches of defences put up by the Germans at various points, and estimates of the strength of garrisons and the calibre of artillery mounted in defence positions.

It is true that much of this information was inaccurate, for it was gleaned by peasants who had had no training in the art of collecting intelligence. It was usually rather exaggerated in favour of the Germans, which on the whole is a fault on the right side. It helped us tremendously in our preparations for offensive raids, though I must add that it was our invariable practice to send at least one patrol of officers to any area in which we intended to do a landing before final plans were made.

The fact that we were isolated on an island in immediate proximity to enemy-occupied islands and mainland ports made it inevitable that we should be subject to rumours of invasion at frequent intervals. At one time, about the beginning of February 1944, the Germans did succeed in collecting a lot of landing craft in the coves at the western end of Hvar island which was certainly the prelude to an invasion attempt. There were many other signs of this shipping build-up in the Neretva River and at Split and other ports, and it was only nipped in the bud by some excellent bombing by the RAF who managed to sink more than sixty per cent of the craft. This was the nearest we ever came to being invaded (so far as one can judge), though there is no doubt that the enemy continued to retain his intention to land on Vis for many more months and was only prevented by the incessant vigilance of the Navy and RAF and the offensive tactics of the Vis garrison.

A few days after the Solta raid, news was received from the partisans that the Germans were pulling out of Hvar island. There was great excitement as they thought this might mean that a general evacuation of the islands might be beginning. We were not so optimistic, for there seemed no real reason from the enemy's point of view as to why he should suddenly alter his policy, and it looked to us as though he was up to one of two courses: either he was afraid we might do the same thing to Hvar as we had done to Solta, and he was merely moving away from the western part of the former island as his garrisons there were the nearest to our base; or else it might be a typical German military ruse to get us to occupy Hvar in a hurry, and as soon as we got there and before we had had time to organise ourselves he might counter-attack with superior forces from Brac and Korcula and catch us on the hop. However there seemed a chance to attack him while he was on the move and therefore vulnerable, and we decided to send a combined force of commandos and partisans at once to Hvar to try and catch his garrison, or what part of it still remained, before it sailed from the port of Jelsa.

While we were making these arrangements and Commander Morgan Giles was collecting the necessary shipping to make the move that afternoon, we asked our airman, Squadron Leader Le Hardy, to get some bombers from the mainland to bomb Jelsa and the shipping in the harbour.

No 43 (RM) Commando under the command of Lieutenant-Colonel Simonds and a partisan force of about 3000 sailed in daylight for Hvar escorted by the Navy and with a fighter escort overhead. It had been a great rush to get them off so quickly but we had reason to think, from partisan information, that unless we got to Jelsa before midnight, the last of the enemy garrison would have sailed. On the way over the attacking force saw our bombers swoop down on Jelsa, and though the port was on the far side of the island, columns of smoke and dust were seen to rise from the port as the result of the bombing.

The objective at which the commandos and partisans were aiming was the port of Jelsa which was situated on the north coast of the island. They landed at coves on the south coast just before dusk, and had to make a forced march across country to reach the port before midnight at which time the Germans were understood to be intending to sail. The ground between the two coasts consists of a high plateau which falls steeply to the sea and the attackers had therefore to climb stiff slopes as soon as they disembarked in order to reach the plateau. No 43 Commando was the first ashore, and it set off at once, leaving the partisans to follow on behind as soon as they had completed their disembarkation.

When Colonel Simonds reached the heights overlooking Jelsa, the first thing he saw was enemy shipping still burning in the harbour from the afternoon's bombing, and local peasants told him that the Germans had run out of the port during the bombing and sheltered in the hills to the north-west of the town. He decided therefore to send his Commando down into the port to make sure it was clear, and asked the partisans to remain on the heights overlooking the port for the time being. They were not very anxious to adopt this role as they are impatient fighters and they wanted to rush down into the port after the commandos.

It was just as well that the Colonel managed to persuade them to adopt his plan, for about two hours before dawn the Germans issued out of their hiding places in the hills and attempted to surround the Commando by occupying the very hills on which the partisans were waiting. A battle followed in the dark in which there was an immense amount of unaimed fire on both sides, and the Commando hearing the firing decided to come up on to the high ground to see if they could assist the partisans. For a few minutes the latter hotly engaged the Commando but this possibility had been foreseen and No 43 advanced very cautiously managing to avoid casualties from its own side and soon made their identity known. In the ensuing engagement the Germans were caught as dawn broke in a heavy fire which caused them many casualties, and they gave up the field and split up into small parties making for the hills. They were followed all day by the combined forces of the Commando and the partisans, and by nightfall over a hundred prisoners had been taken and about half that number killed.

There was a submarine cable between Vis and Hvar, and it was typical of the partisans that they had managed to conceal the terminal at the Hvar end all the time that the Germans had been in occupation. Now that they were driven out, the cable was rapidly brought into use, and we were able to get news of the fighting very quickly. By nightfall it seemed that only isolated bands of the enemy remained, so I ordered the Commando to return with half the partisan force, leaving the remainder to complete the mopping up. Unfortunately we could not occupy Hvar without seriously weakening our garrison on Vis, and as the enemy always had greatly superior forces on the coast of Yugoslavia and in Korcula and Brac with which he could easily mount an invasion, we had to be careful that we did not fall into the trap of weakening our garrison so much that he would be tempted to overrun Vis.

I had just seen Morgan Giles about the re-embarkation of the Commando that night, and was getting into a jeep on the waterfront of Komiza with my brother when we heard a whistle and a salvo of bombs exploded without any warning in the town and harbour. A second later six enemy aircraft screamed over our heads and out over the harbour about a hundred feet above the sea. We leaped under cover, he into the porch of a house and I into a crevice of a wall when the next salvo fell, one bomb bursting in the water about three yards from the sea-wall and covering us with water. Splintered glass was flying all over the place and smoke and dust was rising from the port. In the middle of the confusion I remember seeing Admiral Sir Walter Cowan walking straight out on to the breakwater with the bombs throwing up columns of water on both sides of him. He went to assist the crew of a motor torpedo boat which was alongside and which had received a number of splinters in her hull.

The bombing lasted about fifteen minutes, and was a short sharp raid timed to utilise the last quarter of an hour of daylight. It undoubtedly caught our AA defences napping, and they did not start to get any rounds off until the third enemy flight came into the attack. The German airmen came in over the island from the north-west, swept over the shoulder of Mount Hum and dived on Komiza releasing their bombs from a very low altitude. They were obviously expecting to find the harbour full of the craft that we had used to take the raiding parties over to Hvar, and they hoped no doubt to sink them before they could go out again to bring our forces back. There had been an enemy reconnaissance of the island as usual that morning, and they would have seen Komiza harbour crowded with shipping.

As it was, however, all except two of the craft had left Komiza some hours before, and of the two that remained, an ML at a buoy was untouched though its buoy was sunk, and the RAF crash boat which was alongside the quay was holed by splinters. In the town about five houses were damaged and in one which was used as a billet for men of my headquarters, one signaller was killed and five others wounded. Two civilians were killed and one or two wounded, but many of the bombs fell in the vineyards just outside the town and did no harm.

It so happened that the hundred odd German prisoners that had been taken in the Solta raid were in a house in Komiza under guard during the bombing. Their evacuation to Italy had been postponed owing to the necessity to use all available shipping for the Hvar expedition. As soon as the first bombs fell the Huns ran screaming into the street crying, 'Luftwaffe! Luftwaffe!' and it says much for the commando guards that they did not open fire. Instead they kept their heads and calmed the Germans telling them to lie down in the street under the walls of the houses. None of them came to any harm, but after the bombing was over I ordered them to march out of the town and up on to the central plain of the island, as I quite expected that we should get another dose later on in the night.

Rather an odd incident occurred when the Germans arrived at their destination on the plain. When they were halted, their officer was told to fall the men out and dispose them in the rooms of a cottage which we had had evacuated to accommodate them. Before he did so, he addressed the men and said in German, 'I want to express to our captors our sense of appreciation for their humane act in marching us out of the town to avoid casualties amongst our ranks if the Luftwaffe should return. But it is not only an humane act; there is another adjective that I wish to apply. Can anyone supply me with the word I want?'

Someone suggested, 'Considerate'. Someone else suggested, 'Correct'. 'No,' said the officer, 'those are not the words I want.' Then someone said, 'Chivalrous.' 'That is the adjective,' he said triumphantly. 'It has been a very chivalrous act and we thank our captors accordingly.'

In point of fact no further bombing took place that night and the raiding parties returned safely from Hvar in the early hours of the morning bringing their prisoners with them.

This was the first raid that we had carried out in conjunction with the partisans, and was therefore the first opportunity our soldiers had had of judging their fighting qualities. All our officers and men were unanimous in declaring that their physical bravery in advancing under fire was magnificent. They had gone forward to the attack singing the partisan songs that we had so often heard them sing in the streets of Komiza and Vis, and one woman had been killed in a bayonet charge.

On the other hand Colonel Simonds told me that it was a little hard to dissuade them from acting recklessly on the first bit of information that came in from a peasant, instead of checking it, as it often turned out that the information was at least twelve hours old. Also their lack of signal equipment made it hard to control and coordinate their efforts. They relied on runners for communication, usually using young boys who covered big distances remarkably quickly and without apparent effort.

The technique of committee government which was inherited from the democratic nature of the partisan movement was also adopted in the army, and the political commissars had a say in all decisions. After an action, the whole proceedings were subjected to review by the forces taking part at an open meeting at which any soldier was entitled to criticise any action or phase of the battle. If serious casualties had been sustained, the officer responsible was required to justify them. An officer whose decisions were frequently questioned and who failed to justify himself would soon lose his appointment and rank. Criticism cannot be silenced on grounds of discipline – a custom which we could emulate with advantage in our own army.

During and after the bombing of Komiza my headquarters had found that so many telephone lines were cut that the town was virtually isolated from the rest of the island. We had of course alternative wireless communication, but this took a little time to start up and all messages had to be encoded for security reasons so that quick messages were virtually impossible to send. On the other hand our main telephone switchboard was located at Borovik which was the partisan headquarters, and it would usually be possible to bypass a broken line if one was near the switchboard and could talk to the operators.

This factor combined with the obvious advantage of always being in close proximity to the partisans made me decide to move my headquarters from Komiza to the less hospitable slopes of Mount Hum, for there were only five houses in Borovik, and of these only one could be made available to us. Accordingly we used the house for our offices, and slept in bivouacs on the mountainside until the extra tentage that we had urgently indented for arrived. In the end we provided ourselves with perfectly adequate quarters and a mess under canvas. I mention this move because in a way it marked the passing of a phase on the island. From now onward our garrison began to increase rather rapidly as the authorities began to appreciate the advantages that the holding of the island conferred, and consequently, we began to lose the family atmosphere that had prevailed since the early days when only a handful of No 2 Commando and the Navy 'held the fort'.

The flat in Komiza which Colonel Jack occupied with his adjutant, Captain Ray Keep, and, for a short time, Major Hamilton-Hill, his administrative officer, had become a meeting place in the evenings for officers who were visiting Komiza and had been invited to enjoy his hospitality, and many will remember the famous cocktails which he concocted on the piano in the corner of the tiny little room which he used for the entertainment of his guests. Surrounded by jugs and bottles he would produce a mixture which basically consisted of naval rum and tinned pineapple or orange juice, and he would serve the island anchovies on ration biscuits as savouries. When I arrived the flat was stretched to house Admiral Cowan and myself, but when I moved up to Borovik with my staff, the flat once more became Jack's private mess, though the Admiral remained to share it with him and Ray Keep.

CHAPTER FIFTEEN

Enemy View-point, and Further Island Raids

Ever since we landed on Vis in the autumn of 1943, I wondered how the Germans would react to our presence there. I thought that an enemy attack on the island was more than likely, and I was confirmed in this view by warnings from Allied Forces headquarters in Algiers, based on Ultra decrypted signals.

Thanks to German documents captured at the end of the war, we now know exactly what the enemy thought of our occupation of Vis, and what he intended to do about it. These documents include the War Diary of the Army High Command; the Combat Calendar of the 118th Rifle Division; the War Diary of the German Naval Staff Operations Division, and the Minutes of the Führer Conferences on Naval affairs 1944 held at Headquarters Berghof.

One document dating from the beginning of March 1944 stated that the British Brigadier-General Tom Churchill took over supreme command on Vis. Towards the end of the month the strength of the occupying forces on the island was reckoned at 10,000 Tito-followers and 700–800 English and Americans. The number of small boats varied, but often exceeded a hundred; the communist naval staff, which was known to have been on the island since the beginning of the year, was responsible for activity in this shipping area.

The dominating factor in the German attitude to the Dalmatian Islands situation was the overwhelming Allied air superiority which, coupled with the already scanty German naval and air forces in that area, robbed them of all prospect of securing these islands which were regarded by the Navy, in particular, as a bridgehead for a possible Allied invasion of the eastern Adriatic coast.

As early as September 1943, when the war in the Adriatic was growing in intensity, Vice-Admiral Lietzmann, the admiral in command in the Adriatic, realised the importance of the Germans occupying the Dalmatian Islands, especially Vis (which the Germans always called Lissa, its old Austrian name). It was also realised that, while the naval forces available were unable to carry out this task, the Army was likewise unable to undertake it without the Navy's help.

The native partisans were causing the Germans considerable embarrassment and the naval officer in charge of Split said in his October report: 'Railway communications were cut and land transport, already complicated by a shortage of vehicles, is further hampered by the continuous activities of partisans who completely surround Split to landward and whose artillery occupies commanding positions on the islands.'

The Naval War Staff asked the opinion of Admiral Adriatic on the occupation of the islands. His reply advocated the occupation of all the larger islands on the east coast of the Adriatic, because the enemy might at any time infiltrate and use them not only as bases for small naval craft and submarines, but also as jumping-off points for commando operations.

He was convinced of the strategic necessity of occupying the Dalmatian Islands, and he made the suggestion early in December 1943 that all available naval forces, cooperating with strong forces of fighter aircraft, should attempt the operation. On 11th December, the importance of such an undertaking was recognised by the German Naval War Staff and the naval authorities accordingly began concentrating their shipping for the capture of Korcula, Hvar and Brac, to be followed by Lagosta and Vis.

The Germans occupied Korcula on 23rd December, and as the partisans evacuated Hvar Island the next day, the Germans took it over. According to army opinion, the navy's needs were now satisfied, for the sea-route from Dubrovnik to Cattaro was clear. In order to stamp out supplies to the partisans, the army was prepared to clear the island of Vis and use it as a base, as well as for the defence of the coast; but the navy was required to produce a garrison of at least one battalion and three coastal batteries. This was impossible, but Flag Officer in charge of Group South pointed out that a continuous occupation of the island was in the interests of all the forces in the whole coastal area, and not of the navy alone.

After much discussion on the garrisoning question, a date was fixed for the attack, viz. between 20th February and 1st March 1944. Admiral Adriatic managed to gather together the following vessels: 2 large and 2 small torpedo boats, 1 escort ship, 2 corvettes, 6 E-boats, 3 R-boats, 4–6 Siebel ferries, 14 landing craft and 25 other craft. The Supreme Commander South East expressed the view that resistance against a landing on the island (code-named Operation Freischutz – the folk-lore marksman with magic bullets) would presumably be stronger than on Leros. Of the Germans troops, participation was mainly planned for parts of the 118th Rifle Division, additionally a Sapper Landing Battalion, a detachment of Coastal Riflemen 'Brandenburg' and the SS Rifle Battalion – with torpedo boats, assault boats, Siebel ferries, one strengthened pursuit group, and one dive-bomber squadron of the Air Force.

The attacking group was to concentrate gradually after 1st March on the island area of 118th Rifle Division, and, sailing from ports on the east of the Peljesac Peninsula, would approach Vis between midnight and 02.00 hours a.m., steering to the north of Korcula so as to evade observation from Lagosta. Landings would be made on the south-east of Vis. It was pointed out that the chief difficulty was the length of the passage in relation to the speed of the craft, and it was therefore advisable to take as much material as possible over with the first wave of the attack. (It is gratifying to know that we accurately foresaw in our planning the point at which the Germans intended to land!)

After further postponements due to reports of the reinforcement of Vis garrison, the Chief of the General Staff of the Armed Forces briefed the Führer on the latest situation on 9th April. The Führer decided that no decision should be taken until Guards Lieutenant Colonel Ziervogel, who had been sent to the General Staff of the Armed Forces to discuss Operation Freischutz with the Panzer HQ Staff, returned; and in the meantime, the Air Force was to bomb the island heavily, and attempt to destroy the airstrip which the British had built.

The Colonel presented his report on 19th April, and his conclusions were that the chances of success were slim, and expressed doubts as to whether the Air Force could provide sufficient protection from the RAF. If the operation failed, the loss would be much more severe than would be the relief gained in the event of success, especially as in the course of the operation the majority of the German Adriatic shipping resources would be destroyed. The Führer thereupon decided on 23rd April that Operation Freischutz was to be postponed for the time being. In fact it never took place.

*

One morning shortly after the Hvar attack Cerni and Millic came to see me to say that a general from Marshal Tito's headquarters on the mainland was coming to visit them, and to ask if they might bring him to see me when he arrived. He came the following day, and we ordered a guard of honour from No 43 (RM) Commando to receive him outside my headquarters.

He was a magnificently built man over six foot three in height with a swarthy complexion and fine clear-cut features. His name was Sreten Zujovic and he had recently been appointed to the rank of lieutenant-general in the partisan army. He was noted as an old friend of Tito's and as one of the most forceful and vigorous of the partisan leaders. He came of a well-known Belgrade family and had been one of the prime movers in the Serbian rising in June 1941, and now was a member of the High Command and Acting Minister for Transport in the National Committee of Liberation.

He brought with him a Colonel Milojevic who was a thickset little man with a black patch over one eye and a protruding lower jaw, who was reputed to be the only surviving holder of the highest partisan distinction for bravery, Hero of Yugoslavia. He had been wounded 32 times but apart from his eye one would not have guessed that he had suffered at all.

Zujovic, who was in his forties and spoke French very well, was anxious to carry out a large scale attack on the enemy-held islands, and pointed out that as both the Solta and Hvar raids had been of short duration and had only involved one island as objective, he thought of attacking one island and then moving direct from that island to another to perform a second attack. He chose the island of Mljet as the object of the first attack, and Korcula as the second objective. He said he intended to use the three Yugoslav brigades which had been on the island ever since we arrived, and also the 'Overseas' brigade which had recently come to the island and had not yet been in action. We offered to cooperate with him and send our forces as well, until we discovered that he intended to start the following night!

Apart from the fact that I was not allowed to mount a raid of more than 200 men without first asking permission of the authorities on the mainland of Italy – a strange restriction for a commander of a brigade – we could never have got the sea and air support arranged in time with Italy as they always wanted to know minute details before they would provide any assistance, and in the end we always had to send an officer over to explain everything and press for what we wanted.

Zujovic said that he could not wait, and proposed to start the following night, but he asked for assistance in bombing from the RAF and protection from the Navy for his schooners during the sea voyages. Owing to the rush he was in, all the mainland would agree to was armed reconnaissances over his area and adjacent ones, to stop the enemy bringing reinforcements by sea. He asked for bombing on certain enemy positions on hills, but this the RAF refused to provide saying they were 'unsuitable targets'. We found the same difficulty when we wanted hill positions bombed later on for some of our operations.

We knew from our own experience that there was little hope of getting much out of Italy in the way of help in a hurry, but we determined to do all we could for him on the island, and Morgan Giles went into the naval side of his plan very carefully and gave Cerni an immense amount of help, while we provided each of his four brigades with wireless sets and British personnel to man them, and also a set and operators for his own headquarters. We also sent certain commando detachments with the signallers to look after their safety should a hitch occur in the plans.

It so happened that the weather was very bad at the time, and Cerni pointed out to his general that it was too rough for the schooners to make landings in the little coves that they proposed to utilise; Zujovic however (who was a landsman) would have none of it, and demanded to be taken to sea that afternoon to test the elements. Apparently they had a frightful tossing and Cerni informed us with some glee that the General had been sea-sick. He therefore agreed to a twenty-four-hour postponement, but in fact he had to agree to a further postponement of the same length of time before the sea abated sufficiently for the voyage to become possible. These days of postponement gave the various junior commanders time to explain the plans to their men, and gave our signallers time to get in a little practice with the partisan staffs with whom they were to work, and I think were very valuable; and the General's impatience to get started rather illustrates one of the weak points in the partisan army's methods. They had tremendous enthusiasm but had little experience in operating several forces at the same time, and no experience at all of Combined Operations. It was indeed lucky for them that they had the benefit of Morgan Giles' cooperation and experience in the operations which subsequently took place.

Mljet island, which was the partisans' first objective, is long and narrow and much more thickly wooded than Vis. The centre of the island consists of a high, steep and rocky mountain range in which each summit is separated from its neighbour by a deep valley so that progress in the mountains is particularly slow and arduous. The Germans had occupied positions on the very summits of these mountains, and they had surrounded themselves with barbed wire and mines. They used one port on the north coast of the island by which they brought supplies in once a week; otherwise the garrison remained on the hills perfecting their defence works and only going outside their camping grounds to get water from the wells in one of the villages.

The partisans attacked in two separate columns, one of which invested the port and the other went into the mountains and slowly closed on the enemy in his hill positions. The fighting was bitter and both sides suffered rather high casualties but after three days the port was captured and all except one of the mountain positions were taken. The partisans then withdrew in their schooners to Lagosta, where they reformed and the following night descended on Korcula, making landings on the north and south coasts of that island simultaneously with the intention of cutting it in half and then destroying the German garrison in the western half of the island. Here again they fought for three days and succeeded in achieving the object completely. The Germans were routed, and the number of prisoners taken by the partisans in the two attacks was 180.

Once again those British officers and men who were with the partisan forces bore witness to their great bravery and their enthusiasm in attack. They did of course outnumber their adversaries by more than two to one, but in modern warfare this is far from an overwhelming superiority when the enemy is fighting a defensive battle from prepared positions.

An interesting sidelight on partisan methods of communal welfare was shed by the report of a British officer who was with the partisan artillery during this battle. During a lull in the fighting a commissar called for washing materials and some girls disappeared to the baggage dump returning with a large bundle wrapped up in a waterproof cape. This was set down in the middle of the battery position and untied, and was seen to contain tooth-brushes, soap and towels. Those that wished to avail themselves of these amenities formed into a queue and were handed a tooth-brush, a piece of soap and a towel. When they had done with them they were handed back and reissued to someone else. When all had finished, the bundle was tied up again and put back with the baggage ready for the next occasion. In the same way food was cooked centrally by the women and when ready the men would file past the fire being handed their plates loaded with food as they passed.

The success of this partisan attack naturally had a splendid effect on the general spirit of their troops in the island, and great were the rejoicings and celebrations that went on after all the forces had returned to Vis. Much booty had been captured, including a German battery of howitzers, a number of military lorries and motor-cars and of course an immense amount of arms, equipment, clothing and boots. Every partisan one saw seemed to be wearing some article of clothing or equipment which he had captured, and he would point it out gleefully. There is no doubt that there is something very attractive in being able to use captured material against the enemy from whom it has been taken, especially when the enemy is as genuinely and universally hated as the Germans in Yugoslavia.

One of the days which the partisans celebrate with parades and speeches and ceremonial banquets is Labour Day – 1st May. In 1944 it occurred only a few days after their return from the Mljet and Korcula battles, so the occasion was really a double celebration. A parade of all their forces was held in the island's central plain, and a stage was erected draped with carpets and decorated with the banners of Yugoslavia, Russia, Britain and America. As usual there were also life-size portraits of Tito, Stalin, Churchill and Roosevelt. General Zujovic had returned to Tito's headquarters, so Colonel Milojevic took the salute and made a speech, followed by more speeches by other commanders and by commissars and even by one woman who was, in fact, Millic's wife. A feature of the parade was the display of captured weapons, including the German howitzers which had already been formed into a battery with Yugoslav personnel.

After the parade there was a luncheon given by the headquarters of the Partisan Division, to which Admiral Sir Walter Cowan and I had been invited. There were songs and toasts and an immense number of courses, followed by the inevitable speeches, and both the Admiral and I had to make our contribution. One amusing incident occurred which proves that the infantry of all armies find the same difficulties; a partisan colonel of artillery had concluded a flowery speech in which he expressed the pleasure of the Gunners in being able to support the army in its fight on Mljet and Korcula, for this was the first time that the teams, trained by the Balkan School of Artillery, had been in action. When he sat down, the commander of the 1st Infantry Brigade, one Colonel Bogdan, who was easily the best commander they had, and was a man of few words, rose and said, 'Yes. Good old Artillery. But they shouldn't shell their own troops!' and he sat down amidst much laughter.

The partisans now decided to attack Solta island on their own, as the Germans had reoccupied it since the No 2 Commando raid. We had reconnoitred the island at intervals and had found that the enemy had built a number of concrete pill-boxes to defend their garrison and had laid a large quantity of mines round their positions. They had also increased the size of the garrison and had worked out a scheme whereby guns on a small neighbouring island could fire on to Solta by means of OPs which they maintained on the latter island. It seemed to us to be a pretty tough proposition, and we thought there were better targets elsewhere; however the partisans were determined to go for it, and asked us to lend them wireless equipment and personnel, which we did. They displayed their customary impatience to be off once they had decided to make the attack, and would pay little attention to the detailed defences which we offered to put on their maps for them. They were a little flushed, I think, by their previous success, and seemed to think that from now onwards they would always have things their own way.

They sailed in due course, and made two landings, one on the south coast and one at the west of the island; but they soon came up against very strong defences and suffered a number of casualties on mines. This broke up the attack, and the shell-fire which the Germans brought down from a neighbouring island, combined with the resistance of the pill-boxes, was too much for them. The first plan having gone wrong, they seemed incapable of disengaging, reforming and attacking again to a new plan. Instead, the fight was carried on in a desultory manner by individuals and small groups who fought entirely uncoordinated actions up and down the battlefield; these isolated efforts failed to have any effect on the garrison who remained in their concrete and mowed down any small parties that managed to survive the crossing of the minefields. In the end the partisans withdrew by night, having taken a few prisoners but leaving the enemy in possession of the field. The fact was that strongly defended positions which included wire, mines and concrete, were a new experience to the Yugoslavs, and they disliked intensely the artillery fire which the Germans called down. These were not the conditions under which a guerilla army shows to best advantage, and if they returned somewhat chastened, they probably learnt a good deal in the course of the battle.

The Germans played a cunning and typical trick during the withdrawal of the schooners to Vis. Our MGBs and MLs as usual went out to convoy and protect the returning schooners from prowling E-boats, and the schooners were martialled so that the return journey did not start till they had embarked all the troops from Solta island.

The partisans however thought it would be a good thing to send one schooner off without waiting for the others, in order to get the wounded back as quickly as possible. They said nothing of this to the Navy, who had no idea that one schooner, crammed with wounded, both partisan and German, had sailed by itself.

This schooner was just entering Vis harbour when a heavy air raid developed on the harbour and a large number of bombs were dropped. The Yugoslav skipper, therefore, turned round and coasted round the north-east point of the island intending to wait till the bombing was over, but instead he met an E-boat which had slunk up the channel between Hvar and Korcula and was lying off Vis harbour waiting to attack anything that was unable to get into the harbour owing to the bombing. Unfortunately the schooner was sunk and of all the wounded on board and the crew, only three survived.

There had always been a project to build an aerodrome on Vis, as this would enable the RAF to increase the range of their fighter sweeps over the mainland of Yugoslavia, and it would have got over the difficulty of the different weather conditions on the east and west of the Adriatic. On many occasions when good weather prevailed over the islands and southern Yugoslavia, the conditions over the aerodromes in Italy made it impossible for aircraft to take off. But the space available for a landing ground on the island was limited to the comparatively level ground east of St Vid hill, and it was a moot point whether the heavy bull-dozing equipment could be brought over from Italy and unloaded at Komiza, and whether it could negotiate the narrow and steep road which led up from the port to the aerodrome.

A small emergency strip had been constructed on the north side of the road simply by clearing the vines, but it was very unsatisfactory, and a number of accidents had occurred when the few aircraft that had used it attempted to land and take off. It was decided to bring over from Italy an aerodrome construction surveying party to look into the project thoroughly, and in due course three American and one British officer arrived to make the survey. After careful study of the ground they decided in favour of the project, and recommended certain minor adjustments in the road to enable the heavy equipment to reach the site of the aerodrome.

As soon as the ships arrived at Komiza with the bull-dozing equipment, the main road from the port to the site was closed to all other traffic, and the cumbersome vehicles slowly climbed up the hill above the town and arrived safely at the aerodrome site. The partisans were put on to pulling up the vines, which was a sad necessity as it involved the uprooting of some very ancient plantations, thereby depriving the islanders of some of their best wine-producing land; but they were very philosophical about it and made no complaints, realising the necessity and the benefit to the war effort that would result from the construction of an aerodrome.

The American construction team went about their work with a will, and in exactly seven days the landing strip was made. I was astonished at the speed and efficiency with which they completed their task. In less than no time fighters were based on the aerodrome, and a sector operations room was organised on the island. Heavy bombers were soon using our landing strip, particularly Fortresses and Liberators from the big air armadas which went out from Italy to bomb the oil-fields in Roumania and targets in Hungary. For the crews of aircraft that had been hit by flak Vis offered a convenient stopping place on the eastern shore of the Adriatic, and we soon had bombers limping in, or their crews bailing out over the island.

I took a keen interest in the fate of the first crew to bale out and land on Vis, as it had always been a point of conjecture as to whether parachutists could land safely on the rocky slopes of the mountains. I was surprised to find that none of them so much as twisted an ankle, and the many other crews that landed from parachutes later all seemed to escape very lightly. It pointed the moral that if the enemy had used parachutists to attack us, the majority would have made safe landings, though to look at the barren slopes of the hills one would never have thought it.

My garrison had now been greatly strengthened by the arrival of a regiment of 25-pounder field guns from Italy. This battery was an Eighth Army unit – the 111th Field Regiment, under the command of Lieutenant-Colonel J. Elliott. Though they had been sent primarily to strengthen the defensive fire of the island, Colonel Elliott made it clear from the first that he hoped we should be able to take his guns, or some of them, on our raids against the other islands, and one of the first things he did was to devise a means of stripping his guns down so that they could be fitted into a landing craft, and trained his men to reassemble the guns in the dark. This was not an easy thing to do, for the 25-pounder is not designed for this use; but Elliott's enthusiasm overcame all the snags and his officers and men were as keen as he was to take part in offensive operations.

We had also been sent the headquarters of a Beach Group to assist my hard-worked brigade administrative staff with the administration of the now considerable island garrison. We could now boast two batteries of 3.7-inch AA guns, two batteries of Bofors guns, a Field Company of Royal Engineers, a Searchlight Battery, a Works Company RE, a Bomb Disposal Section RE, and a Boring Section RE, while a battalion of The Queen's Royal Regiment was sent to us for a short time to strengthen the resident garrison in the island, and when they went we got the 2nd Battalion of the Highland Light Infantry. The total strength in British officers and men of the garrison had risen from a hundred to over five thousand between January and May; it will thus be seen how grateful we were to see Colonel Hugo Meynell and the headquarters of his Beach Group who henceforward relieved us of all the administration of those troops which did not strictly belong to my Commando Brigade.

As has been mentioned already, the increase in the garrison brought about a change in the atmosphere of the island and a loss of the old intimate spirit which had existed during the early anxious months, but this was inevitable; and it must be remembered that the new regime brought many advantages with it. Colonel Meynell was able to devote much time to the welfare of the troops on the island, and it was not long before ENSA entertainment parties visited Vis to cheer up the static units whose routine life had till now been dull in the extreme. He also organised island Sports Meetings and Football Matches and Swimming Galas, for all of which we were very grateful.

As the summer months came, an acute problem began to exercise my mind: this was the shortage of fresh water on the island. Many of the small wells upon which we had drawn during the winter started to dry up, and the cessation of the rainfall cancelled the value of the water-catchments which had been a valuable source of yield.

To remedy this deficiency a number of resorts were adopted, each of which played its part in relieving our predicament. The Boring Section, after working in many areas, discovered two new but small sources of water which were at once developed; an old Austrian well which had been sealed for nearly a hundred years was reopened, and its yield increased by the excavation of new galleries; and certain landing craft were specially modified to carry water over from Italy which was pumped out into storage tanks at Komiza and Vis, and from there distributed to other storage tanks which were erected all over the island. At first this distribution was carried out by water-vehicles, but in the course of time a pipe-line was constructed which performed this function more economically; but these remedies only sufficed by the strictest economy in water-consumption which had to be enforced in every unit.

An attempt to relieve the feeling of isolation on the island was made by my resourceful Intelligence Officer, Captain Clifford Jupp. He started an island newspaper which he called *The Daily Vis-à-Vis* which was distributed each morning to every unit of the garrison. This reproduced a digest of the BBC news and also reported any local events which would be of interest to the troops on the island. It had a Sunday edition which was called *The Vis of the World*, and this went in for editorial comment on current world affairs, readers' contributions in the shape of verse and correspondence, topical comments, generally with a sting in the tail for some individual or unit, and full reports on any major sports fixtures which had taken place during the week. The verse was usually in the form of doggerel but occasionally contributions in more serious vein were offered, and I quote one such contribution which was entitled 'Death Passed Me By' and was initialled 'A.M.' though I never knew the identity of the author:

Death passed me by, but I
Caught his swift glance and knew
He saw me too.

When shall we meet again –
In the soft April rain?
When the first swallows wing?
In time of harvesting?
It may be then:
When the last lacquered leaf
Falls to the mud beneath?

When, in a time of woe,
All the land lies in snow?
Then, perhaps then.

This do I know, we shall
Meet, but I know not now
What time – or how.

It will be recalled that when, in February 1944, No 43 (RM) Commando had been sent to Vis to reinforce the island, No 9 Commando and No 40 (RM) Commando had been called to Anzio to help out the hard-pressed infantry in the beach-head. Any unit in the perimeter at this time had an uncomfortable passage. No square yard of ground was safe from the enemy's artillery, and when units were pulled out of the line for a short rest, they still suffered casualties and were continually liable to disturbance from enemy shelling.

The Germans were patrolling most actively in front of their outposts and the actual line of contact of the opposing armies was fluid in the extreme. The many *nullahs* that intersected the front, particularly on the north and north-eastern faces of the perimeter, offered avenues of approach which both sides were quick to take advantage of; and it was a common experience suddenly to find a body of the enemy at night to the rear of a battalion or brigade headquarters, intent on doing as much damage as possible during the hours of darkness. In the month that the two Commandos were at Anzio, they carried out numerous patrols on the front of the infantry, and No 9 Commando closed their stay in the beach-head with a spirited attack which bore fruitful results.

When these two Commandos were relieved, No 9, which was much under strength due to its casualties at Ornito which it had had no time or opportunity to make up, and now its further losses sustained at Anzio, was settled into billets at Molfetta where it commenced recruiting and set up training cadres for the instruction of the new recruits when they arrived. No 40 Commando, after a period of rest at Molfetta, was brought over to Vis where it took over some of the defensive positions on the island and also constituted a reserve for the garrison.

During the early weeks of May I had been planning a raid rather further afield than usual against an island called Pasman which was situated well to the north of the group in which all our previous exploits had taken place; but at the last minute we discovered that the enemy had got wind of the various reconnaissances that we had carried out, and had deduced our intention. His immediate reaction had been to occupy some hills which we had hoped to reach under cover of darkness and from which we should have been able to dominate his garrison.

Once we knew we had lost the advantage of surprise it was clear that not only our plan of attack on the island was likely to fail, but our chances of withdrawing in safety after the raid were slender in the extreme as the long sea-voyage back to Vis could be intercepted at many points by enemy E-boats and by aircraft. The Navy was strongly of the opinion that sea-interception was likely, and were naturally reluctant to risk it when their craft were heavily laden with soldiers for whom they would be responsible. As their view coincided with mine, I cancelled the operation, to the relief of everyone concerned except our masters in Italy who were distinctly upset. So they pressed me to put on another raid at short notice against some other objective.

It had always been my view that in our circumstances which

enabled us to chose our objectives and to strike when and where we liked, we should lay our plans so that the chances of success were as strong as we could possibly make them. We had no reserves to rely on, and if we took unjustifiable risks, we might sustain casualties which would make us too weak to hold Vis itself in the face of a determined attack: and as the defence of the island was my over-riding responsibility, I had to be careful that I did not incur serious losses in the troops which formed the garrison when I employed them on offensive raids. The geography of the islands was such that the enemy could always reinforce one of his islands more strongly and more quickly than I could, so that our success depended on good information and a well-executed plan that ran through with speed and without serious hitches. By thinking out every eventuality and laying plans which included them all, we had so far been able to inflict considerable harm on the enemy at a remarkably small cost to ourselves. However, detailed plans of this sort could not be devised at short notice.

When we were pressed to undertake a raid at short notice, as we were when the Pasman project was cancelled, I selected the island of Mljet as our objective, as this was one which had not been visited since the partisans had fought their battle there a month previously. The German garrison was thought to be about two hundred men, and provided the partisan intelligence was correct and the positions of the enemy as reported were accurate, it seemed to offer reasonable chances of success; but there was no time to send our own officers on reconnaissance to check the intelligence – a course which we had always made a point of following in all previous raids.

It will suffice to say that after a successful landing, Nos 2 and 43 Commandos advanced into the hills to attack the summits which the enemy was reported to be holding. The country was particularly difficult and the physical strain in carrying heavy equipment up the mountain-sides and across the numerous valleys that separated the various ranges was more severe than anything we had yet encountered.

It was not until three o'clock in the afternoon (we had landed just after midnight) that the Commandos were in possession of all the heights which were understood to be held by the enemy, but he, though sniping at us and mortaring us from these positions while we climbed up towards him, had retired on our arrival to other positions which owing to the hilly nature of the country, we could neither see nor engage by fire. Further, the local inhabitants whom we contacted could give us no accurate information of his whereabouts, and the only locations they indicated were found on reconnaissances to be devoid of enemy.

This was a predicament which we had previously been able to avoid by taking the trouble to make sure of our intelligence first. Now I had to decide whether to advance further into the mountains in a blind search which would leave me at nightfall more than six miles from the cove from which our evacuation was due to take place, and with no troops available to watch our rear to ensure that the enemy did not cut us off; or whether to break off the attempt while there was still daylight and return to our cove by midnight as agreed with the Navy. If we decided to remain on the island, new plans would have to be agreed by signal with the mainland to provide for an evacuation the following night, and for air cover for a further twelve hours than had originally been requested.

I decided that in the circumstances the best thing to do was to admit to ourselves that the raid had misfired, and withdraw in good order according to our original programme. Accordingly the Commandos were told to return to the cove, and it is some indication of the difficulties of the terrain that two troops of No 43 Commando did not reach the ships until 3 a.m. Later we heard that the island was reinforced early the next morning by the enemy with troops from the mainland of Yugoslavia who were ferried across the Mljet channel, and two Focke Wulf aircraft reconnoitred our cove while we were re-embarking. The net result was that we had neither gained nor lost anything, but I was sorry that the troops had had such an appalling sweat during their twenty-four hours ashore for no positive results.

About four weeks before the Mljet raid took place, Combined Operations Headquarters in London had asked Allied Force Headquarters in the Mediterranean if I could be spared to return to England for a short visit in order to take part in certain discussions, and to pass on such experience in Combined Operations as we had gained during our service in Sicily, Italy and the Adriatic. AFHQ had replied that I could not be spared at the time, but that I could probably proceed to London a little later. A few days after our return from Mljet I received orders to fly to England for a visit of not more than three weeks, and I therefore handed the command of my brigade and of the island of Vis to my brother, and flew home by way of Italy and North Africa.

Two days after I left Vis, the Germans carried out a parachute raid against Marshal Tito's Headquarters at Drvar in Bosnia, on the mainland of Yugoslavia. They nearly succeeded in capturing him, but not quite. The whole of his staff had, however, to take to flight, and serious fighting broke out as the Germans made yet another savage drive to wipe out the partisan resistance. Tito ordered the partisan forces in Vis to create a maximum diversion in the islands in the hope that this would be mistaken for the preliminaries of an invasion of the coast of Yugoslavia by the Allies, and so draw off some of the German pressure inland.

The partisans decided to send all their available forces on Vis to attack the German-held island of Brac, for this island was strongly held as an outpost for the protection of the coastal strip in the vicinity of Split, an area which the Germans always assumed might be selected by the Allies as a favourable landing point for an invasion of the mainland. An attack on this island was therefore more likely to draw off German forces than one on any other island in the Dalmatian Group. It was however strongly held, and the authorities in Italy decided to assist the partisans by sending a British force to cooperate with them in their attack. This force consisted of No 43 (RM) Commando and a company of the Highland Light Infantry, together with some of the guns of the 111th Field Regiment and some 3.7 AA guns of the Vis garrison. The force was put under the command of my brother, Lieutenant-Colonel J. M. T. Churchill.

The total force of British and partisans numbered nearly 6,000 men, and the Navy cooperated valiantly to move and escort this large body, together with its supplies and mule-trains, to Brac. The attacking forces split up into three main detachments, one to attack the German garrison at Supetar, the port on the northern coast of the island; one to invest the second garrison at Sumartin, the port on the eastern end of the island; and the third to attack the German headquarter position in the centre of the island just to the south-east of the village of Nerezisce. It was with this third detachment that the British contingent cooperated.

The main landings were to take place on the night of Thursday, 1st June, but in order to prevent the enemy from shelling the cove to the south-west of the island where the majority of the partisans and the British were to land, a company of the Highland Light Infantry was detailed to disembark on the night of Wednesday, 31st May, and attack the enemy observation post on Vidova Gora, the highest point on Brac, at dusk on the following night.

Fierce fighting continued for three days and heavy casualties were sustained on both sides. The most stubborn resistance was encountered, particularly from the German observation position at Vidova Gora, but after this was captured by the combined efforts of the HLI and the partisans, the German main positions were attacked on three rocky mountains near the village of Nerezisce. My brother had to send for No 40 (RM) Commando and some more field guns to continue the attack, and these units were accordingly brought over to Brac by the Navy.

After a plan had been decided upon between the British and partisan commanders for a night attack on 3rd June commencing at 9 p.m. on the German positions, detailed reconnaissances were carried out of the objectives assigned to the British. When all was ready, orders were issued; but then quite suddenly the partisan commander changed his mind. Although efforts were made to induce him to conform to the original plan, he was adamant.

This was a most awkward predicament, for 43 (RM) Commando were already on the move to their start line, and difficulty was now being experienced with communication with No 40 (RM) Commando, owing to the failure of the wireless sets to get through in the mountainous country. 43 Commando met very fierce resistance and particularly heavy mortar fire, while 40 Commando had to start their attack late owing to the difficulty of getting the new orders to them. Churchill decided to direct the attack himself, and moved forward with 40 Commando to the objective. The enemy positions were on the summit of a mountain, and the punishing advance over the hill-sides in the face of heavy mortar and machine-gun fire resulted in high casualties, particularly as the partisans failed to draw off any of the enemy's resistance.

Colonel Jack had his bagpipes with him and played them continuously during the advance in order to assist in the maintenance of direction of the attack which, owing to the darkness, the enemy fire and the difficult country, became liable to lose direction. Finally, No 40 Commando reached the objective and cleared the enemy from the summit of the hill, but he delivered a heavy counter-attack supported by a furious mortar concentration which enabled him to regain the summit. The Marine Commandos fell back to the lower slopes, now seriously depleted in officers; and the last that was seen of Colonel Jack was in the glare of a shell-burst when a marine saw him assisting Lieutenant-Colonel 'Pops' Manners DSO, the colonel of No 40 Commando and Captain Roger Wakefield, both of whom had been wounded while on the objective itself.

The determined nature of the partisan attacks on the north and east of the island, together with the fierceness of the British attack against the main positions near Nerezisce evidently caused considerable alarm at the German Headquarters in Yugoslavia which resulted in the diversion of certain forces to the coast to meet what was now assumed to be an Allied landing near Split. This was precisely the object for which the Brac attack had been undertaken, and greatly eased the predicament of Tito's forces on the mainland.

The partisan and Allied forces were therefore withdrawn to Vis, the Navy as usual rendering the maximum assistance, but the Germans had been so hard hit on Brac that they were unable to interfere in any way with the withdrawal, which was carried out methodically and successfully over a period of 24 hours. To harry the enemy, however, detachments of No 2 Commando were landed on Brac during the withdrawal, and continued to operate on the island in isolated bodies for fourteen days, thereby prolonging the uncertainty of the enemy as to the Allied intentions, and interfering with his efforts to reform his shattered garrison. These small raiding parties succeeded in bringing in a number of wounded who had been left on the battlefield.

CHAPTER SIXTEEN

Naval Operations

The more one reads of the doings of our great forebears in the Adriatic at the time of the Napoleonic Wars, the more one is struck by the closeness of the parallel between their activities and ours. It has been seen how the frigates of Nelson's day used the island of Lissa as a base to harass the enemy's shipping, and how in time the Navy came to realise the advantages that would offer if the island was securely held by a British military garrison. It was in fact at the request of the Admiralty that the War Office (or War Department as it was called in those days) issued orders to Lord William Bentinck to garrison this small Adriatic island. So in our day, the light craft of the Navy used Vis as a base several months before the military came on the scene; and one of the reasons for the garrisoning of the island by the commandos was to facilitate the work of the Navy in operating from it.

It was in the autumn of 1943 that light naval forces commenced to operate from the Dalmatian islands. At that time the Germans had not occupied the islands, nor indeed were they in the port of Split on the mainland. The partisans operated their schooners between the mainland and the islands, and the British craft based themselves on the two islands of Hvar and Vis, with their headquarters with the partisan naval headquarters at Hvar.

The task of the Navy was twofold: to maintain a flow of food and war material to Tito's armies from Italy, using the islands as a forward base and marshalling point, and to attack enemy shipping using Dalmatian waters. To do this, naval officers were stationed on all the major islands to maintain contact with the partisans in the harbours. Schooners and MLs were used to run the stores in to the mainland, while MGBs and MTBs patrolled the sea-lanes and offered battle whenever the enemy could be found.

The conditions in which the Navy operated were not easy. The Germans had undisputed air superiority over Dalmatia using the many aerodromes which they had captured in Yugoslavia. If a schooner or naval craft attempted to operate during daylight it was certain to be seen by the constant air patrols which the Germans maintained, and a fierce dive-bomber or fighter attack followed as a matter of routine. Our craft were therefore obliged to hide themselves in harbours and coves during the day, covering themselves with camouflage nets and branches of trees to make themselves as inconspicuous as possible. At Vis they used a large cave or grotto on Ravnik island which enabled the boats to be completely hidden from above; they took advantage of a funnel in the roof, which nature had provided, to erect an aerial which projected out of the top and enabled them to keep in touch with their headquarters in Hvar.

At the end of 1943 came the German drive to the coast, the capture of Split and its magnificent harbour, and the invasion of the Dalmatian islands. The Peljesac Peninsula was first seized, and then Korcula, Brac and Hvar were occupied in rapid succession. The partisan military forces on the islands were in a poor state of organisation and were ill-equipped, for their needs had so far been regarded as secondary to those of the main armies in Yugoslavia itself. Rearguard actions were fought, and on Korcula Lieutenant K. J. (Spider) Webb RNR, one of the original band of naval officers who had made the islands their home for the preceding four months, acquired a great military reputation with the partisans for his able conduct of the retirement, and his military skill. But the enemy as usual had ensured that he had an overwhelming superiority before he undertook the campaign, and the partisans were no match for him. All the islands previously held were evacuated with the single exception of Vis, to which the British and partisan naval forces retired. At the same time, the first hundred commandos arrived on the island, and from then onwards the soldiers shared with the sailors in the defence of this historic island outpost.

Lieutenant-Commander Morgan Giles OBE, GM, RN, was sent over to Vis to become Senior Naval Officer. As he had already visited the island and had been working in Italy on the Naval Staff which was concerned with the supply of stores by sea to the partisans, he was well aware of the conditions and he lost no time in taking control of the naval situation. In this he was ably assisted by Lieutenant-Commander Merlin Minshall RNVR who until the evacuation had been with the partisans at naval headquarters on Hvar, and he remained at Vis for several weeks to assist Giles before returning to Italy. In one of the earliest raids carried out by No 2 Commando on Hvar, Lieutenant-Commander Minshall rendered invaluable service to the Commandos.

Morgan Giles set up his Naval Headquarters in Komiza, taking over a house on the waterfront overlooking the harbour with a convenient verandah which was used for signalling to craft in the bay. His total operational craft at this time amounted to about six MGBs and MTBs, though he was reinforced for limited periods by occasional units of Vosper MTBs. Spider Webb became his second-in-command, and he was given a staff which included Lieutenant W. L. Clinton-Baker RN as Staff Officer Operations, and Paymaster Lieutenant R. Harrari RNVR as secretary. They used the top flat of the building in which Colonel Jack was established as a naval mess, and the two staffs worked in the closest collaboration.

The constant enemy threat from the air made a strict dispersal of craft in daylight an absolute necessity, and the boats anchored themselves in the coves near the harbour as close inshore as possible, using camouflage nets to conceal themselves. Ring-bolts were let into the rocks, and later, buoys were anchored as moorings. Petrol dumps were established at various points on the island, and a wireless station was set up on Mount Hum.

Having established themselves at Komiza, the sailors set about their task of harassing the German shipping which was using Dalmatian waters. The increasing success of Tito's forces in cutting rail and road communications in Yugoslavia forced the enemy to make increased use of sea-transport in supplying his coastal garrisons, his occupied islands and his armies further to the south in Albania and Greece. His main sea-route commenced at Fiume and ran close to the shore inside the island belt via Karlobag to Zara. This portion of the route was performed by big ships and was largely out of range of our craft based on Vis.

From Zara the cargoes were carried in schooners and landing-craft which proceeded by way of Biograd, Sibenik and Split to the mouth of the Neretva River. Thence the sea-lane continued round the Peljesac Peninsula and through the Korcula channel to Dubrovnik, and thence southwards to Albania and Greece. Broadly speaking it may be said that the light naval forces based on Vis took as their happy hunting-ground that portion of the route that lay between Zara and Dubrovnik, and made it their task to make this portion of the journey as unhealthy as possible for the enemy.

The German reaction to these marauding tactics was quick, and took the form of increasing the escorts which accompanied the schooners and craft, of increasing their E-boat patrols in these waters, of establishing shore-batteries at points which commanded the route, and of increasing their air patrols by day and by night. We replied by increasing our own air cover in this area, which resulted in the enemy having to cease operating by day, and his convoys consequently would hide away in coves just before dawn, continuing their journey the following night. Our craft when performing long patrols would often have to adapt this procedure too, and this applied chiefly to operations at the extreme northern limit of the patrol area. Generally speaking it was the Vospers which took on the big ships in the routes north of Zara, while the large MTBs (Dogboats) and MGBs seldom operated much to the north of Murter island.

The strategy of the naval problem would alter from time to time as the enemy altered his habits and defences, but two principles were adhered to by our forces in their operations; first, they always endeavoured to carry out their patrols differently each night, so that the enemy could never foresee their tactics; and secondly they always tried to keep closer to the shore than the enemy. Visibility was always better outwards from the shore than inwards, and our craft would utilise the shadow which on fine summer nights the cliffs cast on the water to conceal their presence, and by so doing they were able to discern more easily the enemy boats against the faintly lighter background of the sky. This consideration was found to outweigh almost all others, and became a cardinal point in the tactics adopted.

Naturally the phases of the moon directly affected the operations undertaken, for in the Adriatic the moon is particularly bright and visibility becomes possible at surprising distances. For instance, on a bright moonlight night patrols would operate on the north rather than the southern shores of the Peljesac Peninsula in order to take advantage of the shadow of the cliffs. But in deciding on the operations to be undertaken on any particular night Morgan Giles would have many considerations to weigh up. Apart from the weather and the visibility which invariably influenced the problem, there was the highly important factor of partisan intelligence which was available in profusion and often indicated areas which might offer good targets. Thus they would report the routes which the Germans were using, or the number of craft in a harbour, and they would watch the arrival and departure of boats noting how long the enemy remained. They might report that the German troops from a barracks had all moved out and were waiting in a harbour, obviously foreshadowing a move by transports. All these stories would be reviewed daily, and if a particularly hot bit of news was received, Cerni would often ring Morgan on the phone and the two would concert plans.

The difficulty of the dual control of partisans and British was no easier for the Navy than it was for the army on shore. The partisans had to go from the island to the mainland each night: partly to deliver stores or personnel, partly to obtain information, and partly to evacuate sick or wounded, or homeless families who were in danger of starving to death. These journeys would be performed by their schooners without signals, lights, navigational aids or wireless. We had to carry out our patrols often in the near vicinity of the partisans, and the danger of clashes was considerable. This was minimised as much as possible by agreement each evening between Morgan Giles and Cerni, when each would indicate their night intentions, and the two plans would be coordinated. Normally each would agree to avoid the water in which the other was operating, and when the two had to coincide, due warnings were issued to the captains of the craft concerned. The partisans were on the whole very good, obliging us when we urgently wished to carry out a special patrol which would interfere with their nightly journeys; but in spite of every precaution, on several occasions clashes did occur between partisan patrol boats and our craft.

The partisans maintained ceaseless touch and contact with the neighbouring islands. Every night boats would go out to land two or three men, perhaps also a sack of flour or some rations, and would bring back wounded or persons who had become compromised and were therefore unsuitable for continued use as informers.

These journeys were carried out every night and regardless of weather. On one occasion Morgan was in the harbour chatting with a partisan schooner captain, and bemoaning the weather, as a 'Bora' was blowing which seriously interfered with our naval operations. The captain on the other hand was grateful for it, for he pointed out that he had been out on journeys for the previous 28 nights without a break, and preferred the fearful weather to the danger of a clash with E-boats, which would be compelled to stay in harbour in such weather conditions.

Many of the partisan boats were very well armed and constituted a formidable foe when met with on the seas at night. They would be fitted with British two-pounder guns, Oerlikons, Italian anti-tank guns and captured machine guns, and they used to make up for their lack of armour-plating by building bulwarks of boards about a foot or so apart with shingle in between. Most of the boats had compasses which were used to some extent for navigation, but all the skippers were Dalmatian sailors who have long been famous for their skill as seamen in their own waters.

They have of course no modern methods of navigation, and to a partisan, a compass either works or is broken! They do not worry themselves about compass errors or such frills, but their resource is unbounded and on many an occasion enabled them to extricate themselves or their boats from situations which seemed hopeless. Their movements were, however, always somewhat uncertain, and when a schooner went off on a mission, there was never any telling when it would return. It almost invariably did come back, but in its own time, and often after incredible adventures.

There were one or two so-called partisan dockyards on Vis where they used to carry out repairs to their schooners, working under the most primitive conditions imaginable, but with the highest standard of workmanship. The most famous of these was in a cove on Vis harbour, and Colonel Jack always referred to it as 'John Brown's'. Here they had constructed two slipways and installed a primitive winch by which the boats were drawn up on to the beach for repairs. Minor repairs were even carried out to our naval craft on these slips, sometimes just sufficient to make the boat watertight for the journey over to Italy.

The dockyard workers were mostly shipwrights from the town of Korcula on Korcula island who had been famous in times of peace for the building of yachts and sailing boats. They would haul a schooner up on the slips, hoist out its engine, repair it in the 'engine-shops' in the anchovy factory nearby (which had been converted into a primitive workshop), refit the engine and relaunch the schooner. They used any kind of material they could get hold of – ration tins, the wood from packing-cases, metal from aircraft which had crashed on the island – anything in fact which was available and which ingenuity could make serviceable.

I cannot possibly attempt to describe all the numerous patrols which our naval craft carried out during the time that we cooperated on Vis, but I will just mention some of the more outstanding events in a naval chronicle which will I believe become as famous in this war as were the actions of William Hoste and his fellow frigate captains in the Adriatic at the time of the Napoleonic Wars. But I must point out that the lot of the crew of a MTB, MGB or ML while on duty at Vis was hard and monotonous and often punctuated with periods of great anxiety, and the few incidents which I shall mention by no means illustrate the much longer periods of unremitting work which did not always have the luck to lead to such excitements.

On one occasion Lieutenant-Commander Tom Fuller DSC, and two bars, RCNVR, was patrolling off Murter island with three or four MGBs when he saw two large German schooners approaching. Advancing boldly up to them, he hailed them in German and said that unless they surrendered immediately they would be torpedoed. Fuller did not mention that he had no torpedoes. The Italian crews panicked and jumped overboard, and the German guards put their hands up, although these schooners were heavily armed and their guns would have been a match for the MGBs.

Fuller took the two large boats in tow and started on the return journey to Vis, but on the ay he had to pass over a minefield which was safe for his light-draught boats but was dangerous for the heavily-laden schooners. He was loath to lose his prizes, so rather than cut them adrift, he put them on the end of a long wire so that if they struck a mine, the resulting explosion would not damage his own craft too much.

In point of fact he managed to get them over without mishap, and he then lashed them alongside and completed the voyage to his base. One of these schooners was the *Libbechic*, of 200 tons, with a cargo of military stores which included 65 barrels of Danish butter addressed to the German Mayor of Split. The Navy very kindly divided up the spoil between the various units of the Vis garrison, and we all lived on this delicious butter for a month.

The enemy soon took to escorting all his convoys with E-boats and I-boats (the latter being tank-landing craft with a low silhouette and very heavily armed). The job of intercepting these convoys became harder and harder, and called for the exercise of the maximum amount of ingenuity combined with the taking of considerable risk. At one time our craft made a habit of concealing themselves between two wrecks off one of the northern islands, stretching camouflage nets between the masts which projected above the water. Another favourite trick was to land an officer in a dinghy with a wireless set to observe the approaches to a channel, and when a convoy or an enemy patrol was seen to be approaching, the officer would warn the boats who would then station themselves in convenient positions to ambush the enemy.

It must always be remembered that the crew of an MGB were on top of many thousand gallons of high octane petrol which might be exploded at any moment by one incendiary bullet, and when one realises the extremely short range at which many of the encounters took place, it is easy to appreciate how easily such a mishap might occur.

Lieutenant-Commander Tim Bligh DSC, RNVR, in *MGB 662*, was operating off Vir island with several other MGBs in company when he came upon what appeared to be two converging convoys of 'F'

Lighters (large German tank-landing craft with a formidable armament). The gun-boats immediately attacked at short range, and in the fierce action which ensued they sank all the craft that could be seen. Bligh thought that some might have escaped and beached themselves during the engagement, so he closed the shore to have a look, though this was a dangerous move as his craft would have been seen by the enemy before he could have discerned them in the shadow of the land. Sure enough the Bosch opened up, and Bligh, uncertain of their position or their number, lay off and waited for the moon to rise. As soon as there was sufficient light to pick out the enemy, Bligh torpedoed one craft which was close inshore, and the flash revealed two more which he engaged with gun-fire and sank also. In all he accounted for nine 'F' Lighters in this one engagement.

Another of Tim Bligh's victories occurred when he was patrolling off Murter and saw a fast vessel, apparently a destroyer, leaving Sibenik and making north. This was too good a chance to miss although the enemy greatly out-gunned Bligh's unit, so he immediately attacked and apparently took the enemy unawares. The ship turned out to be the ex-Yugoslav torpedo-boat destroyer *T7* manned by Germans, and Bligh's audacious attack so damaged it that it ran ashore on Murter island and became a total loss.

On another occasion off this same island Tom Fuller found what he at first thought was a destroyer, and attacked it with his heart in his mouth. It turned out to be a tug alongside and towing a larger lighter, the hull of the latter and the upper works of the former giving the impression of a destroyer in the half-light. After a gun attack he boarded and captured the crew, but in the fight the safety-valve was blown off the boiler. This resulted in a fearful noise of escaping steam which the captors were powerless to stop; however they tried to take the tug in tow but its wheel jammed, and as it no longer had steam up, it had to be abandoned and sunk. The lighter was brought back after much difficulty as it was so large and unwieldy, but being heavily laden it was hoped that it contained another cargo as succulent as Fuller's former prize with the Danish butter. Alas! when its holds were opened at Vis it was found to contain nothing but mule-fodder!

One of the most notable successes, however, in the whole of the campaign in the Adriatic was secured in the very early days by Lieutenant-Commander D. (Butch) Lancaster DSC, RNVR, when he was patrolling in the northern isles with a unit of Vospers. Near Silba island he saw and torpedoed the German (ex-Yugoslav) cruiser *Dalmatia*, which was the most powerful enemy unit at sea in the

Adriatic at that time. The Germans attempted to salve her, so Lancaster returned a few nights later and torpedoed her again. The partisans spent months on the wreck salvaging everything they could take away, and gained much valuable material and machinery and many guns.

Another valuable prize which the partisans managed to secure was the German vessel *Stella Bianca* which was lying anchored in a storm under the lee of Olib island. The partisans attacked from the shore, and swept the decks of the schooner with machinegun and rifle fire, and killed or wounded most of the crew. They were about to board when a German very gallantly crawled along the deck under heavy fire and managed to slip the cable. The vessel drifted out to sea, but the partisans jumped into small rowing boats and pulled after her and hurled grenades on to her decks from alongside. This was too much for those that remained of the German crew, who surrendered when the partisans swarmed over the side. The partisans lost no time in putting her into commission as an armed patrol boat, and changed her name to the *Stella Rossa* (in honour of the Red Star – badge of the patrisan movement); she became one of the most famous of their vessels operating from Vis afterwards.

The great characteristic of the night actions which our boats used to fight was the closeness of the range and the immediate proximity of the land. This latter point cannot be stressed too strongly. Our craft would creep along within a yard or two of the cliffs, for the Germans too realised the advantage of these tactics and adopted them as well; thus the advantage went to the side which was closest inshore, for they had the better visibility; but it can be seen that this greatly limited the power of manoeuvrability once the battle was joined, and led to many problems which had to be solved in a split second, for there was never any time for prolonged thought once fire had been opened.

Our crews, when on patrol, not only strained their eyes and ears to detect the enemy, but even their noses as well, for sometimes the first indication was the smell of the exhaust of the enemy Diesel engines. A German petty officer, who was afterwards captured, told how on one occasion his craft was one of a convoy which had been attacked by one of our patrols, and he closed the shore to hide. The British boats, having lost contact, also closed the shore where they lay waiting for the reappearance of the enemy; apparently they remained for several hours within a hundred yards of the German boat, which was beached on the rocks and on this occasion managed to escape detection.

Several of the most successful boat captains were Canadians, but a large number of different flotillas shared the hard work in the Adriatic. I shall never forget the reputation that Lieutenant-Commander Tom Fuller built up at Vis amongst the soldiers on the island. We naturally took a keen interest in the Navy's achievement, and were very proud of the team which Morgan Giles operated from 'our' island. We got to know many of them, not only from meeting them on the island, but when they cooperated with us on our raids, and we used to watch the success of their boats, the numbers of which we got to know and remember.

The last time I saw Tom Fuller was in Bari, when, after a long spell of duty, in which he had achieved many more successes than I can chronicle, he was off on leave. He had shaved off his beard, and was in a holiday frame of mind, but his idea of leave seemed to be to get as near as possible to the land fighting, and he begged me to try and get him an air passage to Florence which was then just behind the front line. This was a tall order, but I managed to put him in touch with someone who was able to help him, and he got his aircraft.

Three other Canadians who did well were Lieutenant-Commander Douglas (Wimpey) Maitland DSC and bar, RCNVR, Lieutenant-Commander C. (Corney) Burke DSC and two bars, and Lieutenant-Commander Tommy Ladner DSC and bar, RCNVR.

I have not mentioned the MLs in this story, because their construction and armament made them less suitable than the other boats to take on the offensive patrols; but they did on occasion get to grips with enemy convoys and patrols, though more often they were used for work such as escort duty to our convoys, transporting stores, towing, and air-sea rescue work.

Lieutenant D. R. Romain RNVR in *ML 494* was the senior officer of the 22nd Flotilla throughout the summer of 1944, and other boats with high reputations were *MLs 841, 361* and *218*. On the occasions when I made the journey to and from Italy I was often carried by the MLs, and two captains I came to know well and like were Lieutenants Jimmy Weir and Dick Crighton, both RNVR. The latter performed a last service for me in taking over to Vis a memorial plaque* that I later erected in the old naval cemetery in Vis, to commemorate those who gave their lives for their country in this remote outpost.

* See Appendix.

CHAPTER SEVENTEEN

Tito Arrives on Vis

I have described how it came about that the Brac attack was carried out while I was away from my brigade. The first inkling that I received of the battle was when I read in an evening newspaper in London that the Germans reported that 'Brigadier Tom Churchill, the commander of Lissa island', had been captured. This made me open my eyes, for I realised that the name and description must be a mistake for my brother. I made enquiries in official circles and soon learnt the vague outlines of the battle which had been fought, and almost at once I was recalled by telegram to Vis.

I landed on the island again just over a fortnight after I had taken my departure. In the meantime the Brac battle had been fought, and I was anxious to hear full details from those who had taken part. Not only had I lost two of my Commando commanding officers – one of them my brother, and the other Lieutenant Colonel Pops Manners of 40 (RM) Commando – but also two valued officers of my own staff were missing, my friend Captain Roger Wakefield, and Captain Jim Pirrie. It was not till much later that we heard the melancholy news that the three last mentioned had all been killed in action in South-East Europe.

Pops Manners had commanded No 40 ever since the Dieppe Raid, in which he had been a troop leader and had been cast into the sea when his landing-craft was sunk. He was a veteran of the Sicily campaign and of the Termoli landing, and he had seen hard fighting on the Garigliano and at Anzio. He was a most popular CO and his death was a tremendous loss to his Commando and his friends. Jim Pirrie had joined us in Italy, having previously served with No 12 Commando in England. He became my Staff Officer, Royal Engineers, and his first battle with the brigade was the capture of Mount Ornito. After that he had gone over to Vis to help No 2 Commando with their static defences, and he had been responsible for the siting and laying of nearly all the minefields and wire on the island; it was believed that he lost his life lifting mines on Brac during the battle.

Jack's capture was a great blow to the Vis garrison, for he was known to everyone and was immensely popular. His enthusiastic work on the island in the early days, and his gallant leadership of the first small raids had impressed both the partisans and the British, and the tremendous reputation which he had earned at Dunkirk, Vaagso and Salerno made him one of the greatest commando leaders of the war. We believed that the terms of the enemy broadcasts at the time of his capture indicated that he was taken alive.

Roger Wakefield's death, however, came as a bitter blow, for until this news was received through Red Cross channels, we had had no reason to suppose that he had even been wounded. He was a close personal friend, and had come out to my staff at my request four months previously. I profoundly admired his strength of character and the influence which he exerted by his example of selfless devotion to duty. The men at my headquarters, no less than the officers, realised his staunch loyalty and worth.

The two Marine Commandos had suffered serious losses in officers, for it is always the leaders who suffer when the tide of battle turns temporarily against one; so there was much to do to reorganise and prepare ourselves for further action, and we wasted no time in regrets.

It has been mentioned that the Brac attack was undertaken as a result of the German parachute raid on Tito's Headquarters in Bosnia and the simultaneous drive against the partisan forces. Tito himself had had a very near escape from capture, and had had to undertake a long trek on foot with his staff to avoid the determined effort to catch him and so eliminate once and for all his powerful influence and leadership of the partisan movement.

It was remoured that Rommel himself had organised this attack during one of his lightning visits to the front, and it is true that just before it was carried out, we had received reports that the German general had been seen in the neighbourhood of Split. Although the attempt made had been unsuccessful, circumstances following the attack made it very difficult for Tito to set up his headquarters again on the mainland, and it was Colonel Vivian Street, Fitzroy Maclean's second-in-command at the Maclean Mission, who was with Tito, who organised the latter's flight to Italy.

Street contacted Bari by radio and asked for an aircraft to land on a stretch of flat ground near Mliniste in Bosnia, which was the nearest landing-ground to Tito's position. In reply, the RAF promised to try to land that night, the 3rd/4th June, and in fact, that very evening, a Dakota arrived, and Tito and his staff, the Russian Mission to his headquarters, and his dog Tigger climbed aboard, accompanied by Vivian Street. The latter was surprised to notice after take-off that the aircrew were Russians. The Dakota was supplied under lease-lend, which the Russians were operating from Bari under British control, and somehow the pilot had managed to obtain this particular assignment for his plane. This has enabled the Russian government ever since to claim that it was they who had rescued Tito.

I met the Russian pilot in Belgrade in 1975, at the great parade the Yugoslav government organised to celebrate the anniversary of 'Liberation and Victory over Fascism'. His name is Aleksander Sornikov, and the Yugoslavs made him a National Hero of Yugoslavia, and in the photograph I took of him (which is reproduced in this book) he is wearing civilian clothes with the collar and badge of a National Hero round his neck. I asked him what the circumstances of his landing and take-off were, and if the runway was under fire at the time, but he said it was not, though he implied that there was some fear that the Germans might arrive at any moment. I have not scrupled to suggest to my friends in SUBNOR (The Federation of Veterans Association of the People's Liberation War) that by the same token they should make Lieutenant-Commander Duncan Carson RN, the captain of HMS *Blackmore*, the Hunt Class destroyer that took Tito to Vis, a Hero of Yugoslavia also, but they have never done so.

Tito's decision to make Vis his destination was an acknowledgement of the fact that the island, thanks to its British garrison and all the work and military defences put into it by the British, had now become a nearly impregnable base in which he could, without the inconvenience of continual attacks and consequential moves, settle down to planning the reconquest of Belgrade and the setting-up of a post-war government.

Of course, not long before, Winston Churchill had announced that British war aid, which until that time had been sent to General Mihajlovic and the Cetniks in the Serbian mountains, was now to be sent to Tito and his partisans, because the former had ceased to fight the enemy, and some, at any rate, of his subordinates had been making accommodations with the Germans. The British Military Mission to Mihajlovic was therefore withdrawn, and a Mission to Tito, under the leadership of Fitzroy Maclean, was substituted for it.

At first Marshal Tito established himself in a number of caves high up on the slopes of Mount Hum, above my headquarters at Borovik. The partisans in 24 hours built a road up the side of the mountain to give access to his caves, a road which was banked and graded so that it could be negotiated by Jeeps and trailers. Sentries were posted at all approaches to the locality, and special precautions were taken to guard against a sudden parachute or seaborne raid directed against the Marshal himself.

We, who had been so long on the island, were surprised that he did not avail himself of more comfortable quarters in Vis, where there were one or two good villas which would have suited him; but I suppose he and his staff had so long been used to mountain hide-outs, and had never found themselves protected to the degree which was now possible at Vis, that they automatically adopted their old habits. As a matter of fact, after he had been on the island a month, he realised our strength, and came out of his caves and took up his dwelling in a comfortable villa at Milna on the eastern shore of Vis.

I was invited to meet him shortly after his arrival. The setting was entirely in keeping with the legend of a guerilla chief who was directing his irregular hordes from mountain fastnesses. The Marshal was sitting at a deal table in a cave the entrance of which was guarded by sentries with tommy-guns and grenades. Beside him was a huge Alsatian dog which watched his every movement. Through the opening in the cave, lone sentries could be seen silhouetted against the sky on every hill-top, and in the far corner of the cave some straw on the ground and a camp-chair showed where the Marshal slept.

Tito was a thick-set man of medium height with greying hair which was brushed backwards and was slightly wavy. He was 57, and had aquiline features and a square determined jaw. His countenance in repose was stern, but he had a brilliant smile which lit up his face and brought a pronounced twinkle into his eyes. He did not speak English, though he could read it, but many members of his staff spoke English, German or French. He himself spoke fluent Russian and good German. He smoked a good deal, using a cigarette holder in the shape of a miniature silver-mounted meerschaum pipe.

From the outset, Tito had been the moving force in the partisan movement, both on its military and political side. He was born of Croat peasant stock in the village of Kumrovec near Zagreb, and his real name was Josip Broz. The nickname which he assumed of Tito is a common one in the district from which he sprung. He was conscripted into the Austro-Hungarian army during the Great War but went over to the Russians in 1915. After the Russian Revolution he joined the Red Army and fought through the Civil War, where he gained his early experiences in guerilla warfare.

In 1923 Tito returned to Yugoslavia, where he earned his living as a tin-smith in Croatia. He became a leader of the metal-workers' trade union, and engaged actively in political work. This led to his arrest and imprisonment for some years, but on his release he resumed his political interests and became leader of the underground communist movement. Between 1929 and 1939 he paid a number of visits to Russia, where he came to be regarded as an able and farsighted worker. He was concerned in the Spanish Civil War, being responsible for the means by which Balkan sympathisers were enabled to join the Republican army in Spain.

When the Germans invaded Yugoslavia, Tito was working in Zagreb under the assumed name of Tomanek. He managed to escape to Serbia, though his wife was arrested by the Ustase and interned in a concentration camp; but she later was released without her identity being disclosed. Tito at once set about organising resistance to the invader, and from then onwards he became the recognised leader of the partisan movement, personally directing and taking part in all their early battles. While he had always been Commander-in-Chief of the partisan armed forces, he held no official position in the movement, other than leader of the Yugoslav Communist Party, until November 1943 when he was appointed President of the National Committee of Liberation and was created Marshal of Yugoslavia.

Tito's strength lay in his capacity for organisation; and only outstanding organising ability could have harnessed the diverse national bodies in the partisan movement into one coherent and disciplined whole. He had a flair for grasping the essentials of a problem, and he worked tirelessly and boldly for its solution. His choice of collaborators had been fortunate and shrewd, and his personal courage and participation to the full in all the hardships of the campaigns had gained him the veneration and affection of his followers throughout the country.

To mark his appreciation for the work of the commandos on the island and their offensive raids against the enemy, the Marshal honoured us by inspecting No 2 Commando, the one that had been longest on the island, and had the highest record of successes against the enemy, on 23rd June 1944. The unit was drawn up in a vineyard in review order under the command of Major Ted Fynn who had succeeded my brother in command. The Highland Light Infantry kindly lent their band, and the Marshal was received with a General Salute. He then inspected the ranks, and took the salute at the March Past. The Commando was then formed into a hollow square, and he addressed them from a dais. The Marshal's speech was in Yugoslav, and a translation was read out to the troops immediately after he had spoken. The speech began as follows:

'Brothers in arms; Officers and soldiers of our allies, Great Britain and America!

'I am happy to be among you and to be able to greet you as comrades in arms in the battle for our common aim, which is victory over the greatest enemy of progressive humanity, the German invader and all his satellites.

'On this occasion I want to express my gratitude to you and the gratitude of our people for the sacrifices and efforts you have made, far away from your home, here, on the soil of Yugoslavia, for our common goal, the liberation of the people of Europe from the detested Fascist occupier. The gallantry and self-sacrifice of No 2 Commando in the battles on the islands of Brac, Korcula, Solta and others, is well known and much valued. The blood shed by your brave officers and soldiers in those battles has strengthened still more the links between the peoples of Yugoslavia and the peoples of Great Britain and America, and brought them still closer together.

'I am happy to have been convinced personally, that here, on this island, a perfect accord and comradeship in arms exists between you and our Army of National Liberation. This island symbolises that friendship and comradeship in war which unites all the Allies. Therein lies, above all, the power of the Allies, and that is the gauge for victory over the enemy, who, three years ago, was thought to be invincible, and who believed that himself.

'We have hard and sanguinary battles in front of us still, but we go forward to these battles perfectly certain that we will win. The gallant Allied Armies in Italy are rapidly driving the Germans to the North; in France, one part of the European Rampart has been breached, and the Allied Armies are penetrating the so-called "Unconquerable Fortress". In the far north, the Red Army is giving the final blows to Finland, and it is only a matter of a short period before this satellite will be finally dealt with. The peoples of enslaved Europe are rising to take part in this great battle for the liberation of the European Peoples, and the rapid termination of this terrible war imposed on the world by the Fascist invaders.

'I wish you great success in your future struggle, and personally I am sure that this war will very soon be over.

'Long live our brothers of the victorious Armies of Great Britain, the United States, and the Soviet Union!

'Death to Fascism – Liberty for the Peoples.'

*

After the parade, the Marshal gave a luncheon in a house at Borovik to all the officers commanding units on the island. It was a memorable occasion, and as usual there were many speeches, the first by the Marshal himself. I sat on his right and he told me the details of the parachute raid which so nearly captured him and the whole of his headquarters. He said that about three days before, he had decided to move away from the plain in which the headquarters was situated, to a cave in some hills which bordered the plain. He said he felt that an attack might be made, for the Germans had been over every day obviously photographing from aircraft. He had given orders for the whole headquarters to move, and they would have done so in a day or so's time.

The first development was a bombing raid early in the morning, just as dawn broke. Everyone thought it was just another raid, for they had had so many; everyone went to slit-trenches that had been dug near their offices. Then, just as the raid finished, hordes of parachutists jumped out of the aircraft and floated to the ground. Tito watched them from his cave only a few hundred yards away. Fortunately he was above them, and was able to climb up to the plateau and so escape before they could catch him. The parachutists ran about displaying photographs of Tito and demanding to know where he was. Tito laughed as he said that the Germans always make one mistake. If they had dropped on the plateau, and so dominated the plain, 'No-one would have got away.'

Once, when I visited Tito, he showed me a present which he had received from the Russian Government on the occasion of his birthday. In a beautiful maplewood case, a fine full-sized scimitar was enclosed; the sheath was made of steel, embossed with gold, in an exquisite design of little flowers with blue centres, and the blade itself, which he bade me draw, and which was beautifully balanced, was of fine thin steel inlaid with gold and incorporated the slogan of the Yugoslav National Army of Liberation – *'Smrt Facismo, Slobodna Narodu'*.

When one visited the Marshal, I noticed it was usually his custom to call for wine when the business was finished. Small plates of fish were also brought, and were handed round with bread. The wine was usually prosec, which was sent over to him from Hvar, where one of the best brands in the island was made. He used to feed tit-bits to his Alsatian dog, which he had captured from the Germans. He had taught him a number of tricks, and he accompanied Tito wherever he went. Tito, when in the company of British officers, always appeared in a grey-blue uniform consisting of a tunic with a high collar fastened at the throat, and breeches and black field boots. The badge of rank of a Marshal was a sprig of leaves worked in gold thread on the collar, and an oval of intertwined leaves with a star on the cuffs. It was said that this impressive uniform had been made for him in Russia, and there was a certain amount of light comment that whereas we provided the partisans with large numbers of aircraft sorties and great quantities of arms, ammunition and food, the Russians got equal by sending the Marshal a sword and a suit of uniform from time to time!

As a matter of interest, the fact that the Russians were not at that time providing him with active aid did at first cause us to wonder how it was that the partisans' enthusiasm for that country never dwindled; but when we got to appreciate their outlook better, we learnt that their view was that the Western Allies were responsible for the Mediterranean theatre of war, and that the Russians, with the immense burden of defeating the gigantic German armies that had fallen upon their western frontiers, were in no position to offer aid to Yugoslavia in materialistic form.

Yugoslav admiration for the Red Army was unbounded, and there could be no question that the moral influence of Russia was very great throughout the country. The war effort of the USSR was considered stupendous, and the sufferings of the Russian peasants were regarded as a magnified reflection of the hardships which the Yugoslavs themselves had had to endure. The nature of the German-Russian fighting was well understood by the partisans, since it differed only in magnitude from their own struggle with the invaders, and they felt far more in sympathy with this colossal land war than they did with, say, the war being waged at sea by the British and Americans. This latter war had little reality for them, and while they did not of course disbelieve the accounts they heard, they had not the same significance as the Russian operations, so much nearer home and so much more akin to their own.

Another factor which must be remembered is the immense prestige of the Yugoslav Communist Party throughout Yugoslavia, as a result of the manner in which it had identified itself wholeheartedly with the war against the aggressor. Many of its leaders proved themselves among the most able of the partisan generals. Its prestige led to respect for the USSR since the latter was a Communist state, and Stalin was often described as Tito's teacher, in songs and poems.

The Brac attack had demonstrated clearly that the enemy's policy in holding the islands was purely defensive. He ensconced himself in the strongest positions he could find, such as the tops of mountains, and spent his time making those positions stronger by the laying of minefields and the siting of barbed wire obstacles. He made no attempt to control the islands, and did not in fact issue out of his stockades except to collect supplies from a port or to draw water from local wells. Occasionally patrols would be sent out to search the island for food, the patrol returning to the stockade as soon as its mission was accomplished. These patrols were seldom less than 20 strong, and often were much stronger. These tactics had been imposed on him by our raids which preyed on his small detachments; he had therefore abandoned the small isolated garrison, and concentrated his forces into larger strong-points which were so located that a full-scale attack would have to be mounted to turn them out, and the advantage would in any case lie with the defender.

I had been convinced that this was his policy even before I undertook the Mljet raid, and I felt that unless our own policy changed, and we decided to seize and hold an island, it was folly to pit ourselves against positions which were too strong for us and would cause us unnecessarily high casualties. As yet we could not take and hold another island except at the expense of the Vis garrison, for we still did not have a surplus of fighting soldiers on Vis. I therefore advocated attacks on the patrols which he sent out from his positions, when they could be caught at a disadvantage; for I considered that we were in a position to choose our objectives and our timing, and it was up to us to ensure that these attacks were as expensive to the enemy as they were economical in casualties to ourselves, for this is, after all, the whole principle of guerilla tactics.

Fortunately the Brac attack had demonstrated the difficulties of attacking the enemy's chosen defensive localities, and discouraged the authorities from proceeding with grandiose conceptions for which we had neither the troops nor the necessary supporting arms. It also taught a lesson in cooperation with the partisans. Their methods are not the same as ours, and they are used to undertaking projects without carefully weighing the pros and cons beforehand, because they think nothing of abandoning an action if it fails to produce good results; being unencumbered with equipment other than that which the men carry on their backs, they can easily disintegrate their forces and make for the hills, later to reorganise and try again.

The lesson of course was that in concerted actions with them, they should always be given a task which did not directly affect our own, one which might lie on a flank, for instance, the success of which would further our combined plans, but the failure of which would not

ns under British
ision firing 75 mm gun-
ers

g a 25-pounder on to
t Vis prior to raid on
a harbour

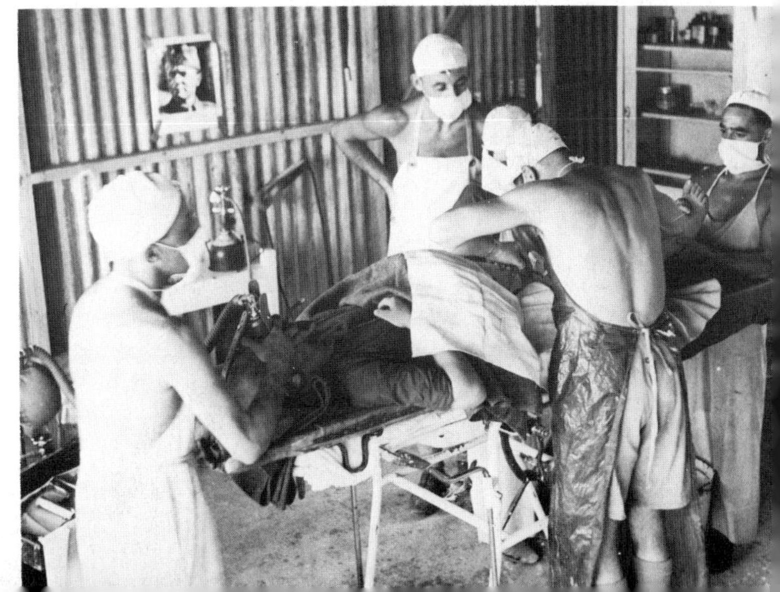

Grey, RAMC operates
ounded partisan – Vis
al

(*Left*) *Hiatus on Vis:* In early July 1944 General Sir Maitland (Jumbo) Wilson sent his aircraft to fetch Marshal Tito from Vis for a meeting at Caserta Palace, but at the last moment Tito refused to leave, fearing he might be confronted with King Peter of Yugoslavia. *Left to right:* The author, Marshal Tito, Brigadier Sir Fitzroy Maclean and Air Marshal Sir William Elliot, commander Balkan Air Force. (The meeting with Wilson in fact took place a few weeks later and was a success.) (*Right*) On left, Major-General Anatolij Gorskov, who was second in command of the Russian Mission to Tito, 1943–45. On right, Aleksander Sornikov, National Hero of Yugoslavia who flew Tito from Yugoslavia to Bari in June 1944. Photo taken by author in Belgrade, 1975

25-pounder in action on Yugoslav soil at Lovisce, Peljesac peninsula, 27 August 1944

jeopardise our immediate operation. I was later able to adopt this method in Albania when cooperating with the Albanian partisans, and found it very workable.

We now decided to station standing patrols permanently on all the enemy-occupied islands. These patrols generally consisted of a couple of officers and twenty to thirty men. They used to split up into small detachments, to watch the enemy, and when they found a likely target, or got wind that one was probably going to appear, they used to wireless over to us stating the nature of the target, and we would rapidly send over a striking force strong enough to deal with it.

The patrols remained permanently, but the personnel were changed over from time to time. They used to take a certain amount of rations with them, and more were sent at night by landing craft or schooners at regular intervals. They contacted the local partisans, who provided guides, and gave them any news that they collected. They used to share their rations with the local inhabitants, for the latter had become extremely short of food owing to the foraging of the Germans and the restriction on imports.

The first success of this new system fell to No 43 (RM) Commando, which was maintaining a patrol on Hvar. This patrol reported that a German party of some twenty men was expected to pass through a shallow defile on its way to pillage and steal from the local inhabitants at a certain village. A troop of this Commando was rushed over under Colonel Bill Simonds, which took up a position overnight on the hills flanking the defile. When dawn broke, a thick fog had set in, and although the road was only some fifty yards from the ambush party, the German patrol somehow managed to enter the defile undetected. The alarm was given when the Huns entered the house in which the Commando doctor had set up a first aid dressing station. As we had control of all the high ground in the vicinity, the enemy was in a difficult position, but he did the only thing which was possible for him, and came up the hills to attack us. Our men waited until he presented a well-defined target and then opened fire. Only two men got away. The Marines took fifteen prisoners, most of them wounded, and a number of dead were left on the field.

Towards the end of August, Lieutenant-Colonel Elliott, commanding 111th Field Regiment RA, made a plan with Lieutenant-Commander Morgan Giles to land artillery on the western edge of the Peljesac Peninsula at a place called Lovisce.

The plan was to land a battery of 25-pounder guns, and four ·75 gun-howitzers of the RSR, while the HLI provided a covering party for the guns.

At dawn the guns opened fire, their first target being an enemy battery near the village of Blato on Korcula. This German gun-position had been carefully reconnoitred previously by an officer of 111th Field Regiment, who, disguising himself as a girl, had wandered close to the battery position with a number of Yugoslavs, taking careful note of its exact position.

A feature of this operation was the use of an improved air observation post. Captain 'Dizzy' Ross, of the RSR, piloted a borrowed Yugoslav biplane of ancient manufacture which he had found on the aerodrome at Vis. He had a signaller with him, who balanced a wireless set on his knees, and transmitted fire orders to the guns. Much damage was done to the enemy positions on Korcula, and by the end of the day, all but one of his guns were knocked out. Four of Elliott's guns received some hot counter-battery fire during the engagement, but managed to re-embark, with the excellent cooperation of the Navy, when the time for withdrawal came; and as the convoy left the Peljesac Peninsula in the late afternoon, a huge fire was burning on the objectives, and a pall of smoke hung over Korcula.

On one occasion it was decided to attempt to intercept the enemy's shipping by means of a land-force instead of by gun-boats. A small force consisting of a handful of American OGs armed with bazookas and automatic weapons set off in landing craft with a detachment of the Raiding Support Regiment and one of the latter's .75 howitzers. They landed by night at a cove on the southern shore of the Peljesac Peninsula, and disposed themselves so that an American party was located on the two small promontories which enclosed the cove while the howitzer was mounted in the cove itself. The plan was for the party to remain for three nights, during which it was hoped that an enemy convoy would pass close inshore. If this occurred, the party would endeavour to engage it. MGBs were arranged to lie off some distance so as not to interfere with the plan, but were in wireless touch with the party, and as soon as an action had taken place, they were to be called to re-embark the soldiers.

On the night that they were due to be picked off, they still had had no target, so the party asked to be allowed to remain one more night. This was agreed, and sure enough on the following night, about an hour after dark, the Americans on the eastward point picked out the shady outline of a craft approaching. This turned out to be a landing craft, and it was followed by another, but behind them they noticed a large schooner. In order not to frighten away the schooner before it came into the sights of the howitzer in the cove, they decided to let the landing craft pass without engaging, and warned the gun-team that the schooner was approaching.

As soon as it came into view, the gun fired, and with its first shot hit the boat fair and square on its port gunwale. As soon as it had fired, the Americans opened up with their bazookas and machine guns at the landing craft. The schooner was sunk, and the landing craft were dispersed and damaged, though in the dark it was impossible to see whether they were sunk or not. Some prisoners were taken from the schooner as they swam ashore, and not long afterwards the MGBs came in and picked the party off. It had been an amusing little ruse, and it worked perfectly.

During our long stay on the island of Vis, we naturally suffered a good many casualties in our raids, though on the whole the proportion of these casualties to the tasks that were undertaken, and the damage inflicted on the enemy, was remarkably small. The medical arrangements to deal with the wounded had, however, to be really good, as the time taken to evacuate men to the mainland of Italy was considerable, especially in the winter months when ships were often held up for a week or more owing to bad weather.

When we first arrived, we were accompanied by a surgical team under the command of Captain Rickett RAMC. He had to set up a hospital by improvisation, for there were no partisan materials to spare, and Italy was unable to send him the essential equipment that he needed owing to a shortage of supplies there and the heavy demands of the Fifth and Eighth Armies. This did not deter Rickett, who set to work to improvise as best he could. He acquired two small houses from the partisans, which he decided to use respectively as a theatre and as wards. For the theatre, he had brought a portable operating table, but he had to make an operating light, lay on a hot-water system, create electric power for the lighting, and construct shelves and sinks, etc., for the washing-up room and the instrument room. The light was made out of biscuit-tins in an ingenious manner so that there were five electric bulb sockets each with tin reflectors; the electric power was provided by a captured German generator which the partisans made available and installed for him; the hot-water system was his own design and was a little Heath-Robinson in appearance but worked very efficiently.

He was of course very short-handed, but because he always treated the Yugoslav wounded or sick however busy he was with our casualties, their gratitude was unbounded and they assisted him to the utmost. He even secured the services of two 'theatre sisters' – the two women who owned the house in which he billeted. These two were always available when operations had to be performed, and turned to with a will however dirty the job or long the hours.

There was another doctor on the island, Captain Lloyd Roberts, who had been sent over to work for the partisans and guide their medical service which were sketchy in the extreme. He normally worked at the partisan hospital down at Vis, but he and Rickett were the best of friends, and they helped each other and shared the island work. Lloyd Roberts was a young lad who threw himself wholeheartedly into his work, and he too was idolized by them. In the early days, wounded would be brought over by schooners from Yugoslavia who had been hit sometimes as much as six months previously, and in the meantime had performed colossal journeys over mountains to reach the coast. All this time the patient would very likely have had no medical aid at all, so the condition of the wounds when they reached Vis can be imagined.

Rickett and Lloyd Roberts had their busiest time immediately after a raid, and when the partisans attacked Mljet and Korcula, they were working in shifts without stop for four days and nights. As the garrison increased, our medical staff had to be augmented, and we were sent over a field hospital to increase our resources.

I was interested to discover the partisan attitude towards religion, and I took a certain amount of trouble to ascertain their official policy within the movement. It is explained, when one makes enquiries on this subject, that the movement is anxious to embrace all creeds whose devotees are taking part in the fight against the invader. They only set their face against a sect if it urges its followers not to join the partisans, or to resist them. It seems that the Orthodox Church in Serbia has always been identified with the movement, while the Catholic Church, particularly in Croatia and Slovenia, has been inclined to hold aloof. Nevertheless certain Catholic clerics have pronounced in favour of the partisans, as have many of the Orthodox faith. Catholics were said to have been active amongst the followers of Pavelic, and even to have been concerned with the Ustase atrocities, and this had naturally set the partisans against them, though the rights and wrongs of the case could not be judged from our position on a Dalmatian island.

I can only say that when we arrived on Vis, all the many Catholic chapels were empty, and the only Orthodox church on the island was used as a dump for supplies. I never saw a partisan attend any church service, but many were billeted in churches which they desecrated to a shocking extent. Most of the Catholic priests went in fear of their lives, though they continued to say their offices in churches empty of a congregation. It was significant that when we arrived and commenced to hold church services, the Catholics in one of the churches, and the other denominations in tents or on the hill-sides, the islanders (as opposed to the partisans) would unobtrusively join our congregations.

Many of us noticed that as the course of the war turned against the Germans, and as the partisan position in Yugoslavia changed from a desperate struggle in the face of appalling odds to a coordinated advance with certain victory in sight, so also did the partisan attitude towards us change. In the early days, we were welcomed with gratitude, openness and friendship; cooperation was unlimited and unstinted. Anything that could be done for us was done, and any help we could give them was accepted gratefully. They were frank and good natured, and our mutual relations could not have been better. We were filled with admiration for their spirit, resource and steadfastness, and sympathetic towards their needs and difficulties. But later their attitude changed, almost imperceptibly at first, but becoming more and more obvious. Old friends suddenly became reserved; facts became harder to obtain. Assistance was asked as a right, and demands which could not be met led to resentment. There was an attitude of truculence abroad, as though a sinister influence was at work.

I do not pretend to be able to give the reasons for this change which we noted, but I should fail to give the whole picture of our relations if I did not record it. There were times when we thought that the new attitude was dictated from above. On one occasion, the Navy decided to give a party to the children of a tiny port in one of the northern islands which had been freed. This was mentioned to the local partisan committee, who demurred, and said they must refer the matter to another and higher committee. Then the reply came that they were unable to sanction it, as permission had not been received from above. They professed to be unable to give a reason. This sort of thing became common – though we did not give it undue attention. I may add that the children had their party just the same, and thoroughly enjoyed themselves.

I am glad that I left Yugoslavia in August 1944 before these new circumstances could cloud the happy memories that I retained of our six months' struggle together. I shall never lose my admiration for their national character and for their determination to free their own country, whatever the cost to themselves. There were times when one almost lost patience with their lack of humour, and a person who always takes himself seriously becomes a little tedious; but if one remembers their privations, and the appalling cruelty of the Germans; the trials of their womenfolk and children, and the magnitude of the task which they took on with their eyes open, one can never cease to admire them.

I left Vis on 12th August 1944, after five and a half months' stewardship. In that time, the island had changed from a beleaguered outpost to a fortified bastion. When we left, we had gained control of the sea, the land and the air about our island, and our work was finished. The Navy gave me a send-off which I shall always remember, and as I watched the hills of Vis sink into the sea from the stern of *MGB 674*, I knew that a part of me was left behind.

CHAPTER EIGHTEEN

The Battle of Sarande, and the Liberation of Corfu

On 7th May 1944, just after the cancellation of the operation for the capture of Pasman Island, and a few days before the commencement of the attack on Mljet Island, a brigadier called G. M. O. Davy arrived practically unannounced on Vis, and came to see me. It turned out that he was the Deputy Assistant Chief of Staff (Operations) at Allied Forces Headquarters in Algiers – which was General Dwight D. Eisenhower's Staff Post. He wanted to inspect the defences of Vis Island, but as those defences had been very comprehensively reviewed only five weeks previously by General Sir Gerald Templer, at the request of General Sir James Gammell, General Jumbo Wilson's Chief of Staff, I wondered what the real reason for Davy's visit was.

I spent two days taking him all over the island and pointing out our battle positions. I introduced him to all my commanding officers but we none of us took much to this unprepossessing staff officer, a renegade Gunner turned Cavalryman who always wore his service cap pulled down too hard on his head so that its rim rested on his large sticking-out ears, and who seemed to have a rather inflated estimation of his own importance.

Soon after his departure I was busy preparing and then leading the raid on Mljet, which I have described in Chapter Fifteen. I then went on duty to England by air, and while I was away, the battle of Brac was fought, and because of the heavy casualties sustained, I was immediately recalled to Vis.

I found that a great many changes in command at the highest level had taken place, in a very short space of time. Firstly, a new air command, called the Balkan Air Force, had been set up under Air Marshal William Elliot, with its headquarters at Bari on the south-east coast of Italy. It took command of all operations by land, sea and air into Central and South-Eastern Europe, and had the special task of ferrying supplies to the Yugoslav partisans, and affording them air support. For control of the land operations, a new formation had been instituted under BAF called Land Forces, Adriatic; and the bad news was that this headquarters was to be commanded by none other than our old friend G. M. O. Davy; and my Commando Brigade was removed from Force 133 of SOE under whom we had operated with contentment for the past six months, under its commander Brigadier 'Bonzo' Miles. Now Miles had been removed from the scene and we found ourselves under Davy.

The victorious course of the war for the Allies had by now made the position of the Germans in the Balkans somewhat precarious. The advance of the Russians threatened to cut off the enemy armies in Greece, Albania and Yugoslavia, and signs were not wanting of his intention to withdraw systematically from these three countries. He had already started to withdraw from the Dalmatian Islands, and No 43 (RM) Commando, the only unit of my brigade that was left on Vis, took part in a number of engagements in the islands designed to hurry his departure, and to inflict as much damage on him as possible in the process. At the same time, another Commando, No 9, was landed at the island of Kithera, off the southern tip of Greece, to be the spearhead of the British forces which were to lever him out of Greece, and a raid by No 2 Commando was mounted against the coast of Albania, where they attacked and damaged a German company which was holding a hill-position at a village called Himara.

For a time Land Forces, Adriatic had a project for my brigade to seize and hold another Adriatic island further up the coast of Yugoslavia, but this was cancelled at the last minute after reconnaissances had been carried out and most of the planning had been completed. Instead, interest began to concentrate on the German garrison in Corfu, which was known to have commenced the evacuation of the island by way of the port of Sarande in Albania.

Originally, the Germans had used two ports on the mainland of Europe by which to supply the garrison of Corfu – one in the south, just inside the Greek frontier, and Sarande in the north, in Albania; but recently Greek partisan action had succeeded in wresting the southern port from the enemy, so that he was left only with Sarande, which he was now using for his evacuation. The country on the mainland between these two ports was either hilly or else marshy, so that no roads reached the coast; and he was therefore forced to rely on Sarande for his escape route.

It was obviously an attractive proposition to seize Sarande in order to cut the enemy off, and this is what Davy ordered the commandos to do; but with so many targets now offering up and down the Adriatic, he decided to allot this task to a minimum force, in order to have others available for other objectives. The capture of Sarande

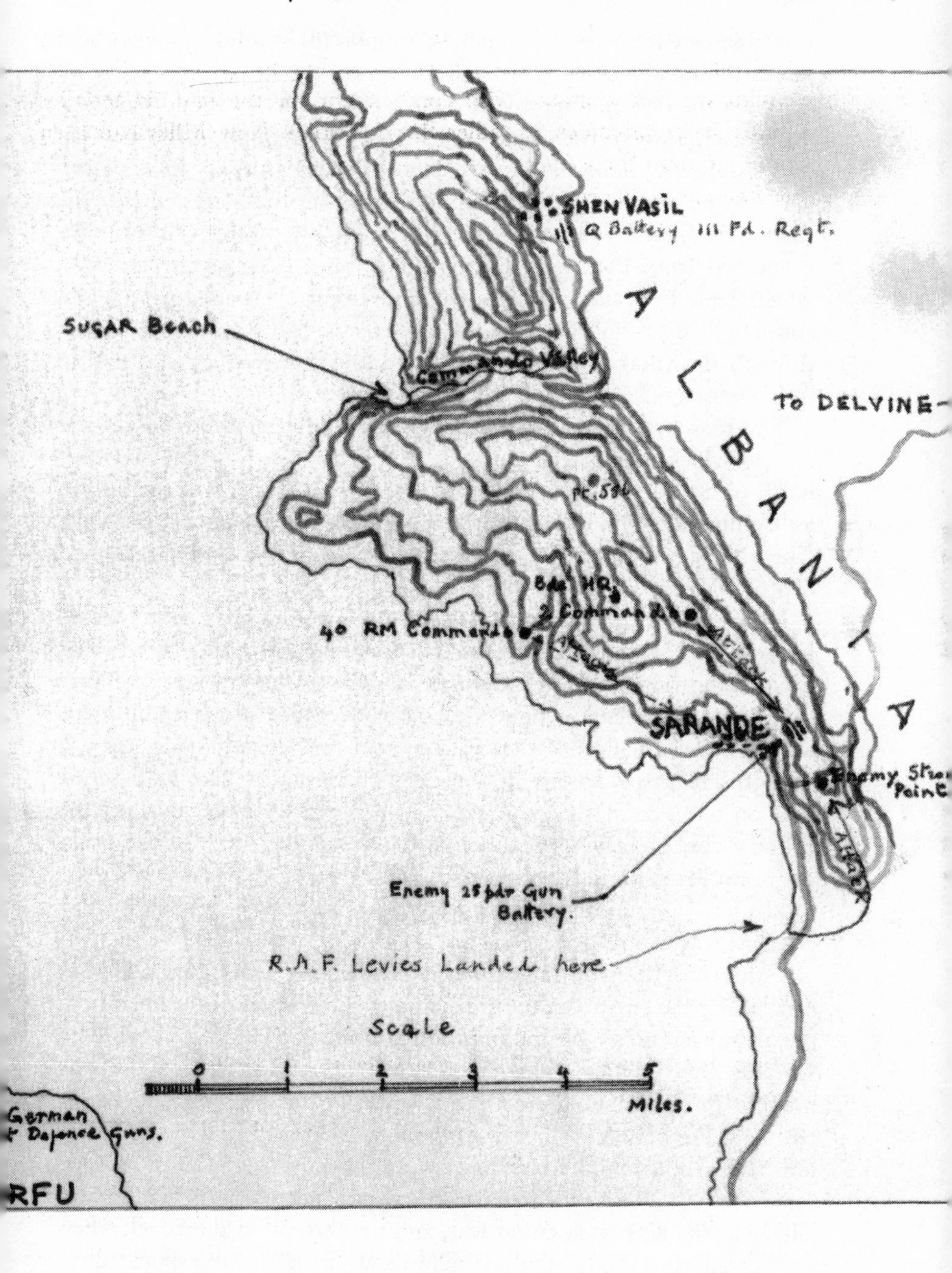

SARANDE ATTACK

was assigned to No 2 Commando, supported by four .75 guns and some additional machine guns and mortars of the RSR.

When the enemy dispositions came to be studied, I found that very little was known of the enemy apart from the strength of the garrison of Sarande itself, and nothing was known of his artillery. All we knew was that he had two or three hundred troops in the port, and that the Corfu garrison, numbering several thousand, were being slowly evacuated from the island by schooners, and a Siebel ferry or two, which came in to Sarande by night. The troops then disembarked and continued their journey inland by mechanical transport, passing through the village of Delvine. In the latter village there was said to be a garrison of seven or eight hundred Germans.

The plan was for the Commando and attached troops to land at a cove which was given the name of 'Sugar Beach', some six miles north of Sarande, and advance up a valley that later became known as 'Commando Valley' until the road leading to Sarande was reached. The troops were then to proceed down this road and attack and capture the port.

I spent a certain amount of time studying this plan with Colonel Fynn, who now commanded No 2 Commando. It seemed to us that it would be very unlike the Germans to have taken no steps to ensure that the approaches to their vital port were not protected in some way, yet the intelligence that we received told us nothing except the strengths of the garrisons in Delvine and Sarande. The map shows that on one side of the road down which we were to advance, the country rises steeply to nearly two thousand feet, and on the other the terrain is flat and marshy. It would not therefore be easy to deploy suddenly if some unexpected snag was met with, as the whole advance was to take place at night.

I therefore pressed that further intelligence should be collected concerning the enemy before we committed ourselves to the operation, but there was an air of optimism abroad and we were told that 'now was the time to take risks'. In the face of this attitude, there was nothing for it but to proceed, but we began to take precautions on our own. We only had three days in hand before the date of embarkation, so I arranged to send an officers' patrol consisting of Captain Alec Parsons MC and two subalterns to the cove by means of an ML, to find out what the enemy situation was, and to meet us on the beach when we landed. We should thus be able to adjust our plans should anything untoward be discovered. I also decided to go with No 2 Commando to see the situation for myself.

We sailed from the port of Monopoli in Italy in landing craft on 22nd September 1944, and met very heavy seas so that at one time it was touch and go whether the craft would be able to complete the journey. However, the wind abated a little as we approached the coast of Albania, and as we entered the cove we were glad to see the torch-flashes of Alec Parsons and his companions from the shore. As soon as we beached, they came on board, looking rather like tramps with a three-days' growth of beard and soaking wet, as by now it was raining torrents.

Alec gave us an alarming picture. It appeared that the enemy had over twenty field and medium guns between Delvine and Sarande, which shelled anything that moved on the road to the port; they had even shelled him when he went out to do a reconnaissance on a mule on the far side of the road, and had pitched a shell so close that the mule bucked him off and bolted. They also shelled the cove at intervals, and had sent a patrol of over a hundred men down the valley the previous afternoon, which had chased the officers into the hills and had destroyed their kit and rations which had been left on the beach.

As this patrol withdrew, however, the Albanian partisans, who were hiding in the hills on the north side of the valley, had descended on the enemy and managed to kill or capture forty of them. The latest news was that the Germans had run a self-propelled gun up the road from Sarande to the head of the valley, where it had shelled the beach intermittently. The partisans had also reported that the garrison of Sarande was not two to three hundred, but four to five hundred strong.

I confess that I expected that the news would not be to our advantage, so this information did not come as too much of a shock. The original plan had of course to be thrown overboard, and I decided to hold the valley in strength. It was also essential to get men up on to the hills on the south side of the valley at once, for if the enemy established himself up there, we could not have got a single craft into the cove, and we should soon have been driven into the sea. Accordingly, Captain Mike Webb was told to get his troop on to the summit marked as Point 586 on the map. The rest of the Commando advanced up the valley in pouring rain, and took up positions at its head, guided by Alec Parsons, who had selected positions for the troops in daylight. I may add that his reconnaissance was admirably carried out, and the information he had obtained turned out to be accurate in every detail.

When day dawned, we adjusted our positions and climbed the hills to get a view of the enemy layout. It had taken Mike Webb seven hours to reach Point 586, but he had got the whole of his troop up there with all their equipment, and so secured our position in the valley. As I looked out over the plain towards Delvine, it was obvious to me that no advance down the road would be possible, and our only hope of taking Sarande would be by an advance over the hills which lay between the sea and the road. This was obviously going to be a very difficult operation, and we should need another Commando and at least eight 25-pounders, for the enemy's artillery was so strong that we should have to have something with which to reply to it. Our .75 guns were not able to reach Delvine, and even the 25-pounders would only be able to touch the fringe of the village. I therefore sent a signal to Italy asking for No 40 (RM) Commando and a battery of field guns.

The other Commando arrived two days later, but the guns did not reach me for over a week. We spent the first ten days establishing three troops up on the hills, while No 40 Commando also held positions on the coast within a few hundred yards of the enemy outposts defending Sarande. During the whole of this time we experienced torrential rain both night and day. I have never seen anything like it before, though I served in Burma during my subaltern days and know what monsoon rain is like; every valley became a torrent, and the soldiers were wet through all the time. There was no cover to be had, for there were no houses, so it was impossible to dry anything. The men had one groundsheet each, and one blanket. The blanket was permanently soaking, and the groundsheet was used in an attempt to provide cover, but this could only be done by attaching it to two boulders, and invariably the weight of water collapsed the 'tent'. The men's boots were soaking also, and soon began to break open owing to the rockiness of the mountains and their dampness.

The expedition had been mounted in a hurry, and as if for a raid of three or four days' duration. Only twelve mules had been sent, and these, apart from being totally inadequate in number, soon ran out of the fodder which had been provided. The hills were so steep and rocky that the mules were unable to negotiate the worst places, and every man of the two Commandos who was not actually manning a forward post had to be used as a porter to carry up boxes of rations or ammunition to the hill positions. This was a most punishing ordeal, and I had 200 cases of exposure and trench feet in the first ten days. As my fighting strength was only 650, this was an alarming proportion.

To maintain No 40 Commando, supplies had to be carried from our cove over the hills and parallel to the coast, to their positions above and not far west of Sarande. To avoid this arduous journey, we hoped to be able to supply them by sea, and we asked Italy to send us some small landing craft to enable us to ferry supplies round the coast. We also needed sea transport to work up to our northern beach, on which we landed the 25-pounders, as they could not shoot from our valley owing to the height and the steepness of the mountains which enclosed it.

The mainland, however, was not very sympathetic to our needs, and replied that no landing craft were available. I knew this was not the case, for I had spoken to the flotilla officer of some LCAs that were based at Bari the night before we sailed, and I also knew that there were some LCPs doing nothing at Manfredonia, as I had visited that port not long before.

My needs were so desperate that I sent a Polish naval lieutenant who was attached to us, and who had been most helpful and co-operative, over to Taranto with a letter to the Admiral, asking that something be done to help us out, and also suggesting that there were excellent targets going begging in the straits between Corfu and Albania, where schooners were evacuating the German garrison every night.

Although the Admiral did not send me the landing craft at once, he appointed a Naval Force Commander for our expedition, and sent him over post-haste in a LCH (a large landing craft converted for use as a headquarter ship). This officer, Lieutenant-Commander Usherwood by name, saw the position for himself when he arrived, and after discussions with me, signalled for landing craft which were then immediately dispatched!

Once we got the small craft, our supply problem was eased considerably, and the field guns, when they arrived, were able to reply to the enemy artillery which shelled us regularly in our valley and on our hill positions. There was however a battery of high-velocity guns on the northern coast of Corfu which gave us a good deal of trouble, as they could see and reach us, and we could not reach them. They used to chase our craft as they came in and out of our cove, and made a habit of trying to lob shells into our valley. We asked the RAF from Italy to deal with them, and after two or three tries, they finally succeeded in knocking them out.

The battery of 25-pounders that came over to us was our old Vis friends 'Queen' Battery of 111th Field Regiment, who had supported us on many occasions in Dalmatia. Major Daniel, their commanding officer, joined me at my headquarters, and he got his guns into position at Shen Vasil, a village some miles from us but from where he could bring fire to bear on most of the enemy gun positions, and also on to Sarande. To do the latter task, however, the guns had to use 'super-charge', in order to get over the high peaks that intervened, and this could only be done to a limited extent as it wore out the springs of the guns.

About the tenth day of our stay on Albanian soil, the rain stopped and the sun broke through. We were a very bedraggled sight, but having managed to hang on so long, and the worst of the weather apparently being over, I was determined to get Sarande. Until now it had only been possible to try and interfere with the enemy's evacuation by raiding the Delvine road at night with small parties to shoot up traffic, and by putting down concentrations of artillery fire at unspecified intervals on the port and on the road and the bridges. We had had a few successes, but we could not cut the road properly as the ground was so marshy, between the road and Delvine, that any parties that we sent out took so long to traverse this difficult ground that they could not remain on the road for more than an hour each night. I had asked for some pioneers to be sent to me, to relieve my fighting troops of the unloading and loading that had to be done at the beach, and some of the porterage, for when the time came to attack, I should certainly have to use every available fighting man that I had.

In the meantime I had had plenty of time to study the enemy positions and decide which was the best way to attack him. Our positions in the hills overlooked Sarande, and it seemed to me that the best method of approach would be a three-pronged attack, two from the north and one from the south. The Germans had established a battery of British 25-pounders that they had captured in Greece on a hill to the north-east of Sarande, and this would certainly have to be assaulted by one prong of the attack. The second prong would be directed at the port at its western end, partly over the hills and partly round the coast; and the third prong would have as its objective the isolated hill on which he had a company, just south of the road that ran out of Sarande. It would be essential to take this hill, as it dominated the port; but its northern slopes were very steep, and an approach from that direction would be bound to meet very heavy fire.

It seemed to me that the way to take this objective would be to land a force at a cove to the south of it, and to advance on it from the rear. I proposed to use my landing craft to get the force to the cove, to put them down at night so that, with any luck, they should have the advantage of surprise and should fall on the enemy unawares.

I had been in touch with the Albanian partisans, who professed themselves as willing to cooperate with us, and conform to any plans that we formulated; so I mentally reserved for them the task of operating on our left flank, with a view to cutting the Delvine road, and I told their colonel, whose first name was Ismail (but whose second name I have now forgotten), that I would let him know as soon as I was in a position to attack.

On 6th October I was informed that I was to receive a reinforcement the following day of approximately a hundred men of a paratroop company of the RAF Levies. At the same time I was told that some pioneers would be sent as soon as possible. Now that our administrative arrangements were on a better footing, and the weather was at last dry, I decided to attack Sarande on the night of 8th/9th October. I called a conference for the morning of the 7th, and a message was sent to Colonel Ismail asking him to attend. We held this conference on board Commander Usherwood's LCH, and orders were issued to the units that were to take part in the attack.

The final plan was as follows: No 2 Commando was to attack and capture the German battery; No 40 Commando was to capture the port of Sarande, and the RAF Levies were to land from craft to the south of the isolated hill and capture it from the rear. The partisans were to cooperate on the left flank, and cut the Delvine road. The attack was to commence at 4.30 a.m. on the 9th, and was to be preceded by half an hour's artillery concentration on the German positions.

As we were still outnumbered by the enemy's artillery, I was anxious to create a diversion in order to draw off some of his fire. For this purpose I had previously asked for, and had been sent, an officer of the New Zealand Engineers who had devised a special 'box of tricks' which, when put into action, made – so I was assured – a noise like a whole brigade attacking. This mystery man appeared on our beaches and only made the modest demand of five soldiers to carry his various contraptions. I asked him to make the maximum diversion on our left flank ten minutes before our main attack went in. Lieutenant McNab, for that was his name, was overjoyed at the opportunity of letting off his wares, and set about his preparations with a will, while his five porters were highly intrigued with the novel role that was assigned to them.

On the afternoon of 8th October, I moved my headquarters to the top of a hill overlooking Sarande, for, by getting up high, one greatly increased the chances of successful wireless communication during the battle, and from my mountain position it was possible to get a good view of the whole battlefield. Telephone lines had already been laid to the Commandos, and linesmen were ready to extend them forward as the battle progressed. I had the partisan colonel with me, and his interpreter who spoke French; and to facilitate communication with his forces on the flank, we had attached to them a commando officer with a wireless set.

All preparations had now been made, and as the barrage was not due to begin until four o'clock in the morning, everyone except the duty officers tried to snatch some sleep. We had built little dry stone walls round our position to break the force of the wind, for it was very cold on the mountain-tops, and I shall always remember the view that evening as the sun set over the hills of Corfu, tinting the channel between the island and the Albanian coast, and the sea stretching away to the shores of Greece.

Promptly at four o'clock the barrage commenced, and twenty minutes later McNab set off his fireworks. I had never seen or heard anything like it. It was a magnificent display of flashes and lights and rockets, accompanied by an astounding variety of noises. What the Germans thought, I have no idea, but recovering from their astonishment, they brought down a severe concentration of artillery in his area. This was exactly what we wanted, but I was a bit worried about McNab. Ten minutes later, our attack started, and I waited anxiously for news.

As dawn broke, I heard from both Commandos. No 2 had overrun the enemy positions covering the battery, and were forming up for the attack on the guns themselves. Their casualties had been light, but the difficult nature of the hills had slowed their advance, and they were faced with three quarters of a mile to cover before they came to grips with the enemy again. 40 Commando had also captured the German outpost line, but they had met much fiercer resistance, and two of their troop leaders had been killed. They were still in very close contact, and the sound of the battle came rolling over the hills to where I was. They were now pressing in to the village itself, and were meeting fierce machine gun, light automatic and mortar fire from the buildings and streets on the edge of the town.